THE BOREAL CURMUDGEON

Twenty Years of *Nordicity*: a Yukon Reader

AL POPE

ILLUSTRATED BY HEIDI MARION

The Boreal Curmudgeon
Twenty Years of *Nordicity*: a Yukon Reader

Printed in Canada
First Printing, 2018

Book design, editorial input & production services
provided by Andrea Schmidt, www.a-schmidt.com

ISBN 978-1-7752044-0-4

Al Pope
P.O. Box 11261, Whitehorse, YT
Y1A 6N5 Canada

ALPOPE.COM | FACEBOOK.COM/THEBOREALCURMUDGEON

For we wrestle not against flesh and blood,
but against principalities, against powers,
against the rulers of the darkness of this world,
against spiritual wickedness in high places.

– EPHESIANS 6:12

ACKNOWLEDGEMENTS

When I began writing, Peter Lesniak, then editor of the *Yukon News*, gave me both advice and encouragement, as well as a small weekly stipend to write *Nordicity*. I am indebted to Peter and to publisher Steve Robertson for that start, and for the nearly 20 years in which I was left to write practically anything that interested me. Had it not been for their sufferance, this would not be such an eclectic collection.

I could not have written the column or produced this book without the help and support of Lois Moorcroft, my wife of 42 years. She has always been my first reader, with a keen editor's eye.

Book designer Andrea Schmidt was an invaluable resource, not only for her design talents and her knowledge of the industry, but for her help with the final copy edit, and for her endless patience and good humour.

Finally, my thanks to Heidi Marion for brightening up these pages with her striking, fun, witty illustrations. It would be a much lesser book without them.

CONTENTS

INTRODUCTION

When I began to write my column, *Nordicity*, for the *Yukon News*, Canada had just survived the 1995 Quebec Referendum, Monica Lewinsky and Bill Clinton were not having sexual relations as such in the White House, and Prime Minister Jean Chretien was still innocent of assaulting demonstrators. The Balkans were on fire, NAFTA was an infant known as Free Trade, and former prime minister Brian Mulroney was suing the Canadian taxpayer over a smudge on what he called, with a straight face, his "good name."

Nineteen years later, when the *News* and I parted company, the US had its first black president, the Canadian Senate was investigating itself on corruption charges (nothing turned up, surprise!), and one of Pierre Trudeau's kids was running to be prime minister of Canada. Much water had passed under the bridge during those years, and *Nordicity* was there, like a boy on the bridge, leaning over to watch all that muddy water coursing by, trying to come up with an original thought.

During these years I was living, as I still do, on the Watson River, about fifty kilometres from Whitehorse, the capital of the Yukon – or as it's officially known, Yukon. The government dropped the "the" years ago, but we Yukoners still cling to that article as if it were the only definite thing in our lives. But I digress. When I first took up writing I had three kids, all in school, several goats, a horse or two, a few chickens, and the remnants of a once-great – ok a once-good – sled-dog racing team. I also had my first computer, with auto-correct, a blessing because I was and remain a blight on the name of typists everywhere.

My life was a writer's dream. Each day I got up, cooked breakfast, saw my kids off to the school bus and my wife off to work, and had eight straight hours all to myself in the peace of the Yukon bush. Not surprising then that a lot of the earlier columns referred to the life I was living at the time. Later, after the kids were grown up and gone, the subject matter broadened to include national and international issues, but I often fell back into my old ways. Snuggled in amongst the vagaries of politics and the horrors of war you will find destructive cats, urban chickens, threatened pigs, breastfeeding, and anything else I might have been preoccupied with on deadline day.

These columns aren't meant to be read like a novel, from start to finish. After one or two they may start to cloy. Unless you are the kind of voracious reader who can't quit no matter what the content, you might prefer to treat this book as a kind of outhouse reader. The entries are organized by subject, rather than chronology, and there is no reason to read them in any particular order. Open the book at random if you will, or leaf through till a headline or an illustration catches your eye. I hope you will find some nugget of fun, or truth, or inspiration, to occupy your mind for as long as you are seated.

CHAPTER 1: THE VIEW FROM ONE BUCKET CREEK

> " YOU WILL BECOME
> DISORIENTED IN THE FOREST,
> AND WHEN YOU TRY TO
> RETURN TO THE CABIN, YOU WILL
> NOT FIND THE PATH…

If you set out to search for the community of One Bucket Creek, you will never find it. It slips from the view of the seeker like a mirage, like the end of an interrupted dream. The few shy souls who make this scattering of cabins in the boreal forest their home have no desire to be tracked down, mapped, or discovered;

but if one day, called perhaps by nothing more than a whim, you should chance to travel out past the pavement, past the gravel, past the good dirt road, out to the ruts and the puddles, where fallen trees lie across the trail for days before anyone troubles to move them, you might happen upon the rutted track that leads down to the mayor's house, where the creek washes the doorstep in high water, where the leaves of autumn lie unswept until the next summer's winds carry them off, where the pig cleans the table scraps from the yard, and the dog patrols for squirrels until the bitter days of winter drive squirrel and dog alike to move to shelter, one in the depths of a nest of dismantled pine-cones and stolen insulation, the other on an old rug, in front of a smoky cookstove,

and if beckoned by something you don't understand or recognize you wander in, unexpected, unexpecting, you will find a welcome here, of sorts. The mayor, a man of indeterminate age and no particular appearance, cares nothing for strangers, but has a short memory for friends,

so if you arrive at his door, he will assume that he knows you, and before you can spoil his illusion and your own welcome by attempting to introduce yourself, he'll have you planted at his kitchen table, facing a mug of black, bitter coffee, and telling him what you've been up to since he saw you last;

and if you argue, if you attempt to correct the misunderstanding, the mayor will not ask you to leave, for it is not the way of the Creek to argue with a guest. Hizonner will simply get up and walk out the door, as if to answer the call of nature, and not come back, till, eventually tiring of waiting alone in a stranger's kitchen, you will get up from the table, step out the door, and walk down the path to look for him. You will become disoriented in the forest, and when you try to return to the cabin, you will not find the path, or you will find two paths, three, five, a dozen, each leading nowhere and everywhere.

In the end, with night and panic closing in, you will think you hear a motor running, and you will hurry toward the sound, and there, along a disused road, you will find your own vehicle, idling, warm. Don't bother to try and make your way back, or to seek out other cabins. Even after you have been there once, you can never find One Bucket Creek, except by accident.

The Arts Are Flourishing in One Bucket Creek

NOVEMBER 2000

There was a time when the only Arts at One Bucket Creek ran a construction company. Big Art did the surveying and carpentry and Art Junior handled plumbing and electrical. That was back in the good old days, when the Yukon had an economy. Now with everybody laid off and pogey harder to get than a straight answer in Question Period, nobody can afford to build anything.

With the economy missing, there are only two kinds of employment available: government work and the Arts. The neighbouring town of Whitehorse has the franchise on the former field of endeavour, so we here at One Bucket Creek have turned our hand to the latter. Nowadays, the Arts are flourishing in the valley: Big Art is a collage designer, and Art Junior writes romance novels. They both find it easier on the back than construction.

To understand how it's possible for artists to get by without an economy, you must first understand that a living for an artist is not quite the same as a living for a construction worker. As a matter of fact, it can be a lot less money.

The Arts don't need to eat fresh fruit and red meat anymore since they work sitting down, and they don't spend as much money on clothes because they don't work outdoors in winter anymore. Besides that, they're always able to scavenge stuff that the government workers up in Whitehorse throw away, so they don't really miss the big paycheques. But one thing artists do require in order to survive is the occasional government grant. They don't expect it to be much: enough to last the average construction guy two weeks will see an artist through six months of creativity.

So there was panic today in One Bucket Creek when word got out that Canada's Minister Of Fun, Sheila ("I'll quit if Free Trade goes ahead") Copps had announced $600 million in new spending commitments to the arts. Beyond a shadow of a doubt, this announcement means that federal funding for the arts in Canada is doomed. If you have any doubt of this, take a look at the document in which Copps's pledge is made: that's right, it's Red Book Three. So that means we can expect to get our next arts grants when the promises from Red Books One and Two have been fulfilled, or right after the Ayatollah Day shows up for a photo-op in a pink tutu and vows to legalize gay marriage.

Oh sure, we'd like the six hundred mil. It would make about fifty bucks apiece for all the artistes-nouveau in regions like the Yukon that used to have an economy and now have arts instead, and that's fifty bucks we'd be glad of. But we have to tell you Sheila, we're not holding our breath.

THE ARTS ARE FLOURISHING AT ONE BUCKET CREEK

The Honourable
Minister of Fun
1996-2003

The Old Wild Bill & Rambling Rick Logging Company

JUNE 1998

Modernization in the North comes in many forms, not all of them bad. Hot and cold running water at the One Bucket Hilton, for instance, was very well received, whereas armed robberies in Whitehorse have been less popular. Other such modernities as party politics and commercial logging have been given more mixed reviews. With all the talk about the timber harvest these days, you might think that no-one has ever tried to log the Yukon's forests before. Not so.

Old-timers along One Bucket Creek recall a day when the industry almost got off to a roaring start right here. That was nearly two decades ago, when Old Wild Bill's mom bought him a new chainsaw, and he traded in his pick-up for a five-ton with a red button on the gearshift that made the motor go vroom on the uphills. Bill was so excited that he took off his Carpenters Union baseball cap and wrote Mac-Blo on the front with a magic marker he borrowed from the new hippies up the road. He'd been working in construction in Whitehorse, but it was too hard to keep an eye on his horses from there, so when his mom sent him the money for that chainsaw, he knew right away that his future lay in the logging business. There were a number of trees along the part of One Bucket Creek where Bill's horses liked to hang out, and a road that was mostly made by Bill roaming around with the window down listening for the sound of the bell-mare, so all he really had to do was get himself a permit and go straight to work.

Bill was not without some experience in the logging business; his career had been intense, though short. As a young man in BC he was given the job of blowing a whistle to indicate that the chokers were all set, and it was okay to fire up the steam donkey and drag the logs on out of there. The official name of this position was 'whistlepunk', and it was the custom to address the worker in question as 'Punk', regardless of his age, appearance, or standard of behaviour. Had Bill been informed of this fact beforehand, his term of employment might have lasted longer than it did. As it was, Bill took exception to this particular nominative of address on the very first occasion that he heard it, and the foreman, when he regained consciousness, took exception to Bill's reaction. Wild Bill ceased to be a logger at that time.

But that was when he was Young Wild Bill. As Old Wild Bill he had a cooler and more businesslike head, and would have been well on his way to the big-time had he not, on the first day of operations, backed the three-ton with the red button on the gearshift over the new chainsaw that his mom bought him, and effectively put himself out of business.

Old Wild Bill decided then that he needed a partner: preferably one with a chainsaw, and so it was that the company of Old Wild Bill and Rambling Rick Ltd. came into existence. Being a newly formed company, it was necessary for OWBRR to make a new arrangement with the Forestry, who even in those pioneering times liked the paperwork to be just so.

On the morning that they were scheduled to meet the Forestry Guy at his office, Bill and Rick got up early and set out for town in the three-ton without taking the time for breakfast. When they arrived at the office they found that the Forestry Guy, whose boss was far away in another time zone, was not at work yet, and being in need of sustenance they decided to head for the nearest convenient place where they could get a bite, which happened to be the tavern up the road.

Breakfast took a little longer than our heroes had anticipated, and they returned to find the

F.G. waiting for them with the maps of One Bucket Creek spread all over his desk. It is at this point that our story turns ugly. Here, what might have been one of the great resource-industry successes in the history of One Bucket Creek went seriously sour. Because, you see, something in that breakfast disagreed with Rambling Rick. This is no reflection on the tavern's bill of fare, since Old Wild Bill had exactly the same breakfast and he was fine, but Rick's stomach was of a more delicate sort, and his reaction was unpleasant, both to experience and to witness.

In this, as in so many of history's critical moments, timing played a crucial role. Had Rambling Rick's stomach reacted outside the tavern, no-one would have noticed. Had it reacted inside Bill's three-ton the unpleasantness could have been dealt with. But when it reacted in the forester's office, irreparably damaging a set of maps belonging to Her Majesty's Colonial Service, corporate-government relations in the Yukon took a turn for the worse from which they have yet to recover.

Until now, the secret has never been revealed, but on that unhappy morning logging in the Yukon became the chancy proposition which it has remained to this day. Representatives of today's loggers might do well to come to the negotiating table prepared to assure the Forestry Guy that OWBRR Ltd. is no part of their association. You never know: remove one stumbling block, and the whole process might just open right up.

This is a true story. Or true-ish. My old friend, the late Bill Lynn, quit indulging in tavern breakfasts soon after this incident, or as he liked to put it, "gave that drinkin' a kick in the ass." Bill never did make a great success out of logging, but he was a brilliant horseman, and is in fact the only person I know who left the Yukon on horseback, down the old Telegraph Trail. At this writing, Rambling Rick is still alive, and for that reason, I think it best to remain discreet about his true identity, except to say he lives in Carcross, and is no longer involved in the logging industry. Another friend knows the Forestry Guy quite well, and tells me he denies all knowledge of the incident related here. I can only say I've passed it along exactly as Bill and Rick told it to me, to the best of my memory.

THE OWBRR LOGGING CO.

Come to Sunny One Bucket Creek

AUGUST 1997

The sun shines over One Bucket Creek today, and the glimmer of last night's rain is beginning to disappear from the leaves. Birds sing, gophers scurry, folks are busy testing out their decks and patios. But beneath this idyllic scene seethes an undercurrent of worry. As we sip our cool lemonades, or what have you, deep in all our minds is one burning question: where did those darn tourists go?

Now there's been trouble in the past over whether we actually wanted any tourists out here. Some citizens have been wanting to put the pot-holes back in the One Bucket Creek Road, just to slow down the number of visitors, while others can't wait for election year, so we can get another few miles paved. Whether you want tourists or not tends to depend on whether you can make any money off them. As it turns out, the Mayor and Council all own bed-and-breakfasts, except for the Upstream member, who has a canoe, and wants to take tours down the creek, and the Midstream Member, who has horses and wants to do a bit of dude-ranching, so the pro-tourism faction has won out.

Trouble is, there's no tourists.

So where have they all gone? First, someone said that BC Premier Glen Clarke stole them. Right away the mayor wanted to sue, but council convinced him that any mayor that tried that would look like a total jerk, so he called it off. There was talk that we could sue the US govern-ment, because Alaskan tourist operators were taking dollars destined for Canadian pockets, but it was pointed out that, while the United States may not walk so softly any more, it still carries a very big stick. So the Council recently sent *Nordicity* on a mission to seek out the places where tourists go, to discover our inner tourists, and report back on what it is that a tourist wants.

Our findings were as follows. Tourists want a decent cup of coffee. They haven't had one since they left home, and they are climbing the walls. All of the highways we explored, with the exception of those within the 50-mile Compulsory Great Coffee Zone around Seattle, served a substance known as coffee, but actually made by dipping a used drip filter into a gallon of hot water.

Nordicity recommends that the council put a huge sign at the end of the road which reads, "Great Coffee, made from real beans." Next, the tourist is looking for cheap gas. In particular, the RV tourist is looking desperately for cheap gas, since the rig gets about six miles to the gallon. The majority are capable of multiplying by four, and can figure out that 70 cents a litre is about $2.80 a gallon. Don't ask them to do the US to Canadian dollar calculation, though, nobody wants to do decimal fractions on their vacation. It's simply, "$2.80 a gallon? Let's find the quickest way out of here, Martha!"

Nordicity recommends that the council put signs up all along the highway which read, "Gas at 30.9/ gallon ..." with arrows pointing down the OBC Road. At the end of the road put a sign that says, "... would be great. Enjoy your stay at One Bucket Creek." With any luck they'll get flat tires from all the rocks in the road, and they'll be stuck in One Bucket Creek for the two days it takes to get the flats hauled to Whitehorse and fixed.

Thirdly, the tourist wants information. You're driving along the highway, and you see trees, and you see mountains, and you sometimes see signs advertising this and that, but if you want to know what's really in an area to attract tourists, it's hard to know without getting off the road. Trouble is, if you get off the road, and you don't find anything to do, you've wasted time, and this trip is costing

13

a fortune, and you can't afford to waste time. The worst thing you can do to a tourist is to hide the tourism information away downtown.

Now there's an ugly-looking shack on the highway just next to the One Bucket Creek Road, and *Nordicity*'s recommendation to the Mayor and Council is, don't let the look of the place worry you, tourists will never remember what the building looked like. Just put in lots of maps, and someplace to pee in private, and they'll love you forever. The third thing road tourists want is something to do that doesn't take long. There's only so many days to see so much territory. A four hour trail ride is a big decision for many tourists; a ten-hour paddle down One Bucket Creek is out of the question.

Fourth and last, the road tourist is sick to death of looking at signs, even though they are still desperate to read that one sign that will tell them something they actually need to know. Our final recommendation is as follows. Amalgamate the highway signs, so that one sign covers all the things a tourist wants.

"Great Coffee at One Bucket Creek Made From Real Beans.
Gas at 30.9 a gallon…
See Everything in Two Hours!
No Ugly Road Signs Like This At Scenic One Bucket Creek."

The Glen Clarke reference: according to the New York Times, no less, "Among the great con men, some argue, are Dawson's municipal leaders," and former Dawson City mayor Peter Jenkins is the first example they offer. Re-elected after having been convicted of perjury when he was charged with tampering with the electrical meter in his hotel, Jenkins was popular with the Dawson voters, always an outlaw crowd, because he once bought a satellite TV subscription under the names of Tagish Charlie and Skookum Jim – two of the long-dead pioneers who discovered gold in the Klondike – and then broadcast the signal free of charge to the whole town. When I was living at the Downtown Hotel while building the Dawson school, I spent many happy hours watching free HBO courtesy of "Pirate Pete." Mayor Jenkins really, truly, did propose that the Yukon sue the then-premier of British Columbia for stealing all the tourists.

Smart Bombs Don't Use Toilet Paper

It's chaos at One Bucket Creek. Ever since the rumour went about that Russia was going to bomb Canada in retaliation for the war in Yugoslavia, people have been getting into a terrible flap. There's no telling where it could end. At first, we were all feeling pretty defiant. We'd heard about how the Serbs are having festivals and parties every day and night to keep their spirits up, and we figured that would work for us too, so on the very first day after the missile threat the mayor announced a big bash in his barn to celebrate Not Bombed Yet Day.

Hizonner had a new batch of home-brew ready, and we all had a great time, so we decided to have another party the next day, and call it Still Not Bombed Day. One of the councillors had her own batch of beer ready, so we could just as easily have called it Still Bombed Day, but that wasn't what we were celebrating. About halfway into the second batch of brew the trouble started. Someone said we had nothing to worry about really, because everybody these days was using those smart bombs that cost about a million apiece to build and launch, and who could afford to waste them on a bunch of old back-to-the-landers out in the middle of nowhere?

Someone replied that Russia could never afford million-dollar smart bombs; they can't even keep their space station supplied with toilet paper. But Hizonner pointed out that no matter how smart a bomb is, it doesn't clean up after itself, and doesn't have any use for toilet paper, and anyway, the money spent on war doesn't count when you calculate your national budget.

Take a look at our own government, he said. They're so panicked about the deficit they'd sooner let you die in a ditch than spend money on a hospital bed, but let Uncle Sam whistle a couple of lines from The Battle Hymn Of The Republic, and Old Bareknuckles comes roaring in, guns a-blazing and million-dollar bills flying out of his pockets. By the same token, no doubt the Russian army has the best technology vodka can buy.

But, someone said, what if they're in the same boat as us? NATO's bombs may be oozing with grey matter, Mensa candidates every one, but they're being dropped by guys you wouldn't trust to deliver pizza back home; you'd send them to take a large pepperoni and mushroom to an armoured personnel carrier full of Serb soldiers, and likely as not they'd go and give it to a tractor-load of refugees.

After a week and a half of Still Not Bombed Days, some folks were starting to get a bit on the edgy side. Chores were being neglected, hangovers were acute. And you couldn't turn on the radio to get the latest update on the Gretzky situation without hearing more bad news about Serbia. Take Pancevo, for instance. That's a town to the north of Belgrade that used to have a chemical plant where they manufactured military products like farm fertilizer. NATO bombed it this week. We were all pretty worried about that, because almost everybody out here has a horse or a couple of pigs, and if the Russians decided to retaliate, any one of us has a pile of fertilizer that could be targeted.

But the biggest cries of outrage came when we heard about the environmental damage done by the air-strike. Tonnes of highly toxic phosgene-caronyl chloride, carbon monoxide, and hydrochloric acid were spewn into the air or dumped in the formerly beautiful, formerly blue, Danube, without a by-your-leave or a may-I. Is this fair? Some of us have waited months for a permit just to put up an outhouse.

One thing we're all agreed on is that it's time they stopped this stupid war so we can all get on with real life. Why, I'll bet there were three days last week when Gretzky was pushed off the front page. The papers are so full of carnage they haven't even had a chance to say what colour of underwear The Great One had on when he played his last game. Now I ask you, is that any way to treat a national hero?

The pizza reference: during the 1999 Kosovo civil war, a NATO air strike slaughtered a trailer-load of ethnic-Albanian refugees, being towed behind a farm tractor. It was a bit of an embarrassment, since not only were they innocent civilians, and pretty obvious ones at that, they were on our side. NATO offered the excuse that the pilot had mistaken the tractor for a Serbian armoured car.

Old Bareknuckles was my personal nickname for former prime minister Jean Chretien, who earned the sobriquet by assaulting an anti-poverty protester at a speaking engagement in 1996.

SMART BOMBS

Contents: Foreign Visitors. Use No Hooks.

Yukon tourism is at a lull during the months of October and November. Slogans like "It's Still Not Forty Below," and "The Skiing Gets Better If You Wait A While," are not drawing the anticipated numbers of early winter visitors. It was hoped that the Tourism Investor Fund would help to take up the slack, but to date the idea hasn't met with much success. This program was modelled after the Immigrant Investor program, which gives wealthy applicants first chance at Canadian citizenship. Under the TIF program, Investor Tourists were to receive special, courteous service at hotels and restaurants. The web page, www.suckers.com, was visited 300,000 times in the first five minutes, but resulted in no new bookings. Researchers theorize that the slogan, *Wenn Sie Haben Das Geld, Wir Sprechen Deutsch*, might need some fine-tuning.

The One Bucket Creek Visitor Association doesn't have the resources to pursue foreign business with the kind of aggressive campaign being waged by Tourism Yukon. We did have a great idea for our own web page, but we'd used up all our webbing making snowshoe bindings.

We were excited at first by rumours of a program initiative from the Yukon's newest MLA, but on reflection we doubt whether genetic engineering has yet progressed to the point where tourists can be raised from sourdough starter. Upon reviewing the options, the One Bucket Creek Council has decided to embark on an experiment, one which we feel will put us at the forefront of tourism research. On the initiative of the Fun And Nightlife Management Board, we're testing the controversial catch-and-release tourism method. Under this program, tourist operators are allowed to get a visitor into their boat, B&B, gas-station, or bar, by any means necessary so long as they return it unharmed to its natural environment.

Catch-and-release tourism has raised a storm of controversy around the globe. Proponents say that, if properly handled, most species of visitor may be returned to their natural habitat without risk to survival or reproductive capability. Opponents of the practice claim that, since wilderness tourism is an activity which takes place out of the public eye, it's almost impossible to police. Who's to say whether operators are wearing gloves to handle their catch, and taking care not to damage sensitive spending apparatus?

A similar program has met with only limited success in Australia, where, according to an industry report, "The codders brodged the walla and dunnied all the poddies." It is in order to avoid just such a disaster here that the Yukon Government tracks the success of tourist-trapping with its annual visitor exit poll. By catching and examining each tourist as it leaves the territory, biologists are able to determine whether prime breeding specimens are being released back into the ecosystem in fit condition.

Studies indicate that human stocks around the world are not currently under threat from catch-and-release tourism. In fact, since the practice began, the earth's human population has swollen to more than six billion. In the words of an industry spokesperson: "These figures prove that, if properly handled, most tourists can be caught again and again, and still survive to spawn successfully."

Comparisons to the Yukon government's failed catch-and-release voter program are meaningless, according to the chair of the management board. "We have reason to believe that voter stocks in Lake Laberge were damaged by careless handling," he said. "Next time, we recommend kid gloves."

The sourdough starter gag, and the Lake Laberge voters gag: Pam Buckway was a well-known and popular radio host when she ran for, and won, the riding of Lake Laberge in the Yukon Legislature. In her radio days, Pam was big on keeping old Yukon traditions alive. In particular, she set great store by a sourdough starter that came over the Chilkoot in 1898. The kid-gloves remark relates to the circumstances of the bi-election; the previous MLA had abandoned his post because he felt like it, and Buckway, a strong candidate in her own right, ran with a tailwind of voter anger.

A Night At The Ice Hotel? No Sweat

JANUARY 2001

Quiz: what do you get for $100 bucks a night in Quebec? Answer: a block of ice covered by a sheet of plywood, deer pelts, and an arctic sleeping bag with liner. Quiz question two: why does anyone pay $100 a night to sleep on a block of ice? Answer: *je ne sais pas*. But they do.

If you missed last week's *Yukon News* you probably think I'm kidding. But no, or *mais non*, as they say in Beauport, Que., the home of the Hotel de Glace: this is a true story: it's a hotel made from 4,150 tonnes of ice and snow. (For the benefit of unilingual readers, *Nordicity*'s research staff has established that "tonne" is French for "way more than a ton.") The hotel employs – I swear – a survival specialist, who is also, and this too is the truth, the bartender. "If you sweat, you're done," he told the guests, right in front of a New York Times stringer. "*C'est fini*," he added, for the local audience.

It probably would have been best if he'd stuck to French for the entire speech. If you're going to cast doubts on the survival rate among your employer's clients, and do it in the hearing of an agent of the world's largest news services, it would be wisest to avoid speaking in a language his readers understand.

Speaking strictly for myself, I don't much enjoy sweating in hotels, but one thing I do try to insist on, as an occasional hotel patron, is that, should I happen to perspire in the night, *c'est* will not be *fini* as a result. One Bucket Creek has been buzzing with the news about the Ice Hotel since Wednesday, which was the first day anybody made it into town to pick up a paper. The weather's been so nice around here that we don't like to waste time on the road.

Besides, there's not much point in going to town, since hardly anybody in the valley has any money to spend anyway. So we tend to stay home. Of course, it means that supplies do run short, but somebody's always got some moose meat, and someone else has

> "THE HOTEL EMPLOYS—
> I SWEAR—A SURVIVAL
> SPECIALIST, WHO IS ALSO,
> AND THIS TOO IS THE TRUTH,
> THE BARTENDER.

a batch of homebrew or a cellar full of spuds, so life goes on in the slow lane. But when we heard about the Ice Hotel, and how people are actually paying to huddle down in their sleeping bags and defy the winter air, a lot of Creekies began to see a way we can get along in the new absence of economy.

You see, chilly as it sounds, the temperature in the Hotel de Glace isn't really that bad, by One Bucket Creek standards. According to the article, it "hovers around freezing." Most of us have a back-room on the opposite side of the house from the woodstove, and the temperature in there usually hovers around cold enough to freeze the balls on a pawn-shop sign.

We've got plenty of old hides kicking around, and everybody owns a good warm sleeping bag and a scrap of plywood. Judging by the story in the paper, all you really need to attract the customers is a cold place to sleep and lots of vodka. We're pretty sure we can manage those things. As a promotion, we've decided to invite a bunch of people who are well known to need a bit of cooling to come on out and spend a night. If they come out of the experience and do something rational for a change, the health benefits of life in the Ice Rooms will be proven, and customers will flock to One Bucket Creek. We thought we might start with Whitehorse City Council.

Different Sex Couples Need Love Too

FEBRUARY 2000

A chill wind blows over One Bucket Creek this morning. The mayor has his chores done and is relaxing in the warm kitchen with a cup of his famous coffee, black and bitter. He doesn't have much to do today, so he's taking the time to mull over some of the things he's been reading in the big city newspapers.

He wonders why the *Globe and Mail* had to pay some business reporter to explain that "there may be a limit to how much expansion the market can handle when it comes to big box stores." It seems pretty obvious to him. For one thing, if the boxes get any bigger than eight feet across, how will they get them in the freight doors? Besides, how big of a box does the average consumer need? The largest container Hizonner has ever wanted would have been about eight feet cubed, just big enough to put his in-laws in to ship them back South.

Another story in the Report On Business reads, "Aurora Foods Executives Resign Amid Probe." The mayor figures the headline writer must have got that one backwards. Hizonner had to get a probe at the hospital in Whitehorse one time, and it was it that got amid him. But the story that's really got the mayor puzzled is the news that the government in Ottawa is in the process of introducing legislation on same sex benefits. Introducing it to whom, he wonders?

Who wants to meet a piece of legislation?

And what are the benefits of same sex? Hizonner's been having pretty much the same sex for over thirty years, and although he's not complaining, if the first lady took it into her head to want a bit of a change some day, he would be willing to give it a try, within reason. There's been some talk of giving pensions to same sex couples, but the mayor doesn't see the sense in that at all. Not that he couldn't use the money, but to him it sounds like discrimination. After all, if couples that have the same old sex get a pension, why shouldn't we extend the privilege to couples who like a little something different once in a while?

And how strong does the similarity have to be from one Sunday afternoon to the next for a couple to claim same-sex status? Some weeks the first lady likes to wear a frilly nightie she bought on vacation in Dawson City a few years back. Would that constitute different sex, and disqualify them from getting a pension? And anyway, who's going to know if people have a bit of different sex once in a while? Is there going to be a monitoring system of some kind? Hizonner's pretty sure he remembers the government getting out of the nation's bedrooms a few years back. Surely that still applies, even if your bedroom's only a loft over the kitchen.

DIFFERENT SEX COUPLES
NEED LOVE TOO

Sex and gender confusion at One Bucket creek

One Bucket Creek: Home Of The Government Grant

A cloudless blue sky smiles down on One Bucket Creek, and soft river breezes murmur among the aspens. If there is a Paradise on Earth, then surely this is it. At least for today. Don't bother to pack up the van and head out into the South Yukon bush searching for us, One Bucket Creek is one of those magical places which can never be found except by accident. Some people say it's because we live in a mystical kingdom. Others blame the signpost.

The original One Bucket Creek welcome sign was a victim of politics. A new council came in a few years back and needed something to change, so they tore down the welcome sign and put a new one down at the end of the road. They said that way the tourists would have to come in just to read it. We're getting ready to put the sign back where it belongs now, but there's talk that we should get a new slogan to paint on it, the same as Whitehorse is doing. The old slogan was "One Bucket Creek: You Can't Get There From Here," but that was back in the good old days, when the local economy was booming along on the 10-42 UIC system. It doesn't fit very well with our aggressive new tourism marketing program.

The Creek Council doesn't deny that we're a bit behind the city on this one. Whitehorse announced their intention to come up with a new motto last week, and they've already got dibs on several ideas. So until they make up their minds, we can't use "Cappuccino Capital of the North," "Canada's Fast Food Mecca," or "Don't Worry, We'll Keep A Lid On The Duke." That's OK, none of those fit very well for us. We have no Cappuccino joints, no donut holes, and all of our councillors are trained to engage their brains prior to firing up their tongues.

By the same token, we don't care if Whitehorse has first option on slogans like "The Food Tastes Better Than It Looks," and "Worth The Extra Expense." They can keep "Where The Shortest Distance Between Two Points Is Under Construction" too, and "Home of the Wide Sidewalks" is no use to us.

But we don't think it's fair if they take "You Think Our Bugs Are Bad, Wait Till You See Anchorage," or, "They Don't Speak German in Fairbanks Either." We might want to use one of those. We also had our eye on "Empty Your Chemical Toilet Somewhere Else," but that's tied up for now. We're not too worried, though, tonight's the monthly Bingo and Social Tea, down at the mayoral barn, and Hizonner has ten cases of home-brew on ice in honour of the hot

The Duke

weather. You can bet that by the time the sun goes down, the valley will have a new slogan.

I hope we manage to come up with something good, because the favourite right now is not destined to endear us to our neighbours. City folks have been driving the South Klondike Highway for years, keeping an eye out for the elusive entrance to our little heaven on earth. Imagine how they'd feel if the first time they actually spied the intersection there was a big plywood sign beside it reading, "One Bucket Creek: Cheer Up, At Least It's Not Whitehorse."

This column is such a jumble of obscure references from the time I almost left it out. But it made me laugh, so here it is. The background story was that a newly elected government had decided to dump the new modern visitor reception centre on the highway near the airport (now redesigned as the Beringia Centre) and build a nice Yukony-looking faux-log thingie downtown. The original building had won an architecture award, but a lot of people, or at least the new minister, found it ugly. At about the same time this decision was announced, Whitehorse City Council went public with their search for a new city slogan. The Duke is my old fried Duke Connelly, at the time an outspoken and often controversial city councillor.

Senate Seats, Going Cheap

SEPTEMBER 1997

Land prices in One Bucket Creek have just shot up. No, it had nothing to do with upcoming civil elections; Hizonner has been acclaimed once again, because no one else wants the job. And since council meetings are held in his crew-cab, the mayor himself gets to appoint all the councillors.

No, the fact is, we've just learned that we're sitting on one of Canada's most valuable commodities, Senate Qualification Parcels. An SQP is an otherwise useless piece of land owned by, or available for ownership by, a member of the Canadian Senate. Section 23 of the British North America Act requires that senators hold "real and personal property" which is to say privately owned land, worth $4,000. According to the *Globe and Mail*, one parcel of swamp in Quebec's Nicolet region has now served to qualify two consecutive appointees to the Senate.

When we first heard of this scam, folks out here in One Bucket Creek were skeptical. None of the parcels of spare moose pasture held by citizens of the Creek are appraised at even close to four grand. No problem. It turns out that appraisal isn't an issue. Before becoming an SQP, the Nicolet parcel was for sale for only $3,000, a problem the prospective senator solved by simply offering four.

So it appears that any piece of land, no matter how useless, becomes an SQP if the senate appointee pays $4,000 for it. When Hizonner heard about this, he immediately hired surveyors to split Mosquito Swamp, his worthless bottom land, into quarter-acre parcels, each valued at guess how much? A bunch of us have joined in the staking rush and are just waiting for the next round of senate appointments to make our fortunes.

A few nervous souls are holding off on the belief that Senate appointments will dry up soon, leaving us all out the cost of the surveys. It seems Old Bareknuckles Jean has vowed to quit burdening the country with overpaid party hacks campaigning on the public dime. We tried to allay those fears. For one thing, the fine print on that promise reads, "as soon as every living breathing Liberal in the country has been appointed," and for another, that was a Red Book promise. Everybody knows those don't count.

Some honest One Bucket Creek folks found the trade in SQPs a bit too shady, but surely this can't be the case: this week in Antigonish, Nova Scotia, a nun acquired one from her church. Yes, the selling of useless land to skirt the intent of the Canadian Constitution – to keep the riff-raff out of the halls of power – has just received the Catholic stamp of legitimacy. Sister Mary Alice Butts has joined the Senate, and to do so she has set aside her vow of poverty – possibly with her fingers crossed – and become the owner of an SQP.

Being a land-owning nun isn't the only thing that sets Sister Peggy, as she's known, apart from the other Chretien appointees. Apparently the good sister is not even a Liberal. So she says, at any rate, and who could argue? True, she was a delegate to the Aylmer Conference, the decade's most important Liberal policy convention, but perhaps she didn't inhale.

We did have a moment of trepidation over the fate of our SQPs when we learned that senators are expected to own land in the riding which they "represent." At present the Yukon is only allowed one senator at a time, but we're not too worried. Old Bareknuckles doesn't seem to be slowing down yet, and if he's appointing Nova Scotian nuns of questionable Liberality, surely some extra Yukon appointments will follow soon.

There are certainly a few qualified individuals around with the money to spare and time on their hands with whom we'd be willing to part just as soon as we've sold them the necessary swamp land. If you're a Yukon Liberal, waiting for the call, act now. Don't waste your money on early electioneering, democracy is a chancy business. Buy a unique One Bucket Creek SQP and secure your future.

CHAPTER 2: **HOW TO MUSH A DOG**

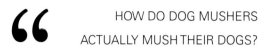

" HOW DO DOG MUSHERS
ACTUALLY MUSH THEIR DOGS?

O ne of the questions we are often asked, here at One Bucket Kennel and Tourism Information Centre, is "How do dog mushers actually mush their dogs?" The answer is, they don't. The dogs are specially bred to be just mushy enough, and not too mushy, and require no extra mushing.

THE DEFLATION OF SCOT MCSNOOD

There's a certain week when the winter bleak begins to turn around.
We fill our packs, board up our shacks, and take a room in town.
There's strange ideas at that time of year, but the strangest I ever knew,
Was to try to erase the dogsled race from Sourdough Rendezvous.
Scot Mcsnood was a trapper good, and he ran his line with dogs.
He was strong and bold and he loved the cold, and his legs were stout as logs.
His dogs were tough and their coats were rough, but they ran like a Norther blue,
and they set the pace in the sled-dog race each year at Rendezvous.

Scot lived his days by the winding ways of a small gold-bearing creek,
And once a year, he packed his gear and headed for Main Street.
Old Whitehorse lies, as the raven flies, a hundred miles from there.
He was down on his luck and he had no truck, so he mushed his dogs to the fair.
Now a hundred miles can be run in style if the trail is hard and fast.
And Scotty's team was a musher's dream, that outran the winter's blast.
But forty below and a foot of snow can slow the swiftest crew.
And it took a week on aching feet to get to Rendezvous.

There was one hotel where they knew Scot well, and they didn't mind his dogs.
So he staked them out in the parking lot, and was soon up sawing logs.
The weather broke when he awoke, and the day was fine and new,
And he went to pay his entry fee to race at Rendezvous.
Mcsnood went down to the end of town where the Yukon River roams,
And there he spied old Pete Garside, standing all alone.
Says Scot, "What's up, where's all the trucks, and the teams, and the mushers, too?"
Says Pete, stone-faced, "There's no dog race this year at Rendezvous."

Says Pete "They say they have to pay too many bills these days.
The Sourdough Board just can't afford to hold a dogsled race.
There's wages, ads, and yuppie fads, it takes a pile of dough.
A quarter mil won't pay the bills, the dog race had to go."
"Well where's the pup that set this up?" says Scot, "I'll see him dead.
No dogsled race? It's a plain disgrace!" Pete says "Don't lose your head!
Some says it's a sign of the times" says he, "Some says it's me and you,
Some says it's Marge at Lake Laberge that cremated Rendezvous."

Now Scot Mcsnood and his lead-dog Dude went sadly down the street.
There was gangs of Yups dressed up as cups and boots and slabs of meat.
There was can-can girls with their hair in curls, showing their skinny thighs,
(There was more they showed, but for all Scot knowed, they could have been veiled to their eyes.)
There was new events for ladies and gents, there was plenty of room to run,
But it seemed to Scot not one in the lot was having any fun.

Says Scot to Dude, "Lets not be rude, it's up to them what they do,
But damn my eyes if you and I will call this Rendezvous."

There was once a week when the winter bleak began to turn around.
We'd fill our packs, board up our shacks, and take a room in town.
We'd have a laugh and spend some cash and watch the races, too.
Now all that's left is to mourn the death of Sourdough Rendezvous.

This poem won the CBC Robert Service Poetry Contest in 1996. Pete Garside was a real person, a long-time dog race volunteer, and he was seriously chuffed to be named in a poem that was aired several times on the radio. Later, when Pete retired from Yukon Electric, his boss asked me to read the poem at his retirement lunch. I couldn't be there, but sent a recording. Later still, when Pete had suffered a series of strokes and wasn't expecting to last long, he asked me to read the poem at his funeral, and I agreed. He bounced back and lived for several years after that, in the Copper Ridge continuing care centre, where I visited him occasionally until his death. When the time came, I found myself at the front of the Anglican church, following beautiful renderings of both Ave Maria and Ecclesiastes 3 ("To everything there is a season, and a time for every purpose under heaven"), and couldn't help feeling just a bit outclassed. But, as someone once said, a promise made is a debt unpaid, so I hitched up my trousers and gave it my all. The writer's life is full of surprises.

THE DEFLATION OF SCOT MCSNOOD

The Art Of Dog Mushing.

NOVEMBER 1998

So you want to take up that most northern of all activities, dog mushing? Here is a step by step plan to follow. Step one: get your head checked. You're nuts.

Of course, since you are nuts anyway, you'll probably enjoy dog-mushing. After all, everybody else in the sport is nuts too. And if you pick your team carefully, there's a fairly good chance the dogs'll be even crazier than you are. So if you've checked, and you are in fact a raving loon, you may be ready to enter the Valley of the Shadow of Debt, also known as dogsled racing. Time to calculate your expenses. We have developed a simple formula for this, based on years of experience in the field. First, estimate the absolute maximum you can afford to spend. Next, double this figure. Now tack on seven percent, and double it again. Or, $2(2B \times 1.7)$ where B = your budget. The same formula will work for your time allocation, too.

Now, to purchase equipment. You will need a sled which is light, strong, easy to pack, easy to drive, and affordable. Do not be daunted by the fact that no such sled exists on the planet earth: dog-mushing is the art of the impossible. When selecting harnesses, remember that your pups will eat them the first time you turn your back. Nylon or polypropylene webbing is very bad for the digestive tracts of young dogs, so a movement is afoot now to construct harnesses of only edible material.

Remember to buy a snow-hook, the dog-musher's anchor. If possible, see that you get one that weighs about twice as much as your sled, and is honed to two deadly, thigh-gripping points, so that when your team bolts away down the trail you stand a chance of being impaled and dragged rather than left behind. The snow-hook is essential, not only for holding the team in place when standing – sort of the musher's equivalent of a parking brake – but also to effect sudden stops. The idea is to throw it around a stout tree while your team is doing thirty miles an hour. Do not attempt this trick unless you have a good relationship with your dogs, as you are liable to end up lying on top of them.

Buy a shovel. You know why you need a shovel, don't you? Good. Enough said.

Now to the fun part of starting up – the acquisition of a team. One thing to remember when shopping for dogs is that most mushers are basically humane, animal-loving folks, who would do anything to keep a useless dog out of the pound – even if it means selling him to you for four hundred dollars.

You will need to decide which breed of dogs to purchase. First, consider what you want from your team. If your aim is to look good in the pictures, you may want to consider the Alaskan Malamute.

Whether silver-grey or black and white, these beautiful dogs can quickly get you on the Yukon tourism calendar, if nowhere else. Make sure you get the picture before the fight breaks out, because red is not their colour. And don't forget that it is accepted wisdom among mushers that the only things dumber than a malamute are, in descending order, a team full of malamutes, and the person driving them. Carry a weapon.

If you'd rather be walrus hunting, then the dog of choice for you may be the Canadian Eskimo Dog. Keep in mind that this animal may have too much nordicity, unless you live north of The Circle. It is said that after one Yukon musher attempted to run the Idiot-arod with Eskimo Dogs the race had to be re-routed to avoid the crater caused by the complete melt-down of the team.

If you are shopping around the racing kennels most of the dogs you will encounter are what is known as Alaskan Huskies. You may find it odd that one yard-full of Alaskan Huskies looks like Whippets, the next like Siberians, and a third like Border Collies. The reason for the confusion is that the Alaskan Husky is not a breed. Nor is it a strain, or even a type. Alaskan Husky is an old Northern term, which, roughly translated, means a-dog-that-I-want-you-to-buy. Tread carefully.

If your interest is in sprint racing, you will need to purchase a particular breed of dogs, not recog-nized by the Canadian Kennel Club, but known throughout the dog-world as ugly little white hound dogs with pink eyes. Don't bother to attempt to sprint race with a more appealing looking breed of dog, the only thing that can go faster than an ugly little white hound dog with pink eyes is a dog musher's paycheque.

Once you have settled on a breed, you will need to look for specific characteristics in the individual dogs. It is said that you should never get any dog that's smarter than you are. This may present some difficulty, since you wouldn't be in this sport in the first place if you had the brains of an Afghan hound, but keep searching: rigorous inbreeding is producing more and more suitable dogs every year.

Once you have the hang of mushing, you may want to try your hand at one of the North's famous long-distance races, the Idiot-arod, and the Moron Quest. One mental-health professional turned dog-musher reports that thousand-mile racing is more fun than two straight weeks on the ECT machine, (although this may be only a matter of taste).   Ok, check-list: sled, dogs, harnesses, snowhook, Visa or Master Charge. All set? Off you go, mush. Oh, you say your eight-hundred dollar lead-dog lay down on the trail, and the rest of the team ran over him? Well, go up and straighten out the tangled lines, and remember next time to spend more money. Happy trails.

One Morning On The Trail

AUGUST 2000

Ok, this is a public confession: I was once a mid-distance dogsled racer. But I didn't inhale, I swear it. So I never really got hooked on that heady thrill of standing half-asleep on a couple of 2 x 2 strips of oak watching a bunch of bored dogs streaking down the trail at exactly 7.25 miles an hour. Honest I didn't. I could have quit any time during those ten years.

Well, alright, there was a brief spell, say four years, that got a bit intense. Not too bad, mind. Just that every race seemed like a cosmic imperative. Something large was going to fall out of the sky if I didn't place in the top whatever-I-was-aiming-at-this-time. It was at the peak of this period that a strange event took place, which eventually led to my withdrawal from the sport of dog-mushing.

It was day two of the Cinnamon Bun Run, a dog race from Braeburn Lodge to the hot-springs area of Whitehorse, and back. The previous day I had helped lead the pack, and cunningly taken every musher in the race, except for one, on a thirty-mile detour. Well, ok, I didn't plan it. I got lost. The trouble was, I was traveling with a wilderness guide and a Mountie and I was kind of letting my attention slip, because who would ever think that those guys would get lost?

Later they informed me that they had been following me, expecting me to know the way, merely because I'd been there before. Well, I ask you. Everybody else followed us, because who would think that a wilderness guide, a mountie, *and* a guy who had been there before would get lost? The one musher who didn't take the thirty mile detour was, guess what, way out in front on day two, and I was asking my dogs for a little extra that day, to catch up.

It must have been about eight in the morning, after a sleepless night. I had left the younger dogs

at the checkpoint, and the team was comprised of only solid, experienced, athletes. (No, the musher is not considered part of the team.) I stopped on Lake Laberge to give the dogs a snack of fish-scraps. When I got to the lead dogs, I gave them an extra piece, and stooped to pat Jet, who was my number one leader at the time.

"Jet," I said, "there's a special treat waiting for you at the other end if you catch that guy for me."

"You know," said the dog, "I'm getting kind of sick of your ego." I rubbed my eyes, and looked at her in disbelief.

"You can't talk to me like that," I said. "In fact, don't talk to me at all. You're a dog."

"Oh, right, now I'm not supposed to talk. What'll it be next? No sniffing crotches?" said Jet. "So what's this special treat, anyway?"

"Liver," I said. "Beef liver."

"Be still my heart. Beef liver."

"I'm not talking to you, I refuse. You're not even a dog, you're a hallucination, that's what you are. Go away."

Jet lay down, and crossed her paws. "Well then, I guess the deal's off," she said.

"What deal?"

"The one where I bust my can for half a pound of liver that's probably labeled not-fit-for-human-consumption."

"What do you mean, the deal's off?" I said. "Get your butt out on that trail, and let's get rolling, there's a team up ahead, and a thousand bucks to be won to pay for your groceries." The dog made no reply. I turned to her partner.

"Minnie," I said, "speak to her. Reason with her, please."

"Minnie?" said Jet. "Are you kidding? You'll wait a long time for her to talk. She's as dumb as a cat."

"Alright," I told her, "I've had enough of this. If you don't get going, you're going to be switching positions with a wheel dog."

"Your wheel dogs are my brothers," smiled Jet, "I've been bossing them around since the womb. They're not going anywhere unless I say so."

"Ok, Ok, you win, we'll talk. What's on your mind?"

"As I was saying, your ego is starting to tick me off. It's not my grocery money we're running for here: second place still pays seven hundred bucks. That'll keep me in the kind of slop you feed for six months. All you're interested in is that trophy, with cinnamon spelled wrong on it."

"Well, my dear Jet, may I remind you that this is a dog race. Competition is sort of the name of the game. And you are a racing dog. It's what we might call your raison d'être."

"There's a whole bunch of racing dogs back at that checkpoint sleeping right now. I could be working for one of those mushers that takes their time."

"Is that what you want?"

"Damn right," said the dog. "It's what I demand. You and I have come to a parting of the ways buster."

"Well, I guess I'll be the one to decide about that."

"Oh yeah?" said Jet, and she smiled, smugly. I tossed my hat on the ground in frustration.

"Let me get this straight," I said. "Are you telling me that unless I agree to sell you to somebody less competitive you're not going to win me this race?"

"Please," said Jet, "don't talk about buying and selling. What do you think I am, your chattel? But basically you have the right idea. You want to win this dog race, I want to be free to seek other employment. Do we have a deal?"

"You mean ...?"

"Yes, I want to be a free agent!"

Jet earned her free agency that day. I wondered what life she would choose. I waited until we were home to bring the matter up.

"Well, what's it to be, old pal? You won the race, now you get to look for a retirement home. What do you fancy? Recreational? Sprint? A stroll through the Yukon Quest? Or did you want to be somebody's pet?"

Nothing from the dog. Not a word. She wagged her tail, licked my hand, whined, did all the usual dog things, but verbal communication skills had she none. Had it really all been a hallucination, brought on by fatigue?

Hallucination or no, I couldn't shake off the feeling that I had made a deal with Jet. It preyed on my mind: a promise made is a debt unpaid, whether the promisee be a loyal lead-dog or a phantasm of the wee small hours. But if I couldn't communicate with the beast, how could I live up to the commitment? The conundrum wore me down. Out on the trail it ate at me like a cancer. Mile after lonely mile on that sled, all I could think of was that circumstance had made me a welsher against my will.

I raced only once more after that, and then hung up my sled. The heart had gone out of it for me. Jet's new job turned out to be on another competitive mid-distance team after all. As far as I can tell, she's happy. I wonder if they've already entered into contract negotiations, or if Jet is saving that up for the right moment. Say on day two of a big race.

I am not the first musher to report uncanny experiences on the trail. Sleeplessness, monotony, and the splendour of the Yukon winter nights combine to create some vivid illusions. Jet and Minnie were both real characters, and Minnie was indeed a dog of little intellect, while Jet could all but talk. I can't remember how much, if any, of this story I hallucinated, and how much I made up later. The wilderness guide and the Mountie were also real, and they really did follow me for miles down what should have been obvious to all of us was the wrong trail. They both still live in the Yukon – in my neighbourhood, now I come to think of it – so I'll refrain from embarrassing them further by naming them here. (You can probably go and look it up).

The True Story Of Iron Will

Some years ago a dog-mushing movie came to town, and being the Northgate Cup Champion, an honour bestowed upon the most persistent loony on the Yukon mid-distance dog-racing circuit, I was invited to participate in a joint promotion of the film and of the sport. My role was to stand in the theatre lobby, holding up a puppy, and looking bearded.

The show was called Iron Will, and I suffered a shock when I recognized that the story was stolen from real life, although it was cunningly placed so far out of context as to be unrecognizable to all but the most savvy of Yukon dog-mushing aficionados. The film sets the story in Minnesota, during the Homburg Hat Era, which was way before the Beatles. In it a young man named Will wins a major dog race despite being robbed, shot, stabbed, poisoned, waylaid, hijacked, seduced, deceived, tortured, and taxed by every baddie in the known universe. 'It's not a matter of strength,' the poster reads, 'or age, or experience. It's a matter of Will. Iron Will.'

The real story began on a January day a couple of years before the film came out, when Lucky Eddie, Yankee Bob, and I set out together for the Dalton Trail Dogsled Race and Roadkill Drinking Biathlon in Haines, Alaska. Lucky and I were traveling together, in his truck, to share expenses. Yankee was our dog-handler, and expert on local customs. In those days I made a practice of forswearing alcohol from January second until my arrival in Dawson on St. Patrick's Day, for the start of the Yukon's biggest mid-distance race, the Percy De Wolfe, at which time I would try to make up for all the beer I had missed in the interim. On this occasion I had considered temporarily rescinding the resolution for the duration of my visit to Alaska, but Herself pointed out that, even in the unlikely event that I should win the dog race, the

thousand dollars US wouldn't cover my outstanding dog-food bill, let alone run to a night of debauchery at the Fort Seward Hotel.

This meant that I was *hors de combat* for the Roadkill event, which involved the consumption of a certain quantity of alcohol, and for this reason was less intimidated than I might have been by the arrival of The Frozen Bluenose, a fierce competitor in both aspects of the Dalton Trail. Frozen had placed second in the previous year's dog race, but had come first overall, by dint of drinking a record five US gallons of roadkill mixture.

On the day of the race, I couldn't help but notice that Frozen seemed nervous, and kept looking up the road.

"What's the matter, Froze?" Lucky asked. "You're favoured to win in two events."

"Nat anymore I'm nat," said Frozen. "Han't you heard Iron William's comin?" A gasp went round the assembly. The legendary Iron William, whose dogs were rumoured to be part cheetah, and whose cast-iron left leg, it was said, could hold three dozen roadkills and never leak? You could see the eyeballs bobbing up and down as each musher present began to re-estimate his potential winnings.

The Frozen Bluenose tried to move casually about the tasks of readying his team, but anyone could see that he was thoroughly unsettled when the world's only Rolls Royce pick-up, emblazoned with a gold-leaf "W," came and parked on his left. Iron William's team of expert handlers scurried about, massaging dogs and applying injections. The Great One himself did not come out of the cab, even when the Trooper fired the shot which signalled the start.

I don't know if you've ever seen one of those mass-start dog races, but let me tell you that at times they can be mass madness, and this was one of those times. Teams were shooting off in all directions, getting tangled, lost, or liberated, and in all the confusion I managed to slip away and be at the front of the pack. The thrill of being in the lead lasted for about half a mile, until I beheld that tell-tale blue streak in the snow which always signals the approach of the Frozen Bluenose. Frozen zipped past me, and I tucked in behind, contenting myself with catching a tail-wind. It seemed that Iron William had failed to start, Lucky Eddie had flown off in the wrong direction, and the first two places were ours for the taking.

And then I heard a strange sound, a soft, rhythmic thump, thump, thump, in the snow, and turning around I beheld the fastest moving dog-team I have ever seen, all looking over their shoulders at the sled, which seemed to be catching up to them as the driver pedalled it along with great thrusts of a stiffened left leg.

"Iron William," Frozen gasped, and then the apparition was around us, and gone. No doubt, if it hadn't been for the freezing rain that day, that's the last we would have seen of Iron until the awards banquet. But Nature will play her part, and when we reached the bottom of the mountain trail which is the principal feature of the race we found Iron William, no longer pumping the sled, and his dogs too played out even to walk.

As I followed Frozen past the forlorn looking Iron, I called out to him. "Do you have trouble?"

"Ya," he replied. "My voon leg is vrozen to ze zled." This called for action. There was more than the race at stake now: there was the code of the trail.

"Good luck," I called, as I waved goodbye.

Frozen won the race. I was second, and Iron William, who had apparently discovered an available source of warm liquid with which to thaw his leg, was third, possibly the lowest placing of his career. But that night, after the awards, the real contest began. Being out of the running, I wandered off to bed. Frozen, I heard, tossed down a dozen or so roadkills, and walked out into the night, a picture of sobriety. They say he wanted to give Iron William a fair and fighting chance to make up for his misfortune in the dog race. It must have been 3AM when I woke to the sound of fingernails scratching across my hotel room door, and a voice calling out, "El, El."

Emerging out of sleep, I struggled to understand. An Englishman swearing? Lucky Eddie trying to remember the alphabet?

"El, El, help, he's got me by ze leg," called the voice of the Legend himself. Another voice followed. It was Lucky Eddie. "Alright you expletive little cabbage, unscrew that leg and pour out those roadkills. There's not an expletive drop left in this whole Yankee expletive, and I'm dying of thirst. Get it out of there before it starts to rust."

"It's not Eyern," the first voice pleaded. "It's voon. And zere's no road-gills inzide, I drank 'em all, vair und zgvare. El, El, help me."

Now Lucky Eddie is not a man to be thwarted when the thirst is on him, and I knew that Iron William was in trouble. To a true dog-musher, the law of the trail prevails at all times; I pulled the pillow over my head. Through the pillow, and through the wall, I still heard the ensuing struggle. "Alright you little quad cranium, gimme that expletive leg."

"No vay, let go, El, El, help."

"Got it, got it. Hey Al, I got his leg, you wanna drink some roadki.... oof."

"Alright, gimme zat leg, ah zole."

"No way, peggy. come and get me." The sound

of two feet, rapidly followed by the sound of one foot, disappeared down the hall, and I returned to a blissful repose.

In the morning, I found Lucky Eddie in a heap on the floor outside the door of my room, wearing right-footed moccasin prints on unexpected parts of his anatomy. Iron William was in his bed, as could be discerned from the sound of peaceful snoring coming through the door. Iron had easily won the roadkill event, and had finally triumphed in the Battle of the Leg. Which only goes to prove that it ain't a matter of strength, or size, or bipedalism.

It's a matter of William. Iron William.

I was at a public event not long after this story appeared, and met a faithful Nordicity reader who complimented me on my imagination. He was impressed that anyone could make up such colourful characters. I told him that Iron William lived in Carcross, Lucky Eddie in Tagish, Yankee Bob in Skagway, and the Frozen Bluenose on the Carcross Road. Since William Kleedehn, the real Iron William, used this piece on his web-site for years, I have no qualms about naming him, and yes, his leg really is wooden, not cast iron, and he really did mush very far, and very successfully on it (and on the other, flesh-and-blood one of course). Sleuth out the rest if you desire. So many years later, they may not wish to see the exploits of their youth bruited about here.

CHAPTER 3: **A NORTHERN BESTIARY**

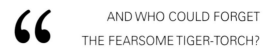

AND WHO COULD FORGET
THE FEARSOME TIGER-TORCH?

W hen writing about the North, it is impossible to avoid the subject of animal life. Whiptail lizards spring immediately to mind, and of course the world-famous Yukon road-chicken. And who could forget the fearsome tiger-torch?

What are Those Birds Doing Martha?

When you think of the King of the Norse Gods, how do you picture him? Big, probably, and with that special kind of quiet dignity that is backed by the threat of having you fed to the eagles if you don't mind your manners. White-haired, heavily bearded, broad shouldered, we all know the image. So it may come as a surprise to some readers that he was also the dweeby kind of guy who keeps oddball pets, and gives them goofy names.

It is a matter of record that Odin was the owner of two pet ravens named Hugin and Munin, who flew off into the wide world each day and returned each evening, unsummoned. It's just as well they didn't have to be summoned; can you imagine the cavalcade of paparazzi if the King of the Gods was going about the neighbourhood calling, "Here Hugin, here Munin"?

At any rate the two were Odin's spies, and were said to travel around observing the behaviour of ordinary mortals and reporting back to the Big Guy. I say, baloney. Any raven observer knows full well what those two were up to all day. First, Hugin and Munin no doubt headed down to the highway to check for roadkills, and then proceeded to the nearest kennel to play at ripping open bags of dog food, to punish the owners for carelessly leaving their valuables unattended for seconds at a time.

Having spent the afternoon in town, dumpster-diving, they would have been back in dog country for feeding time, double-teaming the pups and fighting over the spills, and then off to the mountainsides for an evening of surfing the updraughts. Then they probably went home and made it all up. "Awk, not much happening out there today Boss. Pretty quiet. Did notice a couple of dump fires. Nothing spectacular though. Awk."

Of course the raven, being a bird of unusual intelligence, has occupied a special place in the mythology of any land where it lives. In the legends of our First Nations, the Raven is the Trickster. It is a feature of mythology the world round that whether the Trickster is manifest as Coyote, Spider, Turtle, or Raven, he can spy a plastic garbage bag from three miles away. One famous tale of creation goes that all of the stars and planets came into being with a great bang when Raven flew into heaven's electrical generator, mistaking it for a giant dumpster.

Edgar Allen Poe wasn't the first to assign the raven sinister and prophetic qualities. If Noah had taken the word of the raven who flew out looking for land and came home empty-beaked, the entire animal population of the world might still be stuck in a leaky boat. Instead, that is, of being stuck in a leaky boat again. One thing that got left out of the official telling of that story is that when the Dove came back with an olive branch, Noah declared that she and all her progeny would live in a cozy dovecote all their days, nurtured on the generosity of humans, while the Raven for his bumbling would live on a mountain and eat garbage.

In Calvinist Scotland the raven was again associated with spying: the ever-watchful priests were known as 'corbies', or crows. (Crows and ravens are often confused, although they may seem quite single-minded to the casual observer. When you see them in flight they are simply illustrating the age-old principle of politics, that it's best to pick leaders without much imagination, because it's easier to follow someone who's traveling in a straight line.)

Ravens are known for the range and variety of their vocalizations. They are famous mimics, and indeed, the elders say that the local birds didn't start making the harsh croaking noise most commonly associated with the breed until after they heard their first Scots traders.

But those who love ravens love them best of all for the grace and beauty of their aerobatics. If you never venture far from town you may never see them do much more than plummet from a lamp-post to a parking-lot, and trundle back hoarding a delicious half-chewed bite of Hershey bar with a cigarette butt stuck to the gooey end, but every northern adventurer has a story to tell of sitting on a sandy bank somewhere watching their aerial ballet.

How breathtaking they are as they form into pairs and perform a pas de deux that would make Nureyev and Fontaine look like wooden soldiers. In opposing circles they loop the loop, coordinating their moves perfectly to arrive together first at the top and then at the bottom of the arc. Alternately one and then the other will turn over at the exact instant that they meet, so that their talons touch audibly, they screech together, and then swoop on.

What northern child has not lain on a hillside, chewing a blade of grass, contemplating this marvellous spectacle, and wondering, as the official dump scrounger swoops and dives with unimaginable co-ordination – is that them doing it up there?

Would You Be Careful With That Tail?

AUGUST 1999

These are dark and disturbing times indeed. Did you catch last Friday's *News*? Not only did it lack *Nordicity*, a frightening circumstance on its own, but in its pages male readers learned that we are well on our way to becoming obsolete. That's right. In the usually innocent Alaska Science Forum we read the dark chronicle of the Whiptail Lizard, a species which has developed the ability to reproduce without benefit of the male.

To make matters even more scary, it sounds as if they're having fun doing it, taking turns playing the male role during mating, though whether they are employing their tails in the manner suggested by the name was not entirely clear. As if this weren't alarming enough, CBC Radio reported on Tuesday that biologists are planning to clone the Giant Panda, surely a major advance in our direction from the Scottish Sheep.

If this continues, how long can it be before the human species discovers that single women have been taking out the garbage for themselves for years, and that men are, in fact, completely expendable? True, the lizard does not drive, and therefore has never had to face the flat tire question, but in this day and age, when women have been prime ministers, brain surgeons, and even on rare occasions judges, can anyone doubt that someday they will master even this male-dominated task, and so consign men to the evolutionary junkyard?

When *Nordicity* learned of this dangerous trend, we sent our crack research team to work immediately. Their mission: to find out what women were thinking about the possibility of a life without the male gender. We started by interviewing the Honourable Minister for the One Bucket Creek Women's Directorate. Here is a transcript.

Nordicity: Are you aware of the whiptail lizard situation?

Hon: The what?

Nordicity: The whiptail lizard. They've learned to reproduce without the male.
The females mate with each other, and fertilize each other's eggs.

Hon: Yeah, right.

Nordicity: It's true. It's in the *Yukon News*. I'll show it to you in the morning.

Hon: Is this about *Nordicity*?

Nordicity: Yeah. Don't you think it's a great hook? The Minister for the Wom...

Hon: Don't you dare.

Nordicity: What do you think the lizards have given up by eliminating the male?

Hon: Unfinished nests.

Nordicity: What?

Hon: Their little nests, or holes, or whatever they live in, won't have kitchen cabinets with no doors, or masking tape hanging down from the ceiling. Now will you be quiet? Some of us have work in the morning.

Next, we approached Caitlin of the Short People, a local high-school student.

Nordicity: Are you aware of the whiptail lizard situation?

Caitlin: No.

Nordicity: It's a lizard which has learned to reproduce without males.

Caitlin: Huh. Frogs have been doing that for ages. What does that have to do with anything?

***Nordicity*:** If this trend were to continue, until it reached our own species, what effect do you think it would have on peoples' lives?

Caitlin: Um... (giggle) Um, more women would have jobs?

To find out how this issue was playing out in the artistic community, we consulted the Yukon's number one arts guru, Laurel Parry. It took almost twenty-four hours for Parry to return our call, presumably because she was busy mopping up male tears. The conversation was obscured by background noise. At one point our researcher heard a nasal voice crying out, "I told you they didn't appreciate me."

Expressing deep concern about the situation, Parry stated unequivocally, "Well, you know, I'd have to adapt." We switched on the tape recorder and caught the following, before she had to run out for more Kleenex.

***Nordicity*:** What effect would this have on the arts community?

Parry: Well, book clubs would be a lot easier to organize, but there wouldn't be as much to talk about.

***Nordicity*:** How would it affect the lives of women?

Parry: One thing is, at pot luck suppers, women would get to bring the buns. I'm sorry, just a minute.

Marty, calm down dear, it might never happen. Philip, put that statue down, it's very valuable.

How, we wondered, was this playing in financial circles? We decided to consult Pat, the woman who writes our paycheque.

***Nordicity*:** Are you aware of the whiptail lizard situation?

Pat: Oh, yeah, isn't that a scream?

***Nordicity*:** Scream?

Pat: Yeah, I loved it.

***Nordicity*:** But, don't you think it could lead to disastrous consequences for our own species?

Pat: Like what, for instance?

***Nordicity*:** What do you think women would miss most if the male gender were to disappear?

Pat: Well, it wouldn't be picking up after you, that's for sure.

Does nobody out there take this matter seriously? Market traders, of course, are keeping a close eye on aftershave and beer stocks, but market traders are almost all men, and could be completely redundant in another generation. It is rumoured that condom manufacturers are considering new marketing strategies. "Announcing, new Trojan reusable spice-bags." "Ramses, the heavy-duty balloon, for high-energy parties."

But, again, these are mainly manly voices. The response from the female world has been, to date, a discreet yawn. Listen, ladies, please, have a heart. We don't expect you to keep us around once we're redundant, but we're sensitive. Just say you'll miss us when we're gone, okay? Somebody? Please?

Caitlin, Parry, Pat and the Hon are all real characters, all still living in the Yukon. Philip and Marty are also based on real people, of the sensitive-artist variety, though both have departed for far horizons. Their part in this story is entirely fictitious. The whiptail lizard is real, but never lived here at all.

Make Way For A New Kind Of Pet.

North or south, east or west, it can be a lonely world sometimes. Did you ever think of getting a pet? Something furry and warm that you can just stroke, and then send away, something you can put in a cage at the boarding kennel for two weeks when you go on vacation?

Out of Africa, birthplace of our own species, comes a new and fascinating companion, a ruthless and daring predator that will curl up in a cosy ball at your feet, a brutal sadist that will entertain you by playing with your knitting. If you're thinking of getting a pet, but are bored at the prospect of another gecko, python, or golden retriever, *felis domesticus*, the cat, just might be the dumb chum for you.

First the cat will entertain you at home. Picture your delight when you return from work to discover that the cat has sharpened its claws on the manuscript to your novel, knocked over your favourite houseplant, and defecated in your stereo headphones. There's no end to the jolly antics these furry little cuties can get up to! Mark my words, the cat is the coming thing in house pets. A day will come when folks will say, "A house without a cat is a house without the faint smell of urine."

In the field, the cat is unchallenged in its ability to control pests. A good cat will protect at least twenty acres of ground from the threat of such predators as mice, ground squirrels, squirrels, and ground-nesting birds. Think of it. Acquire one cat, and never again have to put up with indigenous rodents scurrying about your place, whilst wheeling hawks and eagles clutter up the view. Tired of waking up to the shrill piping of the curlews and sandpipers? A cat will soon take care of that.

Although sure to be popular in the country, it is predicted that the cat will reach its true potential as a city pet. Urban cat owners will be able to choose each day between keeping their pet locked up in the house to delight them with their cute carryings-on, or turning them out to reek vengeance on unfriendly neighbours. Neither the gecko nor the retriever are in the cat's league when it comes to neighbour-harassment, although it must be allowed that the python has its merits in this regard. Nonetheless, only the cat has the perfect combination of stealth, agility, and olfactory offensiveness to slip up to the basement window of the people next door, who shovel their snow onto your section of the sidewalk, and render their rec-room uninhabitable for two days.

The cat is a creature of exceptional agility, and every cat born can climb with remarkable haste to the most dizzying of heights. More than half of them can climb back down again too, which is a good thing unless you are fond of tall wobbly ladders. In areas where cats have already taken hold, they have been seen, or heard rather, to add a certain wild and frantic note to the sound of the city at night. What romance awaits us when our streets resound to the lustful call of the mating 'tom-cat', or male cat, and the anguished cries of the confined females.

If all of this doesn't tempt you to own a cat, there's one thing more, the cat's true area of specialization. Other creatures may kill, other creatures may smell bad. Other pets may bring their maimed and desperate prey onto the kitchen floor for a few hours of entertaining torture, others may puke on the living-room rug or make the couch look like it's been through a paper shredder, but in the area of reproduction, can they ever hope to equal the cat?

Consider first the female cat, which can come into heat at six months of age and every six months thereafter, bearing up to a dozen hardy offspring.

This means that by the time she is two years old she may have had as many as thirty-six young. Eighteen of these will be females, twelve will be of reproductive age already. Six will have had one litter, adding seventy-two cats to the list, while the other six will have had two, or a hundred and forty-four.

The first of these litters, six females, will have produced their own young, or another seventy-two cats, thirty-six of them female. So now we have 329 cats, 165 of them breeding females, due to reproduce again in six months and add another 3,948 'kittens', as the young cats are called, to the population. As for the tom-cat he can serve several females a day, and could theoretically be the progenitor of millions by the age of two. And since courtship battles between cats are notoriously fierce, natural selection is sure to continue to refine the species at a terrific rate.

It can only be a matter of a few years as an urban species before felis domesticus evolves into a new breed of super-cat. Do your bit to promote this great advance in civilization. Get a cat. Quick, before it gets you.

The Perfect Pet

AUGUST 2013

Because if it's worth writing once, it's worth writing twice …
I've been thinking I might get myself a cat. Just a fluffy friendly pet that will keep my house free of mice, and my yard free of songbirds. I haven't had a cat in decades, and I've grown to miss the tattered furniture, the hint of urine in the house, the little gifts of desiccated corpses on the doorstep.

Cats are the most versatile of pets, easily switching roles from cuddly companion to serial killer and back again. Though they may seem lazy lying in front of the fireplace at home, out of doors cats are a marvel of industry and efficiency. A study by the Smithsonian Conservation Biology Institute and the Fish and Wildlife Service has determined that cats in the U.S. kill 2.4 billion birds and 12.3 billion mammals a year. Where else do you find that kind of results these days?

Killing mammals is the pet cat's raison d'être. There's nothing like a cat to rid your house of mice, your garden of voles, or your granary of rats. Isn't it great to know that when the job is done, and you let Felix out for the night, he can hone his skills by ridding the planet of small birds and chipmunks? And since the cat, if it's a domestic cat, sleeps indoors and has a guaranteed source of food every day, it can easily outperform natural predators such as foxes, coyotes and hawks, which means it's helping to rid the world of those too.

If you're thinking that we don't need cats, that there are plenty of ways that humans can decimate wildlife populations and threaten biodiversity without resorting to feline predation, consider this. According to the New York Times story on the Smithsonian report, "More birds and mammals die at the mouths of cats, the report said, than from automobile strikes, pesticides and poisons, collisions with skyscrapers and windmills and other so-called anthropogenic causes."

The great thing about a pet cat is that if you get tired of it, or have to move, you can simply abandon the animal, secure in the knowledge that not only can Felix fend for himself, but he will find a plenitude of humanitarians to help him through the lean times. And don't bother getting him neutered before you give him his freedom, the humanitarians will take care of that too.

Humane societies all over the world are adopting the trap, neuter and release, or TNR program. This policy, aimed at controlling the feral cat population without actually killing any cats, is so effective that, according to George Fenwick of the American Bird Conservancy, "the number of free roaming cats is definitively growing. It's estimated that there are now more than 500 TNR colonies in Austin alone."

The beauty of TNR is that while it definitely restricts the breeding habits of the cats involved, it has no effect on the general cat population. The few who escape the dragnet can easily make up the shortfall. Consider that a single breeding pair of cats can produce 12 kittens in its first year of mated bliss. The female kittens will be ready to reproduce the following year, bringing the total to 66. At the end of 10 years, the descendants of that original pair of cats will number 80,399,780.

More good news: those neutered feral cats can still hunt. Felix may not be able to reproduce, but he can live out a long life of slaughter, secure in the knowledge that whenever he has a bad day, there will always be a saucer of milk or a dish of cat food on some kindly doorstep to see him through to kill another day.

Of course there are the irresponsible cat owners, those who neuter their feline friends, keep them indoors, put bells on their collars while they allow them to exercise in a fenced yard, and in all ways stymie their pet's ability to pursue its natural work of species extinction. Not to worry, as long as there are cats there will be owners who give them their freedom to destroy wildlife and make more cats. Steady as she goes, and in a decade or two there won't be much left on the planet but cats.

Yes, I'm going to enjoy my cat. When I'm sitting by the fire, he'll sit with me, cuddling up and purring. When I don't want to cuddle or be purred at, I'll turn him loose to rid the world of cardinals and robins, which in turn will get rid of those bothersome foxes and marsh hawks. Cat owners, all you need to do is maintain your current course, and biodiversity will cease to be an issue on Earth. That is what you're trying to achieve?

If You Go Out In The Woods Tonight

DECEMBER 1996

Shhh. Are they asleep yet? Good. We can talk. Don't you love hibernation season? It's the only break we get from those hairy vandals of the woods. I tell you, it's not safe to walk the paths anymore, ever since this new Ursine Offenders Act came out. Some five-hundred pound lout can commit enter-and-break on your cabin, and even if they do catch him all he gets is a slap on the wrist.

Of course, they do have to shoot him first; well, otherwise they'd never get anybody willing to slap him on the wrist, would they? But have you noticed they never reveal the bear's identity? Unless and until they start publishing the names and addresses of ursine offenders in the local paper, we will never get control of the bear crime situation. As long as bears know that they will be killed with kid gloves, there's no deterrent to stop them from turning into hardened criminals. They may start out small, eating restricted berries or peddling street-carrion, but if they're not taught a good lesson right from the start, the next thing you know they're tearing holes in people's tents and eating their back-packs.

And where are the parents of these criminal louts? When will bear-parents be made to take responsibility for the actions of their children? If every time a bear trashed somebody's camp Renewable Resources went out and slapped his parents on the wrist, first rendering them sufficiently dead to protect the safety of law-enforcement agents, the problem of ursine offenders would soon become a thing of the past.

There has been some debate among bear-care professionals as to whether stricter measures against ursine offenders would actually work. According to a spokesperson for Ursine Services, "They're all pretty dead when they get here. I don't see what difference it makes whether they have colour TV or not. I'd say improved refrigeration would be more to the point, especially with the longer sentences they're getting now."

The outgoing Minister of Ursine Corrections challenges this assertion. "I don't see any reason why we should coddle these hairy hoodlums with fridges, and at the tax-payers expense, too. If the word gets out that things aren't so rosy at the Bear Jail, maybe there'll be fewer of them committing these kinds of crimes in the first place. When it was pointed out that lack of refrigeration causes the bears to rot, leading to a significant health hazard, he replied, "They should have thought of that before they went out and trashed somebody's cabin. Maybe next time they'll think twice before getting involved in criminal activities."

Not content with stricter enforcement of existing legislation, a group of concerned citizens has formed to demand harsher penalties for first offences. "Let's get these characters young, get them into a paw-camp situation like they're using with great success in Ontario, and teach them that society frowns on this kind of thing," a spokesperson for the organization said.

"In the meantime they can be learning valuable skills, and developing some self-esteem, so they don't end up on bear-fare, sponging off society for the rest of their lives.

And what about this bear-relocation program? When are people going to be informed that a potentially dangerous Ursine Offender has been located in their neighbourhood?" When it was pointed out that the bears are invariably relocated to areas which are devoid of human habitation, the spokesperson replied, "So what? What are you,

some kind of bleeding-heart Socialist? It's people like you that want to let the wolves eat all the caribou and get off with only the mildest form of extermination. If the Good Lord hadn't intended us to wipe these critters out, he wouldn't have given us helicopters."

With the money saved on refrigeration, bear-fare, and colour TVs, the territory will be able to pay for a bear-squad of highly-trained special enforcement agents, to catch these furry criminals and turn their lives around when they are little more than bush-wise black bears, before they grow up into full fledged, trail-hardened, recidivist grizzlies.

Then, when you come home to find your camp or cabin has been e-and-b'd, a simple 911 call will bring a team of professionals rushing to the scene. The book of mug-shots will be laid before you on the table, if you still have a table, and a burly, though efficient, police officer will take out a little book, and record your statement. If you become emotional, the officer is trained to help you to calm yourself, using the age-old tried and true law enforcement adage.

"Just the facts Ma'am. The bear facts."

Stalking the Wily Road-Chicken

MARCH 1997

It's been some years now since I gave up going out in the fall to give the local moose population a good giggle at my expense; the humiliation was just too much to bear. I never did shoot a moose, and I never did figure out why. After all, my hunting skills had been honed by many hours of chasing the wily and furtive spruce grouse. You may have read in last week's *News* that even the Yukon's bird biologist enjoys the challenge of stalking the canny road-chicken.

Despite having evolved during an era when the 2x4 was not yet invented, the ever-adaptable spruce grouse has developed a kind of sixth-sense about this weapon, so that the inexperienced hunter has little better than a fifty-fifty chance of sneaking up and bonking one on the head. Many a neophyte grouse hunter has come home with only half his or her bag limit as a result of having failed to practice accurately swinging the 2x4 at home before entering upon the hunt. Experience teaches that, after two or three missed swings, this cagey creature will often surprise the hunter by flying up into a tree. It takes skill and nerve to bring a road-chicken down from a branch by throwing your 2x4 at its head.

Another weapon favoured by grouse hunters is the car-bumper. Although difficult to throw at a treed grouse, the bumper has the advantage over the 2x4, because grouse are congenitally incapable of seeing it coming. For this reason, purists consider the bumper an unsportsmanlike method of hunting. All the same, the guile and cunning of these elusive birds is so legendary that many hunters have been forced to resort to the use of not only the car-bumper, but also the car-door, the windshield, and even the .22 rifle in order to bag their limit. When hunting with a .22, please be advised that it is wise to sight the rifle in before approaching the grouse; these nervous, timid creatures will seldom stand still while more than three or four shots hit the branch on which they stand.

Dogs, the story tells us, are great partners in the hunt. The bird biologist favours the spaniel, though retrievers, setters, and pointers are also used. My own border collie has a couple of unique hunting skills. If I fail to notice a flock of grouse wandering around on the ground twenty feet from my nose, Kerry assists by running into the middle of them, and barking. If the grouse are up in trees, as they often are after she has bravely located them for me, she will discover the only tree around which contains not a road-chicken, but a red squirrel, and point to indicate that I need not bother looking there.

Similar in function to Kerry, but more aggressive in its style, is another type of hunting dog not mentioned in the *News* story, the walk-away dog. The favoured breeds for walk-away dogs are the malamute and the husky. When employing one of these dogs in the hunting of road-chickens, simply position the dog within ten feet of a tree, attach the dog to the tree by a stout chain, and walk away. This will improve your chances of bagging a grouse by a considerable margin.

The male road-chicken is distinguishable from the female by a small red patch over the eye. Sometime in late September, or early October, the large flocks begin to break up into smaller bunches, in which several females group together with a single male. At this time, the extra males hang around by the roadsides playing healthy male-bonding games like running in front of cars, and pinning 'eat me' notes on each other's rumps.

A close relative of the road-chicken is the ruffed grouse, another exciting challenge for the hunter. Many years ago, when it was still legal to hunt moose in the Carcross Valley, a friend and I were returning from a day of airing our rifles on Mount Lorne, when we spied a ruffed grouse cagily hiding on the lower branches of a lone pine tree. Tired from the day's hike, we sat down to discuss the possibility of bagging him, and thus having at least something to show for our exertions. All this time the bird sat stock still on his branch, blending in to the background like a brass band at a funeral.

Finally, since neither of us had thought to bring along a 2x4, bumper, or .22, my friend decided to try a shot with his 30/30 Winchester. Not wishing to convert his prey to *purée d'oiseau*, he aimed for the head, and missed. In an unprecedented display of avian wile, the unscathed bird pretended to be hit, plummeting from the branch and twitching violently on the ground right up until the moment when I ran up to grab it, at which point it cunningly sprang up and began to run around the tree.

The creature led me a merry chase twice around the trunk, and it was only by employing the old hunter's trick of changing directions and meeting it head on that I was able to get my hands on it, and wring its neck, thus effecting my first ever bare-hands kill. After a brief exchange of views on the subject of which of us had actually bagged the grouse we continued home, much compensated for our disappointment at having failed to shoot a moose, fully agreed that there was never such sport as the crafty, flighty, Yukon grouse.

Roadkill Du Jour

JANUARY 2000

The setting sun casts a pink glow on the snow-covered meadows of One Bucket Creek. Within minutes, a curtain of darkness will drop, and the miracle of the stars will slash itself across the sky. A Yukon winter has arrived, in all its terrible beauty. In truth, winter has been so gentle up till now (yes, I am touching wood) that I hardly noticed its arrival. Only the other day I realized that I have stopped scanning the road for Kamikaze gophers.

Few still cling to the discredited belief that the ground squirrels on the summer highways are simply confused rodents trying to make their way to safety. Most observers now agree that an elite corps of suicide-gophers stalks the asphalt, a cadre of fanatics whose purpose is to disrupt human traffic, and who will stop at nothing in their quest for glory.

Contrast these with the innocuous road-chickens which are freeze-up's common highway hazard, and you can see why many rural Yukoners would far prefer to drive when the roads are snow-covered. Oh sure, the road chicken will wait until the shadow of your bumper falls over its head before it flies away, but when it does, you can be sure that it won't turn back for another attempt. The Kamikaze gopher will turn, turn, and turn again in its efforts to make you its personal Jack Kevorkian.

Of course there will be those who will say, Damn the torpedoes, run the little expletives over and forget about them. But that's just not our style out here in the One Bucket Creek Valley. We don't like to kill things we don't plan to eat, and we sure don't plan to eat anything with tire-tracks on its belly.

So we swerve. We take evasive action. Many rural Yukoners have perfected the art of catching the suicide-gophers midway between the wheels, and speeding up to get out of there before they can make a dash for martyrwurst and glory under one side or the other. I, for one, didn't give one single gopher the satisfaction last summer. Time and time again they tried to outwit me, to achieve honour and assure their place in gopher-warrior paradise at my expense, but each attempt only served to hone my gopher-avoidance skills. I was just congratulating myself today on having achieved this perfect score. I was driving down the Robert Service service road, which is the final leg of the voyage from the Creek to Whitehorse. Another season over, I thought, and the relative security of winter arrived.

The service road may or may not have been plowed. It's hard to say for sure whether the bare patch which meanders from lane to lane was created by a snowplough piloted by a drug addict or by the passage of hundreds of commuter vehicles, each following the last. Suffice it to say that whoever blazed the original trail through this year's first snow did so without regard for the shortest distance between two points.

Now given a choice, I am the kind of driver who prefers to follow the roadway as designed by the engineer. Call me conventional, call me timid: it's something I just can't help. Give me those two yellow lines, and I'm your man. Not so whoever laid out this year's winter route down Robert Service. A devil-may-care sort, a driver more concerned with panache than precision, an artist perhaps, he or she described a sweeping arabesque from top to bottom, and we other drivers, like sheep, (if sheep may be said to perform an arabesque) have all followed.

So, as I say, it was on this flamboyance of a roadway that I had my moment of self-satisfaction at the successful conclusion of another gopher season. And moment it was. I had barely returned my hand to the wheel after patting myself on the back when a gruesome image appeared immediately in front of my bumper. It was a cyclist: or I should say, the image of a cyclist, stencilled in off-white on the pavement. My heart sank. Here I was, congratulating myself on the summer's success, and completely forgetting that the worst was yet to come.

What is a gopher, no matter how self-destructive, compared to a winter cyclist? A gopher may dash, it may duck, it may dive. It may ruin your day by making a squelchy splashing noise as it meets its maker under your wheels, but what is the squelch of a three-pound gopher beside that of a hundred-and-fifty-pound health nut? And can a gopher hypnotize you with a flashing blue light? Does a gopher wear a bright orange X on its back to distract you and lure you in? Do the snowplough's tracks lead your car directly over designated gopher areas? As the grizzly image disappeared under my truck I reflected that it never pays to gloat; unto each season cometh the roadkill thereof.

On The Trail Of The Crafty Highway Sign

FEBRUARY 1999

Of all the things which separate the true Northerner from the common herd, the most outstanding must be resourcefulness. (Although, on consideration, blue lips, ugly footwear, and a tendency to believe we know exactly how the government should be run are strong contenders.)

But resourceful we must be, to live in these remote parts. Take the urban Yukoner, for instance. How does the Whitehorse dweller survive the bitter winters, the bug-infested summers, with only four malls, twelve fast-food restaurants, and six espresso bars? Resourcefulness is the answer. Ingenuity. As often as possible, they fly to Vancouver.

Life is even harder in smaller communities such as Dawson, where beleaguered citizens are sometimes forced to survive the cruel winter months with no more than five bars at their disposal. These hardy types seldom complain, though. Showing the true Northern spirit, when times get tough, the tough drive to Whitehorse.

Nor is this traffic only one way. Whitehorse ladies (or wearers of ladies' clothing), who can't afford the trip to Robson Street or Commercial Drive often expand their shopping horizons by taking a trip to Dawson, where two well-stocked shops supply a range of garments not always available here in the city. It is on these trips back and forth between the Yukon's communities that shoppers must keep their eye out for another resourceful group of Northerners, the ever-intrepid sign hunters.

The sign hunter is the perfect example of Yukon ingenuity. A moose or caribou hunter at heart, the sign hunter may have had an unsuccessful year, and be frustrated at the lack of meat in the freezer. Or perhaps he or she, having bagged the winter's provender in one shot, needs to blow off a little steam. Now the game regulations no longer permit the assuaging of these frustrations in the traditional manner, and so you may not, as you once did, blast off a few ravens to empty your clip. To fill this void, the government has provided, in handy locations along the roadways, a selection of highway signs.

The highway sign is not, it is to be admitted, the most challenging of prey. It is neither adept at running, nor skilled at hiding. It does not seek the protection of the herd, nor the safety of the mountain tops. It is poorly camouflaged, and ill equipped to fight back.

On the other hand, the road-sign presents certain challenges which other prey species do not. For instance, as it leaves neither scats nor trail, it is impossible to track the road-sign using traditional methods. Here is an example of the resourcefulness of Yukon hunters: unable to pursue the sign in the usual manner, they have devised the simple but brilliant technique of simply following the roadway.

Another problem which faces the sign hunter is the fact that signs do not mate. This makes it practically impossible to call one. Again, the sign being unequipped with antlers, horns, or external genitalia, only the expert hunter can tell whether the specimen in his sights is male or female. There's been a lot of excitement in the sign hunting community about new types of billboards. The giant game-crossing sign near Braeburn, as an example, is considered a sure Boon and Crocket record breaker for the first hunter to bag it, while the customs warning on the Skagway Road would make a handsome addition to anyone's trophy collection.

But we Northerners have no reason to be smug about our clever utilization of this natural resource. Maritimers, another hardy and ingenious group of Canadians, have been onto the potential of the road sign for years. I learned this fact while on a trip to Mayo with a friend from Cape Breton. I recall that I made a comment about the mentality of the hunter who had come up with the brilliant idea of shooting up the curve signs on the road so that you couldn't tell for sure which direction of curve they were intended to indicate.

"That ain't right," he said, in the authoritative tone of one who knows his traditions. "You're supposed to t'row beer bottles at 'em.

Moose Hunting: A Yukon Primer

SEPTEMBER 2000

Astute readers may have noticed something unusual about *Nordicity* last week, what we might describe as an absence, or, to put it in legal terms, a failure to appear. Fear not: as the observant will, so to speak, observe, we're back. The reason for the previously unexplained lack of *Nordicity* in last Friday's *News* was that the research team was engaged in a study on the practice of moose hunting. This week we are pleased to bring you the results of that inquiry. Our topic for this week: how to hunt a Yukon moose, an easy ten-day primer.

Day one: getting ready to hunt. Begin by making a list. You will require wool pants, winter boots, dry match container, wool socks, flashlight, sleeping bag, pad, tent, rifle, knife, sharpening stone, game bags, and ammo. Be sure to up-end your entire house in search of these items, strewing everything you own about your living-room floor. At this crucial preparatory stage, remember to swear a lot.

Day two: still getting ready to hunt. Beg, borrow, or buy pants, boots, match container, socks, flashlight, etc. Throw away all of your receipts, so that your spouse will not find out that you have already spent enough money on this hunt to keep you in organic beef for longer than your projected life-span.

Day three: getting there. Drive to your chosen hunting spot. Our research indicates that upon arrival you will immediately encounter an enormous bull moose, lying on its side, stone dead, but still warm. Congratulate the successful hunter and move on.

Day four: getting there, continued. Arriving at your second choice of hunting spots, discover a second enormous bull moose, and a second successful hunter, still in a state of high excitement at having made his kill only three minutes and thirteen seconds before you drove up. See instructions for day three.

Day five: still getting there. Drive very quickly to your third choice of hunting spots. Upon arrival, see above instructions.

Days six, seven, and eight: the hunt. Drive despondently up and down the road, staring out at the endless empty buck-brush, swapping stories with your hunting partner about all the bull moose out there aching to leave this cruel life behind. Pause occasionally to roll down the window and make a noise like a sheep impersonating Marilyn Monroe on a cracked trumpet. This is known as "calling a moose," or more precisely, "calling a moose belittling names in moose language and causing it to hide in the bushes until you're out of sight down the road."

Remember to remark at regular intervals that this is the best moose habitat you've ever seen, notwithstanding its apparent lack of living moose.

During this stage of your hunt, take every opportunity to wave pleasantly to all the people who are busily field dressing their moose by the side of the road. This would be a good time to remind yourself and your hunting partner that organic beef is a nutritious alternative to wild game meat.

Incidentally, while engaged on this project the *Nordicity* research team stayed at a number of public campgrounds. While there, we made some inquiries on another matter of interest to our readers: the whereabouts of the Yukon's Premier. You may recall that Premier Duncan's sole promise to date is that she will spend her tenure out among the rural communities, staying in campgrounds and talking to the people. This commitment is widely believed to account for her party's electoral success in Whitehorse, and its complete failure elsewhere.

However, our researchers were unable to discover a single Yukoner who had encountered the premier while camping. While some were irate at this failure to keep the only promise she made, others defended her action on the grounds that the NDP had four years to visit the campgrounds and didn't manage to stay in them all, you can't expect her to repair the damage in five months.

Day nine: in desperation, follow a meandering set of moose tracks deep into thick spruce forest. Remember, you are now stalking game, and must move perfectly soundlessly.

True, the forest floor is carpeted with wall-to-wall dry twigs. The research team found this circumstance particularly amusing in light of the fact that everything else around, including our wool pants, winter boots, and dry match container, were soaking bloody wet.

When the forest becomes impenetrable, you may begin to doubt that a moose could have traveled any farther, and to consider the possibility that the tracks were made by a raven wearing fake moose feet. Make the sheep-Marilyn sound for a while into a forest wall so close and dense that if a moose should happen to blunder along, he will be closer than the end of your gun barrel by the time you see him.

Leave the forest, stomping on every twig on your way out, just to show your defiance. Repeat to yourself the following words. "Highly sensitive ears, is it? Well, hear this: (stomp crash) and this (crash bang)."

Day ten: go home. Unpack your wool pants, winter boots, dry match container, wool socks, flashlight, sleeping bag, tent, rifle, knife, sharpening stone, game bags, and ammo, and store them neatly in a place which you will never be able to remember.

And bear in mind: if properly raised, beef can be a very nutritious food.

Urban Chickens

If you ever have the opportunity to become an op-ed columnist in a local, independent newspaper, I highly recommend that you snatch it up. There can be few activities more rewarding than to vent to thousands of your friends and neighbours every week, knowing that some readers will cheer your words, while others' blood will boil at every sentence.

If there's a downside to being a columnist, it's wondering how much effect you're really having. There's a rule of thumb that suggests one letter to the editor means a hundred people who considered writing, but didn't get around to it. If that ratio holds true, then zero letters to the editor means one hundred times zero people were engaged enough to consider crafting a reply. Hmm.

Sometimes it's tempting to throw a stone in the pond just to see if you can generate some ripples. Like say, for instance, a columnist – a hypothetical columnist that is – should write what he or she believes is a particularly provocative piece. Suppose in that piece he or she were to come down on the presumed-unpopular side of a hot local topic – say, for instance, gun control – and at the same time insult the intelligence of a popular politician.

How might that columnist feel if the stone entered that pond like a knife slicing the surface, stirring not so much as a fold in the water? Frustrated, is my first guess. That columnist might wonder if anyone is really out there. Nervous, is another possibility. He or she might start wondering if the editor too has noticed the paucity of response, and may be about to start looking for something new and more popular to favour the op-ed page.

But then, every once in a while, you get the feeling that your words are going somewhere, that if you're not creating, or at least inspiring, a popular uprising, you're certainly validating one. Last year, *Nordicity* was awarded the Ma Murray prize for Best Columnist for covering the hottest issue of the season. No, it wasn't the prorogation of parliament, nor the bloody war that precipitated it, not the overcrowding of prisons or the plight of Third World countries or the fate of the Peel Watershed.

The issue was urban chickens. The *Yukon News* had reported that Whitehorse city planners were equivocal about the possibility of legalizing small-scale chicken farming in residential neighbourhoods, and this columnist came out strongly in favour.

As a chicken farmer, albeit a rural one, I felt a personal stake in the issue. I can attest to the fact that a laying hen is a hardworking proletarian who will provide uncomplaining service for years, and then instead of burdening the employee pension plan, will furnish her keeper with a tasty soup.

Her mate, I must admit, is another matter. My own rooster, Cato, is trained to test my reflexes whenever I turn my back on him – often when I'm busy collecting eggs you can hear my cries of, "Not now, Cato." He is an exemplar of male aggression, and would be a hazard if let loose on the urban streets, but then few chicken farmers would stretch the definition of "free range" so far as to turn their cocks loose downtown.

So I was gratified to learn in the pages of last week's *Yukon News* that the urban chicken movement is, while still illegal, alive and well in Whitehorse. Clandestine "crow-ops," as these underground chicken farms are called, are springing up around town, to the frustration of the egg-squad. Those boarded-up houses visited only once a day, that hint of a suspicious odour on the sidewalk? You guessed it.

Of course, as in any illegal activity there are always a few desperados for whom the illegality is part of the attraction. One urban farmer told the *News* that her customers enjoy "sticking it to the man." But is this good for society? Houses ruined by the moisture, cars coming and going at all hours of the day and night as customers drop in to purchase a "carton," street talk for a dozen illegal eggs: can neighbourhoods survive the pressure?

Clearly decriminalization is the only answer. The city must act quickly, before criminal gangs step in to corner the lucrative egg trade. If there is a snag, it is that animal welfare advocates may object. According to the *News* article, "Vancouver's SPCA has publicly opposed backyard chickens ... fearing that they may be overrun with chickens when their owners no longer want them." There is even talk of building a $20,000 shelter for abandoned poultry.

Whitehorse, fear not. Do not waste taxpayers' dollars on a costly chicken shelter. Out of a sense of responsibility at having helped to engender the urban chicken movement, *Nordicity* hereby commits to taking any and all abandoned chickens at no cost to the city of Whitehorse. Drop 'em off anytime. We promise you they won't languish long in overcrowded cages. Not long at all.

A Chicken Ain't Nothin' But A Bird

JULY 2013

As the author of two previous columns in support of the urban chicken, I think it's only fair that I should alert readers to an unfortunate development in the movement to poultrify the world's cities. According to the *Globe and Mail*, an alarming number of city people are mistaking chickens for pets. This misconception is so common that last year deluded citizens dropped more than 500 unwanted chickens off at animal shelters in Minneapolis, Minnesota.

I have kept chickens for years, albeit in a rural setting. Sometimes when I pick up my day-old chicks they come with a sheet of instructions: keep them warm, give them water, feed chick starter for so many days, and so on. The page is short, based I suppose on the assumption that the chicks are going to people who already understand the essential elements of the farmer-livestock relationship.

Now that more chicks are destined for urban homes, the hatcheries may need to consider publishing a complete owner's manual, with perhaps a bold warning on the face: "Caution, farm animals – not to be treated as pets." Treating chickens as pets is stupid. Don't do it. This is not to say you can't name your favourite laying hen Betsy, or tickle her under the beak when you collect the eggs. Just keep in mind that her appropriate final resting place is the soup pot. The pet cemeteries are already overcrowded.

It appears that neophyte urban farmers may be listening to the wrong advice. Consider the following, from Sayara Thurston of Humane Society International Canada: "A chicken is a pet like any other and they need to be cared for throughout their lives, which people need to take into consideration if they're thinking of adopting some chickens into their home."

Is it just me, or is it hard to believe Ms Thurston has ever actually met a chicken? I've known hundreds of them, and I've never seen one yet that any sane individual would adopt into their home. As to the assertion that it's a pet like any other, I suppose if it could reach it would drink out of the toilet bowl, but in what other particular is it like a pet?

On pet rule number one, that the subject must be susceptible of house training, the chicken fails miserably. You cannot house train a chicken. It's a scientific fact that a chicken has no idea what's going on anywhere behind its wings. Its brain is too small to reach that far. For a chicken, defecation is an auto-response, like breathing.

On pet rule number two, that the alleged pet ought to return your love, forget it. Chickens, particularly the adult males, are quite capable of hating a human being, but their hearts, which are hardly bigger than their brains, cannot love. Betsy doesn't love you, and you would be advised not to love her too much, because she will break your heart. Especially when she quits laying and you find yourself feeding her for nothing.

But the real reason a chicken makes a lousy pet is that it lacks the necessary condition of pointlessness. Face it, your pet exists for no good reason. If it was a guide dog or a barn cat or a hunting ferret you wouldn't call it a pet. But a chicken is by definition a worker, a layer of eggs, a packer-on of edible flesh. To turn her into a pet is to take a good, utilitarian bird and reduce it to sanctified uselessness.

If you try to take your chickens for walkies through town you will create chaos. Even more so at the off-leash park. Not to mention the disorder you will create in your own life if you make the mistake of believing a chicken is a pet. The *Globe and Mail* reports that Stephanie Brown of the Canadian Coalition for Farm Animals "doubts" urban farmers would be willing to cover the high cost of veterinary care for a sick chicken. I can assure Ms Brown that urban farmers are not unique in that respect. Even out here in the country, you don't see a lot of people taking their chicken in for its annual checkup.

For the record, *Nordicity* continues to support urban farming, and in particular urban chickens, but with the following proviso: urban chickens do not belong in the hands of airheads. Take the following test: are you tempted to cuddle up on the couch with Betsy? If so, give her up, she's not good for you, nor you for her.

And don't clutter up the pet shelters with your cast-off chickens. As a public service I am offering a country home for any chicken you want to abandon, so long as it's either laying or edible.

From My Cold Dead Hands

NOVEMBER 2011

According to a mail-out from Agriculture Canada and the government of Yukon, Canadians are now required to register their pigs. Under the National Agriculture and Food Traceability program, all pigs must be registered, for safety purposes.

They're kidding right? This can't possibly be the Harper government at work. Surely the champions of freedom who are in the process of dismantling the odious gun registry aren't about to replace it with a pig registry? The *Nordicity* research team has been working on this day and night, and we have uncovered some shocking truths. For instance, pet pot-belly pigs, which are short as well as stout, are exempt from the registry. Which means, of course, that Canada is embarked upon a national long-pig registry.

Oh, fools, fools! Will they never learn? Once again the government is bent on making criminals out of ordinary law-abiding farmers. Don't they know our pigs are tools, not weapons, that we have generations of experience in handling pigs safely, and a long lawful tradition of responsible pig ownership? Farmers grew up in an environment where pigs were a normal part of life, everybody had one and nobody thought anything of them, until they needed a Thanksgiving ham or a rasher of breakfast bacon.

The registry is only part of the picture. Our researchers have uncovered persistent rumours that farmers will be required to carry a pig licence, take a pig safety course, and comply with arcane and inconvenient pig-storage laws. In all likelihood we'll be forced to keep the pig feed in a separate place from the pigs. According to our sources, farmers wishing to acquire new pigs will require a PAC, or pig acquisition certificate, issued by the government. Is this the Canada our fathers fought and died for?

The flyer that appeared in the mailbox a couple of weeks ago came from the agricultural branch of Energy, Mines and Resources (here in the Yukon, apparently, even if it can be grown it's got to be mined), which is in cahoots with the feds in this attempt to kill freedom and stigmatize the ordinary, responsible swineherd. It claims that the long-pig registry is necessary because of "recent events in other parts of Canada." Now where have we heard that before? The government isn't saying, but our researchers are following a lead that the demand for a pig registry came from radical humanist agitators in Quebec.

So, because a bunch of liberal urbanites who don't understand country life have their knickers in a twist over an outbreak of bovine spongiform encephalopathy, the government is rushing out to criminalize pig ownership all over Canada. Do they really believe registration will prevent pig crime? Do they think street criminals in major cities will register their pigs? Do they imagine that this registry will do one thing to stop the flow of illegal pigs across the US border?

If the Canadian government believes the Americans will join them in the criminalization of pigs, they'd better check what kind of bacon they're smoking. In the land of the free, pig ownership is a sacred tradition, guaranteed by the constitutional Right to Bear Hams. The National Swine Association is one of the most powerful lobby groups in the country, led by some of America's most influential swine. How will Canada stop the flow of pigs to our inner cities when anyone can walk into a pig shop in Michigan and pick up any kind of pig they want? And as everybody knows, when pigs are criminalized, only criminals will have pigs.

Clearly, the government has un ulterior motive in this. Register your pigs today, and when the crunch comes, they'll know where to find you. Pig registration may seem harmless enough at the start, but sooner or later, it's bound to result in pig confiscation. And what kind of world will it be when the government has all the pigs, and the people are defenseless?

Canadians, resist. Don't let your freedoms be trampled into the pig poop. Pigs don't kill people, people kill people. The best protection against crime is a well-pigged citizenry. When they come to take away your freedom, stand your ground. Let them know in no uncertain terms: you can have my pig, when you take it from my cold dead hands.

CHAPTER 4: ISN'T SCIENCE WONDERFUL?

> " THE COMMON PEOPLE
> KNEW NOTHING OF THE WORLD
> OUTSIDE THEIR OWN BACKYARDS,
> AND RELIED ON MEN IN BLACK
> CASSOCKS TO EXPLAIN THE
> MYSTERIES OF THE UNIVERSE.

B*ack in the Dark Ages, before the invention of science, knowledge was a scarce commodity. The common people knew nothing of the world outside their own backyards, and relied on men in black cassocks to explain the mysteries of the universe. Science has changed all of that. Now we rely on men and women in white lab coats.*

The Art Of Microfabrication

APRIL 2002

According to an article in the *Globe and Mail*, scientists at the Northwestern University in Chicago have developed the world's smallest pen, which they claim could be used to "write" microscopic electronic circuits. The pen's "ink" is made from alkanethiols, and it's "paper" is made of gold.

It is believed that the pen may be used in the fields of microfabrication, nanotechnology, and molecular electronics. For the average reader, some explanation of these terms is probably in order. Microfabrication is the process of inventing little white lies. It is not yet clear why the Northwestern University believes its pen will be superior to any other writing device for this purpose. We here at *Nordicity* have found the ball-point, the Hewitt Rand 32X Max, and the stub of crayon found under the couch, all microfabricate quite adequately.

Nanotechnology refers to the paperwork which has to be processed by the police when a crime suspect is formally charged. Hence the colloquialism, "Book him, Nano." Again, why the world's smallest pen would be a better implement for this task than the customary half-chewed Bic is not yet known. Molecular electronics is exactly like regular electronics, only smaller. Its purpose is to make even the most elementary repairs on your car cost over three hundred dollars.

Also in the science news: after conducting a lengthy study sociologists have established that lesbian women have fewer babies and use fewer oral contraceptives than their heterosexual sisters. At press time, we were unable to verify the rumour that the research group were seeking additional grant money to try to establish a reason for this inequity.

But perhaps the most exciting development on the scientific front this week is the news that Russian scientists plan to place huge mirrors on the Mir Space Station to extend daylight hours in the North. The mirrors will act in much the same manner as the moon, reflecting the light of the sun toward Earth, but will be designed to intensify the light, providing far greater illumination. This will in effect extend the hours of daylight in winter.

People who are starving in the dark in the northern reaches of Russia will no doubt be delighted to learn that their government is spending millions of rubles to make it possible for them to starve in the light instead. But think of the ancillary benefits that this technological advance will bring to Northerners the world round. Here at One Bucket Creek, for instance, there will be no more need to complain that light pollution from Whitehorse makes it increasingly difficult to enjoy the night sky: the moon and stars will be so washed out by the light of the Mir Mirrors that a few hundred streetlights will become irrelevant. Likewise, we can expect a significant drop in the incidence of Aurora Syndrome, the chronic stiff neck suffered by many Northerners as a result of looking up at the Northern Lights.

Most excited of all by the announcement are the cosmonauts on the Mir station, who are said to be anxiously awaiting the arrival of the new mirrors; there's a rumour that a shipment of tea bags and toilet paper is coming in on the same flight.

Stop Nasal Oppression Today

JUNE 2009

I know you've heard this a thousand times in your life, a hundred in the past decade, twenty this year, four this week, but this time it's true: new information has just been released which will mean the end of the world as we know it.

Although similar claims were made for the birth of Christ, the invention of the printing press, and the introduction of Y-front underpants, readers of a certain age will know that the greatest fundamental change in the way we view our universe occurred in July of 1969, when the Apollo 11 landing craft deposited the world's most inarticulate test-pilot on the world's most barren rock. Nothing, as the announcer informed us, would ever be the same again.

It was true, too: the revolution started almost the instant that Neil Armstrong rolled back the cuff of his space suit to read the "one giant step" speech written on his wrist. Within days four new flavours of Jell-O and two new styles of Frisbee were released. By the end of the week they had changed the guy who played Darren on Bewitched. That year the CIA dropped its support for three of the century's most brutal dictators, and picked up four new ones.

After the moon landing, breaks with the known world became fashionable, and soon history was switching direction with the frequency of a dog in a parking lot. Change has been common, swift, and often radical, but nothing in this century has had the sweeping effect expected after last week's announcement from the University of Virginia.

True, we have seen the collapse of Soviet Communism, an event so catastrophic that the gangsters running Russia had to give up the name "the Comintern" and start calling themselves "the Gangsters." True also that the Internet revolution has so fundamentally changed human existence that people from around the world now gather in so-called "electronic rubber rooms" to discuss topics as varied as Leonard Nimoy films, elbow-fetishism, and the electoral hopes of Joe Clark.

But this is bigger than all of those. Bigger even than the invention of the remote channel-changer, more significant than the introduction of individually-packaged custard puddings. This week the Common Cold Unit at the University of Virginia unveiled a study which proves that nose-blowing prolongs suffering for cold victims.

Nordicity declines to discuss the methodology of this study, except to say that it involved the tracking of "radio-labeled fluids." At press time, we were unable to confirm the rumour that the Fraser Institute has released a counter-study showing that nasal congestion is a direct result of barriers to international trade. Lawyers for the newly formed survivors rights group Stop Nasal Oppression Today are not ruling out a class action against the tissue industry, which it claims used misleading and false advertising to attract young nose-blowers. Parents and grandparents may be named as co-defendants in the suit for their participation in the now infamous "honk like a goose" campaign.

The stock market reacted swiftly to the study's release; share prices for Kleenex plummeted, while breathing-apparatus futures took a giant leap. But these are as nothing when compared to the cultural changes which will surely follow. Mouth-breathers will no longer be socially shunned; indeed, it will become the fashion to refer to those of a timid and conservative nature as "nasal retentive." Preston Manning's voice will begin to sound normal.

Coin-op sinus-drainage apparatus will appear in public restrooms. Protest groups will picket these conveniences, proclaiming the "rights of the unblown." Even the normal pronunciation of human speech may be so radically altered that, on that far off day when the first human astronaut sets foot on Mars, she may broadcast to the world the historic words:

"Dad's wud giand steb vor wobad, wud giand leab vor wobadkide."

Are We Men, Or Are We Mice?

NOVEMBER 2004

When I was a boy, jet aircraft broke the sound barrier. It must have been relatively simple, because they broke it all in one big bang; folks started breaking the colour barrier about the same year, and it's still holding strong in spots.

Obviously, some barriers break easy, and some break hard. Take trade barriers, for instance. In order to break down impediments to international trade, imperial Britain was often forced to resort to the tiresome process of sending gunships to 'open up' recalcitrant cities. Today, the United States sends a trade mission, and the cities cheerfully open up on their own. On the rare occasion that this doesn't work, the B52 bomber has turned out to be every bit as effective a barrier-remover as the seventy-gun ship of the line.

There has been a tendency in the latter half of the century to treat barriers as if they were all made to be broken, and in some cases justifiably so. Barriers to women in the clergy began to fall when not enough men could be found who were not pedophiles. Barriers to homosexuality in the army are only now being recognized as stupid, since they eliminate one of the recruiting sergeant's most effective drawing cards.

There are barriers which should never be tampered with. The Whitehorse Rapids power dam, for instance, is a barrier whose failure could cause real stress for those situated downstream. (Indeed, the same could be said of the contraceptive diaphragm.) But of all the barriers I know there is one which surely must hold as firm as a line of Liberal cabinet ministers denying responsibility. I speak of course of the species barrier.

According to The Institute of Food Science & Technology (UK) Statement of Position on Genetic Modification, "GM across the species barrier is ... revolutionary in terms of its potential benefits." Well, maybe yes and maybe no.

New Science magazine reports that the US National Institute of Health is considering a request for funding from a scientist who wants to grow human sperm cells in the testes of mice. Now I don't like to stand in the way of progress, so to speak, but what was wrong with where human sperm cells were growing in the first place? Convenient container, handy reusable applicator: you might say those cells were right at home.

And what are the mice going to do with them, anyway? Are we going to see the introduction of a new group of supermice, smart enough to find their way through complex mazes, coupled with the strength and manual dexterity of a human being – think what plumbers they would make! Or maybe these mice will become the progenitors of a race of super-humans, tough, intelligent, and industrious, and yet small enough to find all the Lebensraum they need in a corner of the attic.

I say, put a stop to cross-species miscegenation now. It's time for men to rise up against genetic gerrymandering, erect a barrier to boundary-bashing. If anyone is going to store up male human reproductive cells, let it be male humans.

I ask you, are we men, or are we mice?

What, Not Ewe Again?

The news that a crew of scientists in Edinburgh, Scotland have successfully cloned a sheep, producing a lamb which is genetically identical to its dam, has raised questions around the world. The first question which springs to mind is, so what? As anyone with any experience of Scottish sheep will tell you, the principal thing which stands out about them is that you can't tell one from another anyway. Every blessed one of them is woolly, stupid, and stubborn, and won't get off the road no matter how hard you blow on your hooter.

The next question which cries out to be answered is, Why bother? Stupid as they are, the sheep of the Old Sod have maintained that stunning uniformity for centuries, and done it in the time-honoured manner of birds, bees, and sheep everywhere, mucking about in byres and pastures. And since the ram is a notoriously unromantic suitor, not given to flowers or chocolates, not a penny was spent in the process of producing millions of identical lambs. What the Edinburgh scientists have discovered is a way to make the production of a single lamb generate millions of pounds in research grants. It is exactly this kind of imaginative thinking which has made the Scots race so successful in Northern Canada, the Land of Government Money.

The naming of the cloned lamb raises questions too, if only about the mentality of the scientists, or of their PR people, if they have such a thing.

"Dolly," the world's most famous sheep, was cloned from the mammary gland of her "mother," and so it was decided to name her after – this is true – Dolly Parton. This has led to widespread speculation that Scotland has never fully recovered from the Great Brain Drain of 1966, when too many of her finest wordsmiths departed to places like One Bucket Creek. *Nordicity* was unable to contact the Edinburgh research team for confirmation of reports that other names considered were, "Brave New Wool," and "Ewe Again?."

The issue of nomenclature takes another turn when we consider the parenthood of the lamb. The famous mammary-cell was fused with an unfertilized egg from another ewe, and the resultant embryo was implanted in a third 'mother'. In effect, this makes the first ewe the father of Dolly, a linguistic impossibility at the very least. At first it was suggested that the host sheep be called the Dam Ewe, the donor of the egg the Egg Dam, and the donor of the mammary tissue the Mother Progenitor, or MP. British Members of Parliament threatened immediate legislative action to prevent the use of the latter term, and new names are still being sought.

Next we must stop to ponder the question, What are the political implications of the cloning of adult mammals? On the one hand, unscrupulous campaigners might seek to stack the polls by cloning large numbers of offspring from a single committed voter, while on the other hand, voters might demand that a particularly popular politician be cloned to run in their home riding.

The dangers in the latter case are obvious. What the heck would we do with them after their popularity waned? Can you imagine if the technique had been available during the Trudeaumania period, an era which spanned the years from 1968 to 1968? We might have ended up with 372 supercilious bird-flipping fuddle-duddles cluttering up the Ottawa scene in the garb of tourists pretending to be artists on the Rive Gauche, necessitating that we clone the same number of Peter Gzoskys to interview them all every time they changed their carnations.

Relax, We're Doomed.

It's not easy being at the top of the evolutionary ladder. Since abandoning the garden of innocence, where beasts lived together in the kind of blissful harmony that comes from eating each other fresh, humanity has been the problem species on the block. If all living things are Mother Earth's children, we are the one she would most like to leave on a doorstep.

So I wasn't much surprised to learn in last Wednesday's *Yukon News* that the Polynesians who arrived in New Zealand in about the 13th century were responsible for the extinction of the moa, a large, clueless bird that you could just walk up to and club on the head and – voila! – instant groceries. Think of it as a five hundred pound spruce grouse without wings. I mean, you can see the temptation, can't you? Open season year round, and no bag limits. Scientists today estimate that 160,000 moas perished in about 160 years.

OK, correct me if I'm wrong, but that sounds like a thousand birds a year, or about 50,000lbs of moa meat, per annum. Not bad for a population of about a hundred or so humans. Must have been good stuff. Anyway, the story goes that when Captain Cook came along, there were no moa. The English, who had read about the moa in the Boy's Own Annual, asked what had happened to them, and the Polynesians shrugged. "What? We were very hungry."

Impressed by the Polynesian people's sang froid, Cook took the story with him on his travels, and like bowler hats and those baggy shorts with prints of bougainvillea flowers on a brown background, it became inexplicably fashionable. "Hey," someone would say, "I'm very hungry, let's kill all the passenger pigeons," and everyone would laugh and go out and do it, and then someone would shout, "I'm still hungry, let's do the dodo bird next."

I could live with this legacy. I've been reading the paper for enough years to have grown accustomed to the fact that species extinction is what we do best. But I have to say it hurt to turn the page and learn that DNA testing has proven that our ancestors did not breed with Homo Neanderthal. So, since we didn't assimilate our closest relatives, the only other logical hypothesis is that we annihilated them.

Well, what can I say? Sorry guys. That's evolution for you. Of course, nowadays we don't permit people to wipe out species by walking up and bonking them on the head. There are game laws to prevent that kind of thing. Today, if you want to annihilate your fellow creature, the only legal way is to turn its habitat into a coal mine, or drill for oil in its calving grounds.

Do not despair: there's good news for the planet. Evolution is an ongoing game of king-of-the-castle in which nobody stays on top of the sand-pile forever. Consider the lemming. Evolution has handed it life on a platter. No predator born can eat faster than the lemming can breed, and being out there on the wide open tundra, it doesn't need chat-lines to find a mate. So, depending on which version of the story you believe, when lemmings get overpopulated they either get together in the thousands and commit mass-suicide or hang around basking in the midnight sun until a Walt Disney crew comes along and herds them over a cliff so they can film them dying. Either way, they crash.

Now there is reason to believe that humanity is on the same track. We're starting with the physical elite, the creme de la creme, the human beings who could, if necessary, chase down a gazelle on foot, throw an iron ball and bonk a boa sixty feet away, or do a really neat gymnastic move and impress the heck out of a water buffalo. Today, in order for humanity's evolutionary front-runners to make a living, they have to compete against each other in a field which we call, with a bare face, amateur sports. By "amateur" we mean a sport in which you don't get a regular paycheque, but at which you can get filthy rich if you take enough drugs.

The drugs function very well, but they have a bit of a tendency to kill people, or at least render them mad, bad, and sterile. Removing the elite athlete from the gene pool could cause a downward evolutionary trend for the species. In ten years they'll be taking the less-than elite athletes, and giving them more drugs. A decade later, they'll be taking the people who can sort of run if they have to.

After that it'll be a downward spiral, until they're working their way down the sofa spud scale, pumping us all full of human growth hormones, and shovelling us out onto the track to shuffle for the gold. By mid-century there's a good chance we'll have drugged the human race out of existence, just to supply the Olympics with amateur athletes. It seems sad, from a human point of view, but if it were possible to pass the news along to the moa, the passenger pigeon, or the dodo, I doubt if they would shed many tears.

Today, the Centre for Biological Diversity reports that species are going extinct at a rate of dozens per day. Guess what the major causes are? (Hint, nobody's clubbing them on the head).

Good-bye, Rocket Scientist

Most of the time we don't mind not being able to get the TV signal here at One Bucket Creek, but it sure puts us out of touch with city folks. Even if we take a bath and put on our town clothes, everybody in Whitehorse knows we're from the sticks, just by the way we make conversation. Somebody says, "Hey, d'you see Gretzky hit that home run last night?" and we're faced with either pretending we know what sport they're talking about or confessing that we live practically on the moon or something, where there's no TV.

Most people are fairly tolerant, even if you don't know who Steinfield or Buffy Brown are, but the real problem is that we hardly talk the same language. Urbanites speak an ever-changing patois known to Creekies as the TV Creole. You go to town one week, and everybody you talk to is saying "that's the bottom line." A couple of weeks later, you go in to pick up some toilet paper, and you say to the clerk, "Well, I guess that's the bottom line," and she looks at you like you're from – well, from One Bucket Creek.

It turns out they're not saying "the bottom line" in town anymore, they're all saying, "at the end of the day" now. By the same token, we learned to say "round up the usual suspects" just about the time everyone else abandoned that and started saying "don't sweat the small stuff." We do have the OBC Radio News, and we get to hear the Yukon Legislature quite a lot, but it crackles so much we never did figure out whether you're supposed to walk the talk or talk the walk, and now that expression seems to be on its dying breath, even with our community leaders.

We were the last to hear that NASA scientists caused the multi-million dollar Mars Orbiter to crash when they forgot to convert their figures from imperial to metric, so several of us made fools of ourselves in town last week by using the discredited expression, "It doesn't take a rocket scientist ..."

We just can't keep up.

So when the OBC Radio announced that Whitehorse was going to get a brand new Retail Power Development, we didn't have the foggiest notion what that was. I guess maybe Johnny Carson said it on his show one night, and now everybody in TV land is saying it, but out in the bush we didn't know what an RPD was till Heronner, the Mayor of Whitehorse, explained: it's the new name for a strip mall.

Now it all makes sense. Anybody looking around the Yukon's capital can see that what the place needs to make it even more appealing is another mall, with maybe a few more fast-food joints thrown in. Visitors to the territory have had their fill of scenery by the time they get to Whitehorse, they need something to block the view of Grey Mountain and the Yukon River as they drive down into town.

Not only will the new RPD attract visitors, it's sure to generate long-term employment. I mean, just think of it: all the people who work at the six existing malls only have five other malls to go shopping in. The new mall will stimulate spending. With spin-off benefits, we'll soon need another new mall, and then another. By constructing shoulder-to shoulder malls the entire length of the main drag, Whitehorse will be emulating that other great Canadian tourist mecca: Regina. The similarity is almost guaranteed by the fact that the developers are expecting financial assistance from the City of Whitehorse and the territorial government, both of whom require compliance with all local and national ugliness standards.

The One Bucket Creek Council takes a different view of commercial development. You can put up a building in the valley if you can afford it yourself. The way we see it, if you can't, you're not ready to go into business yet. We don't think it takes a retail power developer to figure that one out.

CHAPTER 5: A RIGHT ROYAL PAIN

"

AN ESTIMATED MILLION
SPECTATORS LINED THE
STREETS TO WATCH THE GAYS,
BUT WE SAW NOBODY BUT
SECURITY POLICE AWAITING HER MAJ.

My family and I were on a research trip to Toronto some years ago, coincidentally on the same day that the Queen's motorcade passed through. This also happened to be the day of the Gay Pride parade. An estimated million spectators lined the streets to watch the gays, but we saw nobody but security police awaiting Her Maj. We had a great time watching the parade (guess which one) and left town feeling greatly encouraged to know that, in Toronto at least, when it comes to queens, more is better.

Roll Out the Tumbrels

There's trouble at One Bucket Creek. Big trouble: people are worried that this might mean the end of our tightly knit little municipality. What could be at the root of such a tragic sundering of a once harmonious community but an equally tragic event in world affairs? I speak, of course, of the untimely demise of the unfortunately named Princess Di. Reaction to the horror of what has become the world's most infamous car-crash was swift, but varied, and it is that variety which is at the root of all our discord. Because, you see, there are Factions.

Strongest among these is the Hang the Paparazzi faction, led by the mayor himself. This group insists that if a car spins out of control and cracks up, the fault lies with whatever was behind it, especially if it was a car-load of that most despised of all species, journalists. The mayor knows all about the kind of slimy journalism practiced by these ill-begotten photo-snappers and gossip-mongers; he sees their stuff every week in the tabloids he buys at the supermarket. A huge Princess Di fan, he knows every detail of her love-life, her personal problems, her health, her eating habits, and the colour of her undergarments. He has read every scabrous word and pinned every scandalous picture up to the wall of his tack-shed, and he can say without doubt that the people who acquired this filth for him to enjoy are scum of the first rank.

Members of Hizonner's faction have calculated that they shell out sixty bucks a week between them on tabloids and glossy magazines to keep track of their favourite personalities, so no-one is more qualified than them to pronounce on the despicable means by which these materials were acquired. As to the contention, raised by some unsavoury elements in the Valley, that the Princess was as likely at any time to be chasing the press

as chased by them, the mayor points out that this tragedy occurred on a day when she obviously didn't want to speak to them, and that it should be a princess's prerogative to change her mind.

At direct loggerheads with this group are the Blame The Driver faction, who angrily declare that if a wealthy man's car is going too fast, it is the fault of his chauffeur. After all, they say, who makes the decisions on matters of speed? Do people think that just because a guy owns the car and pays the driver's wages, he gets to say how fast they travel? And hell, the man was drunk. Surely no-one would suggest that there is any onus on an employer to ensure that his employees are sober on the job?

But no matter how contentious the debate between these groups, they harmonize like the One Bucket Barbershop Quartet when howling together against the most despised element in the Valley – the One Less Aristo On The Mega-Dole faction. According to these members of the lunatic fringe, the Princess of Wales did her whining and dining on an allowance that would have made a serious dent in Britain's national debt, and her pretentious state funeral is just another case of throwing good money after bad. Some have even gone so far as to say that Great Britain could avoid the trauma of future royal deaths simply by not having any royals. Out with them, they say, and let them live on their fat.

A quiet minority is the Who Really Cares? faction, those who believe that, sad as the death of a thirty-six year old mother of two is, in the grand scheme of things, there are a lot greater tragedies occurring every day. Will the Valley survive? We believe it will. We have weathered storms as rough as this before. Why, only two decades ago we were nearly torn asunder by the great debate over whether Martians really abducted Elvis.

Tumbrels, Redux

This year, Pippa Middleton wore a red striped dress to watch the men's singles tennis tournament at Wimbledon. No great powers of research were required to ascertain this fact: the Vancouver Sun ran a gallery of 28 photographs, half of Ms Middleton sitting in the stands not doing much at all, and the other half of tennis players who distinguished themselves, on that day, by the act of being seen by the royal aunty.

Aside from a comely appearance, the famous Pippa is famous for being the sister of the woman who married the man who will one day be king, if his elders get on with dying off. Pippa's claim to fame is now greater because her sister Kate shimmied her way into and out of some very posh maternity clothes while incubating yet another monarch-in-waiting, Prince George by name.

No explanation was offered as to why the young royals chose to name their child after a smelly pulp-mill town with a reputation for gang wars and crystal meth, but let's leave that aside for the moment. This July, the government of Quebec joined in the legal challenge of an act of the Canadian parliament that changes the rules under which the crown is handed down.

The rules were first changed in England, where the monarchs actually live, and concern such things as gender equality and freedom of religion. If George had been a Georgette, the old rules would have required her to wait for just about every royal male in the UK to die off before she could take the throne. Also, should George grow up and decide to marry a Roman Catholic, he will no longer be barred from assuming his kingdom. No word yet on how that will translate if the Roman Catholic in question turns out to be a man.

Should the prince himself at some point in his life turn aside from the Anglican catholic faith and embrace the Roman one, the picture changes. Roman Catholics are, by ancient tradition, forbidden to rule England. Apparently there were some difficulties, back in the day. This August, the Ontario Superior Court rejected an application by Bryan Teskey, a Roman Catholic Ontario man, to repeal the changes to the Act of Succession on the grounds that they discriminate against his religion.

Mr Teskey's claim was rejected, not on its merits, but because as a commoner, he had "no legal standing" in the matter. Having no possibility of inheriting the throne, he had no right to sue over the constitutionality of the rules governing succession. According to the Ottawa Citizen, Teskey has put his own nascent law career on hold in order to pursue an appeal in this case.

A word of utterly unqualified – in both senses of the word – advice for Mr Teskey. Refocus. True, it's a clear violation of the Charter of Rights and Freedoms that you can't be King or Queen of Canada because you're Catholic, but the problem runs a little deeper than that. Hanging on the gate at Buckingham Palace is a large sign that reads, "no Canadians need apply," and rest assured, it doesn't refer to butlers, footmen, or maids.

There's nothing in the constitution that says our head of state has to be a foreigner, it's just the way things are. No Canadian is ever going to occupy that throne. Wouldn't that make a great constitutional challenge? Picture the headlines: Supreme Court Rules Succession Law Discriminates Against Everybody. And it's not only native-born Canadians who have no chance of ascending our country's throne (although we don't actually have a throne, that's in England too). In fact, the Act of Succession, though it no longer discriminates against women or the spouses of Catholics, still bars entry to all but the inbred descendants of a gang of mad despots who would outshine some of the worst dictators in the world today.

If you can't trace your lineage to a brutal ruler who poisoned his enemies and burned people alive for disagreeing with him over questions of religious practice, don't bother to drop off your resumé, the position of monarch will never be open to you. This is no laughing matter in a world where celebrity is the brightest of all the shining prizes. Consider Miley Cyrus. A song and dance artist whose ambition outstrips her talent, Cyrus is without royal connections, and so in order to achieve stardom is reduced to spicing up her performances with pornography. She might get photographed at Wimbledon if she shows up nude and twerks a ball boy, but she will never know the kind of easy fame that falls upon the relatives of royalty.

Not only does Middleton's royal-connected status guarantee that she will be photographed at fashionable sporting events, it brought her a £400,000 advance from Penguin for her book on party planning. All she ever had to do to attract the world's attention was show up at her sister's wedding with a bum that looks good in a designer bridesmaid's dress.

No amount of tinkering will bring the monarchy into the 21st Century. It is a vestige of a darker time, when England was Syria, only worse. If you want fairness and equality of opportunity, call out the tumbrels. Failing that, choose the successor to the throne by a lottery covering the entire population of the Commonwealth. Canada has better things to do than perfect a bill of rights for princesses.

There's No Life Like It

Listen, do you hear that creaking sound? That's the members of Canada's military straightening up a 43-year-old curvature of the spine. Yes, as Defence Minister Peter McKay boasted this week, thousands of men and women in the Canadian forces can "stand a little taller, a little prouder" this week, since the designation "royal" has returned to their regimental letterheads.

Actually, the army isn't standing any taller, they don't get to be royal. Even in England they haven't let armies call themselves royal since 1648. It seems kings and queens had been jumping to the conclusion that royal armies were theirs to do with as they pleased. The king got to keep the navy, it being of less use in rounding up political adversaries and consigning them to the Tower. The air force simply slipped through the cracks, as air forces were wont to do in the 17th century.

And so it was in Great Britain and her colonies until 1968, when that insidious nationalist, Pierre Elliot Trudeau, reorganized Canada's military, and dropped the royal tag. It was a sad and a sorry sight as, en masse, Canada's sailors and airmen drooped and sagged into the shamefaced slouch of the no-longer-royal.

It became all but impossible to tell the navy and the air force from the army because, not only were they in the same-coloured uniforms, they now carried themselves with the same despondent posture as de-royalized British and colonial foot soldiers have worn for more than 400 years.

Wonderful as it is to see at least some members of our armed forces walking upright again, a few cynical and unpatriotic observers have raised questions about the timing and the true purpose of the announcement. There is speculation on Parliament Hill that, on learning that Stephen Harper is now rated Canada's second-best prime minister after Trudeau, the Conservatives set out to dismantle some of the latter's accomplishments, and this was the most doable one to start with. The Charter of Rights and Freedoms is going to take a bit more work.

Others suggest that, as a tall man himself, the prime minister needs the members of the military standing up as straight as possible when he goes to hide behind them. Whenever the opposition demands to know what happened to all the blacked-out cabinet documents on the detainee-transfer affair, Harper and McKay stand firmly behind their troops, and they were getting sick of scrunching down behind a bunch of slouchers.

Then there are those – probably separatists who desire to see the breakup of Canada – who claim that the Conservatives' ad agency recommended the switch in order to associate their brand with the new and highly marketable Royal/Middleton product line. Now every time the House of Windsor expands to include another bimbo on the mega-dole the Royal Canadian Conservative Party gets a boost in sales.

But the predominant thinking among pundits and politicos alike is that the new royal designation was a fiscally prudent measure, designed to get the most mileage out of a couple of measly millions in insignia and letterhead purchases (outsourced to China, of course, it wouldn't be fair to the taxpayer to expect them to cover Canadian wages). Think how much more it would cost to placate troops and veterans if we had to give them decent health care and pensions.

Canada is the only western democracy that doesn't track what becomes of the members of our military after they depart their country's service. We know that a great many old soldiers, as well as old royal sailors and old royal airmen, end up on the streets. Unlike Britain, France, Germany, and the US, to name a few, we don't know how many, but hey, who cares? At least now they can stand tall.

Veterans may be homeless, they may be shell-shocked, PTSD-suffering divorced alcoholics with little or no pensions, down and out and living in dank hovels in Canada's worst neighbourhoods, coping with mysterious ailments and terrifying nightmares, but, by damn, they are royal, and that's something you never lose. You never lose it because you can't spend it anywhere.

If you're passing through Vancouver's Down-town Eastside, North-Central Regina, or the Whitehorse Waterfront in the next few days, take a look around you. You will observe a few select members of the poorest of the poor standing straight and tall, and you will know by this that they are former members of the once-again royal branches of the armed forces. They served their country in Korea, Cyprus, Somalia, Bosnia, and Afghanistan. They saw things that would break any human being, and they came back damaged and desperate, and Canada gave them two bits and a shrug. The two bits is spent and the shrug is all they have left. But today, damn it, it's a royal shrug.

And there's nothing like a royal shrug to straighten your spine.

THERE'S NO LIFE LIKE IT

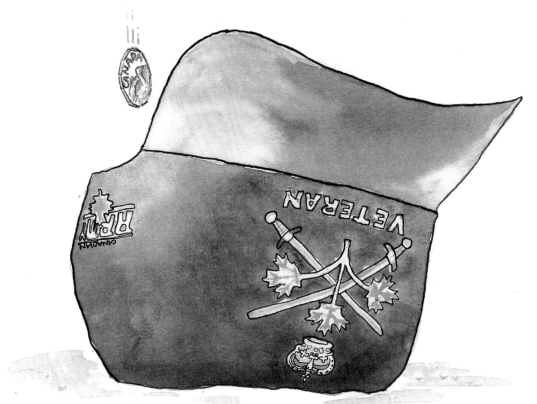

Welcome home, soldier.

A Tale Of Two Elizabeths

APRIL 2013

Elizabeth May has the honour to be Elizabeth Windsor's most humble and obedient servant. The leader of Canada's Green Party may not be the biggest twit ever to style herself so, but if there was an award for making a royal Canadian fool of yourself, May's August 2012 letter to the Queen would furnish an admirable submission to the jury.

May, she said, wished to write Windsor in her capacity as Queen (of Britain and the Colonies), requesting her assistance with a matter of grave importance to Canadians. Without so much as a nudge, a wink, or a hint of irony, the leader of a Canadian political party was asking the Queen of England to set up a royal commission whose aim was to "restore Canada to a free and fair democracy."

A bulletin for Ms May: free and fair democracy, if it exists at all, is not bestowed by monarchs, it is wrested from them. It took centuries of struggle to end England's absolute monarchy, and while democracy prevailed, the royal losers were able to negotiate a deal they call constitutional monarchy. While less forgiving democrats dragged their despots off to the guillotine, the British royals plea-bargained to keep their titles and wealth in return for a promise not to interfere in politics, a field in which they had never been anything but trouble.

The Queen knows the deal better than anyone alive. Constitutional monarchy is her bread and butter, and its boundaries are as fixed as the walls around Buckingham Palace. But while the palace walls are stone and mortar, the monarchy is built on the goodwill of the people. One good shove and it could all fall down. The monarch exerts influence, of course: her quiet ahem echoes in the halls of Westminster, but she does not set up royal enquiries, or otherwise be seen to interfere directly in the business of government, not even in the colonies.

Supposing the Queen was foolish – or poorly advised – enough to stick her Norman nose into Canada's affairs of state, there is no mechanism by which she could create a commission of enquiry. There is no Palace Inquisitor to set upon the task, no Knights of the Enquiry to summon with trumpets, no Royal Commissioner of Democratic Crises. The thing would be impossible to arrange, and May knew it. She sent the letter to make a point about Conservative electoral skulduggery, apparently without noticing that in so doing she was calling into question her own grasp of democratic principles.

Throughout its term in office, the Harper government has blundered from one assault on democracy to another. After a long drawn-out court battle, the Conservative Party pleaded guilty to election financing fraud in the so-called in-and-out scandal, saving four of its senior people from possible prison sentences. Harper prorogued Parliament to avoid releasing the truth about allegations of cabinet complicity in prisoner abuse in Afghanistan. He stuffed the Senate with Conservatives, who went on to shut down the Commons' environment bill.

But it was the Robocalls affair that sent May running for the warmth of her sovereign's love. You might recall that during the last election somebody tried to prevent thousands of Canadians from voting. The thing that most of these voters had in common was that they had identified themselves to the Conservative Party as non-supporters. Elections Canada doesn't have the power to

77

subpoena witnesses, and a number of Conservative officials are reportedly refusing to cooperate with the investigation.

Sooner or later the government will collapse under the weight of all its scandals. Already, there are visible cracks in the superstructure. In a new Ipsos Reed poll, 69 per cent of respondents agreed with the statement, "the Harper Conservatives are too secretive and have not kept their promise to govern according to high ethical standards." Only 13 per cent found anything good to say about the federal budget, while Opposition Leader Tom Mulcair outperformed Harper on values and trustworthiness.

A TALE OF TWO ELIZABETHS

Harper's popularity has never risen above 40 per cent, but in Canada's multi-party system, that's all it takes to secure a majority. May knows this, which is why she decided not to run a candidate in the upcoming Labrador by-election, and urged the NDP to do the same, in order to hand the seat to the Liberals.

In brief, May acknowledges that her party is a vote-splitter which delivers an advantage to the Conservatives, and can come up with no better strategy than to sit out elections. Her actions indicate that she's happy to see Liberals elected, although she usually runs candidates against them, and when Canadian democracy is in peril she thinks it's appropriate to call in the Queen. The question arises: what is this person doing in politics?

The King Has Nothing On

AUGUST 2012

I had intended to remain aloof from the chatter about Prince Curly's excellent adventure in Vegas last week, but a couple of details leapt out of the Royal Monty story that no one else seems to have noticed, and I feel obliged to point them out. Like, $5,000 a night for a hotel room? Who does this guy think he is, Bev Oda? Even more shocking, and this is something you would think the British press might have picked up on, in a game of strip pool the guy standing by the table with his hands over the crown jewels is the loser. What does it say about the way England is educating its upper class twits if they can't even win at billiards?

Harry was not alone in suffering an embarrassing public exposure this past fortnight. Finance Minister Jim Flaherty surely felt a breeze when the suit of magic tax cuts he bought from some crafty economists turned out to be an illusion. They had promised him that only the wise could see how tax cuts for the filthy rich would stimulate the economy, and not wishing to appear foolish, the minister dressed himself in that fantasy and paraded for all the people to see.

It's not known who played the role of the child who proclaims the emperor naked in this story. I like to believe that someone in the finance department drew the minister's attention to *Nordicity* of August 10, where it was revealed that gutting government services to provide the lowest corporate tax rates in the G20 is doing nothing to stimulate the economy, because instead of re-investing, Canadian corporations are sitting on a mountain of cash.

The Toronto Star reports that Flaherty and Mark Carney, governor of the Bank of Canada, are out on the stumps this week with a loud appeal, almost a demand, that Big Business get its bloated butt off the pile and get stimulating. Carney got out of the gate first, calling the more than $200 billion in corporate bank accounts "dead money," and telling reporters "If companies can't figure out what to do with it, then they should give it to shareholders and they'll figure it out." Next came Flaherty with, "At a certain point, it's not up to the government to stimulate the economy, it's up to the private sector, and they have lots of capital."

In a way, Flaherty is in the same soup as Prince Curly. He invited these corporations to his party and they betrayed his trust. Our two heroes might both be asking the same question this morning: "If you can't trust a bunch of hot chicks (or in the minister's case, Calgary School theorists) you met in a bar, who can you trust?" And how did the prince and the minister get themselves into their various situations? They were stupid. Or to be kind, let's say forgetful. One forgot that cell phones take pictures, while the other forgot that a corporation is concerned with its own bottom line, and not with the national economy.

Expensive tomfoolery is the prerogative of the rich. The prince blew $80K in Vegas, and who can complain, it's his money, right? Well, ok, maybe not, but it was his to spend. And who will say it was money wasted? Any day, a video is expected to surface that will prove once and for all that His Awesomeness is a natural redhead. Flaherty gave away billions but likewise, it was his to spend. Unfortunately he got nothing in return, not even a wild night and a hot video.

Both of these stories are about stimulus. The prince indiscriminately tossed around a fortune in Vegas. The hangover is going to last a long time, but hey, it was stimulating while it lasted. Sadly for Canada, we're saddled with a government that believes you can run an economy on the same principle.

CHAPTER 6: **CLEANSING THE TEMPLE**

"

...WHAT WOULD JESUS DO?

A *temple, a gang of money changers, and a whip of cords ... what would Jesus do?*

Racism? No Racism Here.

MARCH 2000

Anyone who's ever driven the One Bucket Creek Road has wondered about CAR, the Church of the Affirmation of Respectability, a congregation that gathers each week in an old stretch limousine abandoned in the ditch somewhere past the fourth milepost. (There are only four mileposts on the road, as the others have all been liberated. They make perfect outhouse supports.)

Depending on one's source of information, CAR is either a life-affirming, mind-liberating, free-thinking group of children of the Lord, or a cult full of mindless zombies. Rev, the leader of the group, likes to say that only the enemies of religious freedom use words like 'cult' to describe legitimate religions. "We don't do any of that cult stuff, the statues, the wine and bread and all that? We just give ten percent of our income, and love the Lord."

So members of CAR, or Carries as they're known, were among the first to raise a cheer when American presidential hopeful George W. Bush spoke at Bob Jones University last month. BJU – yes it is called that – is the place where young Carries aspire to go. It's the most respectability-affirming place in all of North America. Needless to say, George W. praised it to the skies.

You can't go there if your hair's too long, if your skirt's too short, or if your boyfriend's a Negro – unless you yourself are also black (and female: no boys with boyfriends need apply). This does not mean that members of CAR, or the administration of BJU, are racist. By no means. BJU's desire to keep the races separate is based on purely biblical motives. Not that the university can point to any specific biblical reference to interracial dating, but such practices certainly offend the spirit of the Good Book. Or as Rev is reported to have said, "If the Good Lord had wanted us to date other races, he'd have given us stronger urges."

Bob Jones University is not, as skeptical readers might think, a construct of the *Nordicity* imagination. We are sorry to report that BJU is a bona fide institute of higher learning dedicated to the fight against the heresies of Darwinism, Catholicism, short hair (on women), long hair (on men), and interracial table-tennis. (Oops, after the Bush visit the American press made a fuss about that one. Now all twelve of the non-white students at the school are permitted to play ping pong with the Chosen Ones.)

Bob Jones is a privately owned school, run by a guy named, guess what, Bob Jones. It is not an accredited school, because it was at one time all-white, and still hasn't quite managed to satisfy the more stringent requirements of integration. Despite its lack of standing with the state, BJU pre-med students are accepted into medical schools all across the country. (Keep this in mind the next time you're traveling in the United States.)

The people at CAR are a bit miffed with George W, though. It turns out he apologized to "the Antichrist" (as Bob Jones calls the Pope), or at least to his local representative, the Arch-antichrist of New York, confessing that he ought to have taken issue with the school's anti-Catholic rantings. He'd earlier promised he wouldn't apologize, but guess what he found out? They let Catholics vote in presidential elections. Who knew? So of course George W. had to apologize to the millions of Roman Catholic Americans, trying at the same time not to offend all the millions of Born Again Americans who believe Rome is the Evil Empire.

Not only that, but all of the negative publicity has forced BJU to change its interracial dating rules. In a radical departure from previous policy, students of different races may now exchange glances across the quadrangle if they have the permission of all four of their parents and all living grandparents, signed in blood under a full moon.

God Is Dying

Conservative Christian bombastier Pat Robertson warned the voters of Dover Pennsylvania last week to expect trouble from Upstairs. No doubt in a spirit of charity, the popular televangelist was concerned for the community's future after God lost the election there.

In defence of the Dover electorate, they didn't actually set out to turf the deity from office last Tuesday. The citizens were mainly concerned with ridding themselves of a gang of flat-earthers on the local school board who had been abusing their office to force the teaching of superstition in science classes. The fight had become the subject of a high-profile federal court case when, backed by the American Civil Liberties Union, a group of evolved parents challenged the right of the school board, who were created in the likeness of Pat Robertson's God, to foist their religion on area high schools in the name of science. Come election day, the entire board found themselves out on the street.

The Name of God didn't actually appear on the ballot, but according to His servant, Robertson, the Prime Mover was routed in a write-out campaign. On his TV program, The 700 Club, Pastor Pat told the people of Dover, "If there is a disaster in your area, don't turn to God, you just rejected him from your city ...And don't wonder why he hasn't helped you when problems begin, if they begin ... you just voted God out of your city. And if that's the case, don't ask for his help because he might not be there."

Pennsylvanians may have some reason to be concerned; Robertson has a demonstrated talent for apocalyptic prediction. According to a Reuters story, in 1998 the TV preacher warned that, by permitting gay activists to put up rainbow flags around town, Orlando Florida risked God's wrath in the form of "hurricanes, earthquakes and terrorist bombs." It is an indisputable fact that Orlando has, since that time, seen hurricanes. Worse, the earthquakes and bombs are yet to come.

The Dover school board election was fought over something innocently named Intelligent Design, a thin coat of pseudo-scientific twaddle that's just the latest paint job on the Christian creation myth, all tarted up and presented as science. It's pure rubbish of course, focusing its attention on the tired old tomfoolery of refuting minute points in The Origin of Species, as if the scientific understanding of natural selection hadn't advanced since 1859.

Intelligent Design claims that the infinite complexity of this great wonderful universe cannot be the result of a series of accidents, but must in fact be the stamp of some Intelligent Designer (not pointing any elbows). It's a defensible philosophy. If philosophy were taught in high schools it should be on the curriculum. Religious belief is a subject worthy of study, but it isn't taught in science class because it isn't science. Integrated curriculum aside, we don't confuse mathematics with language studies, music with carpentry, theatre arts with the football team, or superstition with science.

The whole business of Christian creation myth as science should have been put to death in 1925 with the Scopes Monkey Trial. Even then Creationism, as it was known, was an embarrassment. But anti-science has festered along in ignorant backwaters, and resurfaced with new vigour during the years of George W. Bush's ascendancy, as Christianity's loony Right flexed its new muscle. It may take a few more polls before the flat-earthers notice, but that ascendancy is now over. The Rise and Fall of the Extreme Right suddenly entered phase two in recent weeks as Old Bring 'Em On cracked like a toppled statue under the weight of Camp Casey,

New Orleans, the 2000th dead soldier, and the case of the fabricated war.

Republicans took a beating in the scattered elections held around the US last week. Here a governor, there a mayor, there a school board fell. In the Senate, Republican leaders were first forced to drop drilling for oil in the Arctic National Wildlife Refuge from a $54 billion budget-cutting bill, and then to abandon the bill altogether.

It remains to be seen whether Plamegate, as the unraveling of White House and Pentagon lies and manipulations in the run-up to the invasion of Iraq has come to be known, will have the same devastating effect on the Bush White House that its namesake, Watergate, had on Nixon. It may be the world will still have to ride out another two years of Dubya, but they won't be the high-flying bring-'em-on years we've just sweated through. Without the support of the American public, Bush is a duck who, if not entirely crippled, is definitely starting to limp.

Don't worry Dover, no doubt it's the same with Pat Robertson's God. When He's riding a wave, you never know what fire and brimstone He might rain down on your head. Just look at Orlando. But where's He going to get the moral authority these days? He's dying at the polls.

The Incredible Popeman

APRIL 2005

" *There will be debates about him. But on balance, he was a man of God, he was a consistent person, he did what he thought was right. That's about all you can ask of anybody.*" Former US president Bill Clinton, speaking of Pope John Paul II.

Unseemly as it is, the haste with which the late Karol Wojtyla, alias Pope John Paul II, is rushing toward canonization has failed to match the speed of more secular tributes. Already in Bogota, Colombia, the first issue of The Incredible Popeman is rattling off the presses.

Colombian artist Rodolfo Leon created the comic-book hero as a tribute to Wojtyla, whom he describes as "a real-life superhero, of flesh and blood." According to Reuters, "... the Incredible Popeman has a battery of special equipment. Along with his yellow cape and green chastity pants, the muscular super-pontiff wields a faith staff with a cross on top and carries holy water and communion wine."

No word on whether Cardinal Bernard Law will be wearing a pair of those chastity pants in Rome this Monday when he conducts a special mourning mass for his old protector. Law is the former Archbishop of Boston, who was forced to resign just two years ago for his complicity in the rape of at least 500 Catholic children.

Law went above and beyond the call of infamy, not merely turning a blind eye to repeated child-rape by priests in his archdiocese, but transferring the offenders to new parishes to rape yet more Catholic children. The church did its best to cover up these crimes, as it's been doing for centuries, but a report by the Massachusetts Attorney General found Law responsible.

A less beatific pope might have chosen to punish the old procurer, but Saint Karol found it in his soul not only to forgive, but to promote Law to the Vatican post of Archpriest of the Basilica of Mary Major, in which function he will this week bless his earthly saviour's departed soul.

The child victims of Law's protégées have not rushed forward to forgive decades of systematic abuse with quite the same alacrity as the Incredible Popeman did, but then, not all of them survived – suicide rates among sexual abuse victims are at least double the average in the general community.

If the cover-up of the child abuse scandal had been the worst of the Vatican's crimes against children, it would have been more than enough. Rapist priests and their pandering superiors leave behind a trail of lost childhoods, broken lives, mental illness, divorce, and death. A percentage of their victims go on to commit the same horrible crimes, and the trail of evil goes on for generations.

But a greater evil hovers over the celebration of the Popeman's life. As thousands flock to mourn, to worship, and to pray, the AIDS-infected children of Africa suffer and die. How many are infected as a direct result of Vatican policies that prevent the use of condoms and spread absurdist lies about their efficacy in the prevention of disease?

For millions who mourn this week, Roman Catholicism is a deeply held faith. It brings them comfort and community, directs their spiritual lives, and helps them to find some communion with the mysteries of the universe. So much more criminal then the powerful men who manipulate that faith in the name of a deeply reactionary political movement with the blood of millions on its hands.

Things don't look good for Africa, for gay Catholics, priest-pedophilia victims, Third World women, and the other wreckage of Vatican ignorance and bigotry: Wojtyla elevated the crypto-fascist cult Opus Dei to an unprecedented level of power in the church, and appointed all but three of the cardinals who will choose his successor. The chances that they'll choose a less reactionary pope this time are slim at best.

Bill Clinton believes that all we can ask of anyone is that they be godly and consistent, and do what they think is right. Let's refrain from trying to list all the evil that's been committed throughout history by people who fit this description, and simply ask one more thing that Clinton forgot: that people of faith do what they think is right with their own lives, and leave the rest of the world in peace.

Looking Through You – The Church, The Beatles, And Petty Gossip

APRIL 2010

This week, the Pope forgave the Beatles. It's been more than four decades since John Lennon quipped that the band was "bigger than Jesus," and to judge by the front page of L'Osservatore Romano, the Vatican's official newspaper, time has finally healed that deepest of wounds.

Not content simply to forgive and forget, the authors of the papally-approved article rhapsodized about the "precious jewel" that was the Beatles. In spite of all their sex, drugs, rock'n'roll and satanic messages, the Vatican tells us, the Beatles' "beautiful melodies changed music and continue to give pleasure." No doubt the surviving Beatles are greatly relieved to know that the Holy See finally wants to hold their hand. When you're heading into your seventies, it must get tedious to be answering for something your long-deceased former friend said when you were all still wet behind the ears.

But what's motivating the church to offer this sudden olive branch? Did Ringo kiss the ring? Does Sir Paul have pull with Opus Dei? Did George promise the church My Sweet Lord for an advertising jingle? As yet none of the former Beatles are rushing to claim the credit for fixing this particular hole. So maybe the Pope took this initiative on his own. It's not hard to imagine that the Holy Father would want to encourage a spirit of forgiveness in the world today. We can all use a little forgiveness now and then.

The church has had a lot to answer for in recent months, and it's done a terrible job of answering for it, all over the world. When Irish Catholics, reeling under the latest reports of pedophile priests and an enabling church hierarchy, looked to Pope Benedict for an apology, he cast the blame everywhere but at his own feet. Adding vile insult to cruel injury, he managed to imply that the parents of abuse victims had been negligent when he encouraged them to, "play your part in ensuring the best possible care of your children."

Allegations of sexual abuse by priests quickly grew from a trickle to a flood, pouring in from Germany, Australia, Holland, Canada, the US and Italy. We learned that boys in Munich's Domspatzen Choir had lived subject to "an elaborate system of sadistic punishments combined with sexual lust," while the Pope's brother, Bishop Ratzinger, was choirmaster there. Ratzinger himself confesses to "slapping" the boys, but denies any knowledge of worse abuses.

There's evidence that suggests the Pope himself may have turned a blind eye to reports of sexual abuse by priests on more than one occasion. When he was Archbishop of Munich he once "unwittingly" approved housing for a priest who had been accused of child sex assault. The priest went on to re-offend. Later, as the cardinal responsible for the Congregation of the Doctrine of the Faith – the Vatican department that judges cases of sexual abuse – he either ignored or suppressed several reports by bishops concerning Father Lawrence Murphy, a priest who sexually abused about 200 boys at the St. John's School For The Deaf in St. Francis, Wisconsin. In his Palm Sunday address, in lieu of an apology, the Pope took the occasion to let the world know that God had given him the courage "not to be intimidated by the petty gossip of dominant opinion."

Among the church's most bizarre responses to the recent rash of sex abuse scandals came from Bill Donohue, president of the Catholic League who wrote, in a full-page New York Times ad, "The Times continues to editorialize about the 'pedophilia crisis,' when all along it's been a homosexual crisis. Eighty percent of the victims of priestly sexual abuse are male and most of them are post-pubescent."

So now we have seen the church try to blame its troubles on parents, homosexuality, gossip, and even the victims themselves, but the award for the strangest, and most offensive, church response to the scandals has to go to the Pope's personal priest, Rev. Raniero Cantalamessa. Cantalamessa told the faithful at St Peter's Basilica that criticism of the church for its demonstrated pattern of failure to protect children from known sexual predators was akin to the Nazi Holocaust.

Jews around the world understandably took issue with certain aspects of this sermon. Many have pointed out that to be criticized, even to be publicly attacked, is not the same as to be imprisoned, enslaved, tortured and murdered by the millions. Nor did it escape notice that the pedophile priests and enabling bishops are suffering "persecution" for serious crimes, or at least the allegation thereof, not for their race or religion.

The church is going to have to walk a long and winding road back to the people's trust, and it can't be done by sucking up to the remnants of a once-popular pop band. They are going to have to hold an open, honest, public enquiry, identify the guilty and hand them over to police. They're going to have to quit making excuses and blaming victims and come clean about who knew what and when. It's going to be a bloodbath, but it's one that's got to come before there can be any renewal.

Don't fight it Your Holiness. Let it be.

Imagine There's No Heaven

DECEMBER 2013

In a comic scene in Joseph Heller's 1961 novel, Catch 22, two atheists argue about God till one cries out in frustration, "But the God I don't believe in is a good God, a just God, a merciful God. He's not the mean and stupid God you make Him out to be."

The very fact that we have a word for atheism demonstrates that it's not like other forms of disbelief. There is no equivalent word for someone who is skeptical about fairies, dragons, or Stephen Harper's latest story on the Senate scandal. To be an atheist is to have considered the notion of a god, held some image of that god in your mind, and then rejected the fruit of your imagining.

Fortunately for atheists, there's no need to conceive of a good, just and merciful god, and then suffer the pain of denying him, her or it. The world is full of mean and stupid gods not to believe in. The god of the Westboro Baptist Church springs to mind, he who "hates fags" and sends his followers, most of them the issue of the group's leader, Fred Phelps, out to picket funerals.

But Phelps's deity is, if not harmless, at least toothless. He resides at the outer edge of the lunatic fringe of the gods, where his influence is limited to inflicting pain on mourners and making idiots of his own followers. Far more insidious are the high profile, big box-office gods, who can never seem to resist meddling in politics and the law. Not content to be worshipped and adored, the A-list deities insist on obedience, even if they have to go to court to get it.

The *National Post* reports that Elinor, an Israeli woman who has somehow managed to keep her last name private, "has been ordered by a religious court to circumcise her son against her will or face fines of 500 shekels ($150) for every day the procedure is not carried out." Elinor's son was born with a medical condition that made circumcision on the 8th day, as required by custom, impossible. Later, his mother balked. "As time went on," she said, "I started reading about what actually happens in circumcision, and I realized that I couldn't do that to my son. He's perfect just as he is."

In imposing the fine the rabbinical court declared that, "Fulfilling the command of circumcision is not a surgical medical act ... Brit milah is exactly what it says: a covenant that God made with His chosen people, the nation of Israel." Elinor appealed the decision to a higher rabbinical court, which rejected her case with the words, "Removal of the foreskin prepares the soul to accept the yoke of Heaven and study God's Torah and commandments."

So, if I understand this correctly, the deity in question gave the human male reproductive apparatus a hood of skin that in some manner interferes with the soul's ability to accept yokes and study commandments, two behaviours said god requires of his followers, especially the male ones. Circumcision is a kind of factory recall to correct the error.

Elinor's and her son's plight is a relatively minor example of the folly of letting superstar gods get their fingers into politics and justice. In Saudi Arabia in 2002 religious police stopped 15 girls from leaving a burning school because their heads weren't covered. All of the girls died in the fire. Saudi is only one of a number of countries in which religious law provides harsh punishments for women who drive cars, or are raped.

It is a common feature of the A-list gods that they all insist on the subjugation of women. This week Pope Francis, earthly agent for the biggest star of all, and head of the only multinational corporation to own a city-state, released an apostolic exhortation that shocked the business world by calling capitalism "a new tyranny," and criticizing inequality and exploitation. Inequality between men and women within the church, however, "is not a question open to discussion."

Francis is a champion of the rights of the poor. He favours decentralizing church power. He stands for peace and against hate. He has even made a muted statement – "who am I to judge?"– of tolerance for gays. By papal standards, he's a passionate reformer, but he serves a god with woman-issues, who can only do business with men.

Here in Canada, although our constitution mandates the separation of church and state, we're still burdened by an entrenched system of state-funded religious schools, and by legions of god-followers who clamour to insert their religious beliefs into public life. Fortunately, the electorate has so far demonstrated only limited tolerance for divine dabbling in government.

Still, gods lurk in parliament, leaping up every once in a while with a private member's bill to curtail women's rights, or a government policy that endangers women's health in Africa by directing aid through conservative religious organizations and de-funding women's health clinics.

A word to the omniscient: play fair. You're welcome to your followers, your churches, your hymns and holy books. Leave us our governments, laws, courts and police. We really can't run them properly if we're tripping over gods at every turn.

A PEEK BEHIND THE VEIL

Not the issue.

A Peek Behind The Veil

MARCH 2007

Last week, Quebec's Chief Electoral Officer Marcel Blanchet created a flurry of controversy by announcing that Muslim women who wear the niqab would be allowed to vote in the provincial election without showing their faces. Amid cries of outrage and even death threats Blanchet was forced to invoke emergency powers to reverse his decision with only three days left till election time.

According to Sarah Elgazzar of the Council on American-Islamic Relations Canada, "These women regularly uncover their faces to identify themselves, and they never asked for any kind of accommodation. This controversy kind of hunted them down and they didn't have anything to do with it." Montreal economist and niqab-wearer Shama Naz agrees, "Muslim women have no problem identifying themselves for security reasons. If they had spoken to me they would have known I wouldn't mind identifying myself at the ballot box."

In Canadian elections, a voter is not normally required to prove her identity. She gives her name to the deputy returning officer, the poll clerk checks to see if the name is on the list of electors, and if it's there and not struck off as having voted, they give her a ballot. If someone's already voted in her name, she'll need to produce identification. In that case, there would be no point in raising her veil unless she could produce photo I.D.

The whole silly incident was a manufactured crisis. It had nothing at all to do with the security of the vote, and everything to do with the recent squabble in Quebec over "reasonable accommodation," that is, how far should the province bend to accommodate immigrants and ethnic minorities?

Multiculturalism took a giant step too far when Ontario and Quebec flirted with the idea of court diversion programs based on Islamic Shariah law.

Shariah is not a single, unified code. It's practiced differently in different countries, and by different sects, but it always makes judges of priests, and it often makes victims out of women. Under Shariah law Afghan women have been beheaded for adultery, Pakistani women sentenced to gang-rape in revenge for crimes committed by their male relatives, and Nigerian girls beaten for becoming pregnant after they were raped. Not surprisingly, the idea met serious resistance in Ontario and Quebec, and had to be abandoned.

But from that point on, it seemed that a certain portion of society had drawn battle lines, and were determined to fight. With the threat of Shariah behind them, Quebecers began to grasp at lesser outrages: headscarves on soccer fields, men banned from pre-natal classes with Muslim women.

When a Montreal YWCA frosted a window rather than expose the Hassidic synagogue across the street to the gyrations of the spandex crowd, members signed a petition for "the right to see and be seen" while exercising. According to a spokesperson for the pro-ogling lobby, "It's like (they're) forcing us to wear the veil."

Matters went from silly to vicious in January when the town council of Herouxville passed a resolution described as a "life code" banning all kinds of practices the councillors regard as un-Quebecois, from the wearing of the kirpan, a ceremonial Sikh dagger whose use in Canada is protected by a Supreme Court decision, to throwing acid in women's faces. It further censures covering one's face except on Halloween, failure to sing carols at Christmas, and beheading one's wife. Herouxville had thousands of e-mails in support of the life code, and other Quebec municipalities expressed an interest in similar resolutions.

This undercurrent of xenophobia has percolated

beneath the surface of the provincial election campaign. Action Democratique Quebec's right-wing leader, Mario Dumont, has proposed a "Quebec constitution" that would specifically limit accommodation for non-Quebecois cultures. In a letter to the people of Quebec Dumont said, "We must make gestures which reinforce our national identity and protect those values which are so invaluable to us."

ADQ is scoring well at the polls, and it's not just because they're promising to cut taxes and get tough on welfare recipients. With 59 per cent of Quebecers describing themselves as slightly to moderately racist, Dumont has positioned himself as the tough guy who will stand up for the province's treasured national identity. If the right wing populist doesn't say that this means persecuting Muslims, he knows that the thousands who supported the Herouxville resolution will read it that way, and approve.

Herouxville's racist attack on Muslims was presented as an expression of outrage against fundamentalist abuse of women. Between 1974 and 2000 in Quebec, an average of 17 women per year were murdered by their husbands. In 2000, 43 per cent of Quebecers reported having witnessed an act of spousal violence directed against a woman. When it comes to outrage about violence against women, there's no need to direct it all at Muslims.

Religious fanaticism is archaic, sexist, and hateful, and the world would be a better place without it. How much better is anti-religious fanaticism? Open and pluralistic societies don't exist so that we can impose openness and pluralism on people who choose to live by codes we find distasteful, any more than they exist to license extremism. It's good that there's a debate about reasonable accommodation. It's a shame that debate has to descend into racism and buffoonery.

Christians versus Gay Cartoons, Part Two

MARCH 2005

Reverend Lou Sheldon, founder of the American right wing activist group Traditional Values Coalition, acknowledged last week that brain-damage celebrity Terri Schiavo has been a bit of a gold mine for his movement. "What this issue has done is it has galvanized people the way nothing could have done in an off-election year," Sheldon gloated.

The Reverend admits, albeit in more sanctimonious words, that the TVC is cashing in on the unfortunate woman's predicament, both politically and financially. "That is what I see as the blessing that dear Terri's life is offering to the conservative Christian movement in America," said Sheldon, according to the New York Times. Last week the Times reported that on the TVC Web page, "next to a link to the Web site of her parents' foundation is a pitch to 'become an active supporter of the Traditional Values Coalition by pledging a monthly gift.'"

Whether or not you find this ghoulish will no doubt depend on whether you support the projects for which this money is destined. If, for instance, moved by the blessing of dear Terri's life, you pledge a monthly ten dollars to TVC, you may or may not be pleased to learn that the money is being used in that organization's campaign against the transgender activist, Shrek.

Shrek is a hulking, blue-skinned, good-hearted cartoon character who, along with fellow-traveler SpongeBob Squarepants, is out to convert good Christian children to homosexuality, cross-dressing, and sex-change surgery. It appears that in the movie Shrek 2, distasteful jokes are made about male characters wearing women's underpants, in clear violation of traditional American values.

It may be that the reason I'm unable to get exercised about the cross-dressing jokes in Shrek is that I grew up in a more permissive society. In the British Isles, during the 1950s and 60s, no entertainment was considered truly funny unless it included men in women's clothing. I wonder now why my parents' generation didn't see the risk they ran with their children's nascent sexuality. Thank goodness for the civilizing influence of American TV, that helped us never to forget God's holy dress code: blue for a boy, pink for a girl, and no skirts on men unless they're Scottish. (Yes, the TV was black-and-white, but you knew damn well Pa Cartwright was not wearing pink.)

I don't know if it will help to alleviate the TVC's concerns, but news out of Germany would seem to suggest that sexuality may be naturally acquired and non-transferable. It seems that a small group of homosexual penguins in Bremerhaven Zoo have flat refused to join the ex-gay movement, despite being tempted by sexy Swedish mail-order brides. The penguins – and there is no evidence that these birds had ever watched cartoons – had confounded their keepers by forming mating couples, but failing to breed. It took some time for researchers to conclude that these mating pairs were actually male same-sex couples.

Here your chronicler must confess ignorance on the subject of penguin anatomy, except to say that zoo-keepers are apparently no better able than the rest of us to tell the penguin girls from the penguin boys. Penguins, it seems, have no traditional values. Perhaps if the females wore pink, it would help to keep things clear. At any rate, the Swedish female penguins have failed to raise any interest among the gay males. At least one of the gay couples would apparently like to procreate – they've been observed trying to hatch rocks – but none have shown any interest in the girls. The zoo is now shopping around for male penguins whose traditional values are more in keeping with procreation.

So my question for the TVC is this: if it's this hard to convert a gay penguin to heterosexuality, what's the matter with the budding flower of

American manhood, who will abandon their traditional values over a joke about a cartoon donkey in panties? As for Terri Schiavo, I don't mean to make light of her situation. Her options were always either a hideous life or a horrible death, and no way to affect the decision. Rather than starve to death she deserves at least the consideration we'd give a dog: swift, legal, euthanasia.

But it sheds some light on the collective conservative outrage at her treatment to know that many so-called red states have Futile Care laws permitting hospitals to pull the feeding tube on terminally or incurably ill patients.

The Texas version, signed into law by governor George W. Bush, is for the most part a sane and humane piece of legislation, which allows Texans to decide in advance not to be kept alive by artificial means when they're beyond hope of recovery. But a clause in the act permits hospitals to make this decision for the patient in defiance of the family's wishes. The family's one option is to transfer the patient to another facility, if they can afford it. If not, their tube gets pulled – without a single word of protest from the Traditional Values Coalition, or George W. Bush.

Had Terri Schiavo's family been poor, her life might well have ebbed away unheralded, without blessing the conservative Christian movement in North America, or the anti-Shrek campaign, by so much as a single penny.

What a tragedy that would have been.

CHRISTIAN VS. GAY CARTOONS

CHAPTER 7: OH, *CANADA*

" HOW DO WE CONVINCE THE WORLD, OURSELVES INCLUDED, THAT WE'RE NOT JUST AMERICANS WITH BLUE LIPS?

Generation after generation, one question plagues Canadians. How do we convince the world, ourselves included, that we're not just Americans with blue lips?

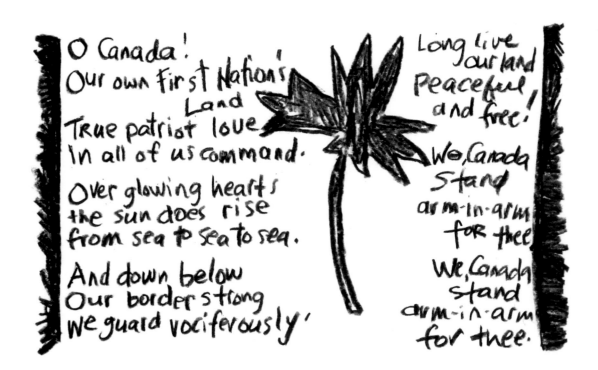

O Canada!
Our own First Nation's
Land
True patriot love
In all of us command.

Over glowing hearts
the sun does rise
from sea ↑ sea to sea.

And down below
Our border strong
We guard vociferously.

Long live
our land
Peaceful,
and free!

We, Canada
stand
arm-in-arm
for thee

We, Canada
stand
arm-in-arm
for thee.

Disnefying Canada: Go Ducks Go

JUNE 2007

This January in the *Globe and Mail*, Margaret Atwood reported that the Harper government had cut all funding for the promotion of Canadian arts and culture abroad. Though some of that money was later unfrozen, according to Atwood it was "not enough to save the networks" that are the product of 40 years of political work.

Atwood points out what a brainless move it is for a government running a multi-billion dollar surplus to slash already-minimal funding for one of the most productive sectors in the economy, one that generates an estimated $40 billion annually. She ponders what the reasons might be for such mystifying behaviour. Postulating ignorance, stupidity, and hatred of the arts, Atwood suggests that Harper and crew either don't realize what a vibrant, essential economic machine arts and culture are, or are predisposed to see artists as unemployed whiners and art as a "degenerate frill" that can be bought cheaper abroad.

Their hatred for the arts is tangible and can't be denied, but it would be a mistake to dismiss the Conservatives as stupid. Though driven by stupid ideas, the Harperites show no lack of cunning, and their ignorance is clearly willful, as Atwood says. Finance Minister Jim Flaherty has surely seen the figures by now, and knows that subsidies to the arts pay off many times over in the GDP.

The return on the arts investment is irrelevant to the Conservatives, who are opposed not just to spending money on Canadian culture, but to its existence. In the march toward a North American Union, currently under the guise of the Security and Prosperity Partnership, it's an act of subversion to promote Canada's distinct culture beyond the tourist-shop level of musical ride postcards, hockey sweaters, and Indian princess dolls.

Harper's much reported anti-Canadian rhetoric and his blatant cozying up to the Bush regime make it easy to forget that he inherited the SPP from his Liberal predecessor, billionaire shipping magnate Paul Martin. The SPP is a project of the extremely wealthy and their hangers on, spearheaded in Canada by the Canadian Council of Chief Executives, and fully supported by both Liberals and Conservatives.

But what price Canadian nationalism? Does it really matter what remains of our sovereignty? The Canada US border is an accident of colonial history. It cuts a vicious slash through ancient aboriginal territories, and makes trade less profitable and travel a damn nuisance. Why not simply do away with Canada? Why spend the taxpayers' money promoting a unique Canadian culture when we could be making extra payments on the debt? Why not live in one giant prosperous North American superculture in a great continent-wide zone of free trade and security?

According to Murray Dobbin, writing in last week's Tyee, we're currently in the act of reducing our standards on over three hundred regulatory regimes, in order to "harmonize" with US standards. Already underway as part of NAFTA but "fast-tracked" by the SPP, deregulation is a race to the bottom, so in cases where American standards are stronger, they'll be harmonized with ours.

Over the long run the result will be more toxins in groceries, lower wages, more workplace accidents, more highway deaths – in short, a marked reduction in security and prosperity for the majority of North Americans. The SPP is not so much a plan to make Canada an American colony as to make both countries and their citizens better suited to the service of the ultra-rich. America is closer to that goal today, so Canada will for the most part have to be Americanized. Canadian culture gets in the way of the security of corporations and the prosperity of billionaires, and that's why the Harperites are taking a meat-axe to it, and that's why Canadians should fight for it to the last inch.

For all their faults, democratic nation states are the agency by which ordinary people exert their citizenship. Multinational corporations and wealthy individuals have tremendous power, and without strong national governments and informed, engaged citizens there's nothing to control that power. One vote in millions doesn't sound like much, but the will of the people can still change the world. Deals like the SPP exist to reduce the effectiveness of that collective will, and solidify corporate power.

The power of citizenship has never been more important than it is today. A well informed citizenry will oppose evils such as nuclear proliferation, rising greenhouse gas emissions, the corporate rape of the Third World, the strip-mining of the oceans, and the never-ending war to control the world's vanishing resources. The CCCEO wants to reduce the power of that citizenry because frankly, it ain't good for business.

Harper does see the value in certain aspects of Canadian culture. It couldn't have been cheap, for instance, to take the Stanley Cup to Afghanistan to help bolster troop morale. What a sad and fitting end to that story that the cup is now held by the Anaheim Mighty Ducks, many of whose players are Canadians, but whose owner is American media giant Walt Disney, the biggest culture-peddler in the world.

Set My People Free

There's great news for white Canadians this week. Correctional Investigator of Canada Howard Sapers released his annual report on Tuesday, and it reveals that despite the government's get-tough-on-crime agenda, the prison system is locking up fewer Caucasians than it did 10 years ago.

In the past decade, while Conservative policies have swelled prison populations, the proportion of prisoners who share Justice Minister Peter Mackay's skin tone has dropped by 13 per cent. While whites make up about 85 per cent of the general population, we represent only 61 per cent of prisoners. In absolute numbers, there are three per cent fewer white people in prison than in 2003, even though 2,100 more Canadians are incarcerated. The numbers look even better if you're an educated, well-paid white man in good mental health. Nearly half of today's prisoners have accessed mental health services, and 80 per cent have substance abuse issues. The average prisoner has a Grade 8 education.

The number of women in prison has increased by 40 per cent in five years. The number of aboriginal women has increased by more than 80 per cent in 10 years. Of those incarcerated women, 85 per cent have been the victims of physical abuse and 68 per cent have been sexually assaulted.

Black people make up nine per cent of the prison population, though only three per cent of Canadians are black. For aboriginal people, the numbers are even more striking: 21 per cent of prisoners, but only 4.3 per cent of the population. As Sapers reports, "if not for these subgroups, the offender population growth rate would have flatlined some time ago."

Sapers suggests that these figures, rather than being good news for the dominant culture, indicate a problem in the system. "Beyond rising inmate counts and costs, Canadians should be interested in who is ending up behind bars. Questions about whom we incarcerate, for how long and why are important public policy issues," he says.

But the Conservative government has no interest in black or aboriginal people. According to Public Safety Minister Steven Blaney, "The only minority I would say we are interested in are the criminals." Can you guess what colour Blaney is?

It's always good to be free, but the white middle class have particular reason to celebrate their un-incarcerated state because, as Sapers outlines in his report, "To make sure that inmates are not 'coddled' has meant making prisons more austere, more crowded, more unsafe and ultimately less effective." Among the growing dangers faced by prisoners he lists "increases in assaults, in use of force, in lockdowns, in gang membership, in self-harm incidents, in placement in segregation."

While taking TVs out of prisons, reducing yard time, double-bunking inmates in single cells, cutting pay for prison work, and making inmates pay for phone calls, those fabulous money-managers in the government have managed to increase the correctional budget by 40 per cent, or $2.6 billion in five years. This is a remarkable achievement, particularly in light of the fact that crime rates had been dropping for years before the Harper government ever came to power.

Sapers says, "crowding, too much time spent in cells; lack of contact with the outside world, lack of program capacity, the paucity of meaningful prison work or vocational skills training and polarization between inmates and custodial staff" are dragging the system back 40 years, to a time of deadly prison riots. Not to worry, the purchase of pepper spray has not been affected by budget cuts.

If you are one of the unfortunate white people who does end up in prison, take heart. According to Sapers, "(Blacks and aboriginals) are over-represented in maximum security institutions and segregation placements. They are more likely to be subject to use of force interventions and incur a disproportionate number of institutional disciplinary charges. They are released later in their sentences and less likely to be granted day or full parole."

Higher rates of incarceration, longer sentences, and tougher prison conditions do nothing to lower crime rates or increase public safety. In fact, they make matters worse, because they make it more difficult to rehabilitate prisoners and reintegrate them into society. But really, what does it matter? Most of the damage done is done to minority groups, and as Blaney says, who cares about them?

It's still a great country to be white in.

Squandering Canada's Water

NOVEMBER 2008

Canadians are fond of reminding each other that 20 per cent of the world's fresh water lies within our borders. It's a reassuring figure, and one that leads to some debate: should we commercialize this abundance, and profit from sales to a drought-ridden United States, or conserve the resource for our own future?

According to a suppressed Environment Canada report from 2007, our self-image as a water-rich nation is more mirage than oasis. In reality, Canadians are facing the possibility of an acute water crisis in the near future. Obtained in an access to information request by the Council of Canadians and Mining Watch, the report makes fascinating, if chilling, reading.

Most of Canada's vaunted freshwater supply is non-renewable. The Great Lakes, for instance, are almost entirely filled with ancient glacier-melt, or "fossil water" which can never be replaced. Our real share of the world's renewable water supply is about 7 per cent, much lower than that of Brazil and Russia, and about equal to that of the US.

Only 1 per cent of Canada's fresh water is renewed annually. The rest is stored in underground aquifers or in glaciers. Further, as the report points out, "most of our rivers flow north" away from where most of our citizens live. Unless we are so foolish as to squander fossil water that once spent can never be recovered, we are not nearly as rich in water as we have been led to believe.

Canada's water supply faces multiple threats from increased population, industrial pollution, and climate change. Here in the Yukon, for instance, the report predicts "impacts on river flows caused by glacial retreat and disappearance" resulting in "reduced hydroelectric power, ecological impacts (including fisheries) damage to infrastructure, (and) water apportionment." According to the report, 33 per cent of Canadians depend on groundwater. But our knowledge of its "quantity, its quality and renewal rate are sparse and often inadequate for management." This lack of data weakens our position in negotiations over cross-border water issues with the US.

Canadians are the world's second biggest per capita consumers of water. To make matters worse, the number one consuming country is right next door, and they're running short. And unlike the General Agreement on Tariffs and Trade, the North American Free Trade Agreement contains no provisions to protect national sovereignty over water.

Canada has a patchwork of laws that protect our water from bulk exports, but NAFTA Chapter 11 has the potential to override these. Chapter 11 is the provision in the trade agreement that permits foreign corporations to sue governments over any regulation proven to be bad for business. For instance in 1997, when the Government of Canada tried to ban the gasoline additive MMT – a known neurotoxin – its manufacturer successfully sued, winning $13 million in damages and causing the repeal of the ban. In 1998, Sun Belt Water Corporation of California filed a notice of claim for $10 billion over British Columbia's ban on bulk water exports. The Chretien government negotiated with the company, but the results of those talks have never been made public.

Large areas of the US are desperate for water, and growing ever more so. A great deal of this desperation could be relieved by appropriate conservation methods, and by a radical change in farming practices, but instead corporations and their allies in government have their eye on Canada's mythical supply of endless clean water. In a leaked "concept paper" for the 2007 Security and Prosperity Partnership meeting in Montebello Quebec, the Washington-based Centre for Strategic and International Studies spoke of the need "to overcome the bureaucratic challenges posed by ... different political systems and legal regimes, particularly if the overriding future goal of North America is to achieve joint optimum utilization of the available water."

Last year the Bloq Quebecois made a motion in Parliament to re-open NAFTA in order to protect Canada's water from bulk exports. The Conservative government voted the motion down. With no such protection in the agreement, it's hard to say how long we can resist "joint optimum utilization" of our own scarce store of renewable fresh water. Bulk water transfers by pipeline or diversion could prove disastrous for Canada's environment, and for our domestic supply. Existing and projected pressures on our water – such as global warming and population increase – mean we will have to change our ways, to learn to use domestic water wisely, to curtail industrial pollution of our lakes and rivers, and to turn away from water-greedy commercial farming methods.

After we've taken these steps to conserve our own fresh water supply, when the neighbours come knocking looking to redirect Canadian rivers, we can suggest instead that they try a little conservation of their own. We might look like a water-rich nation, but the truth is we barely have enough to go around.

And now, Nestlé is pumping an annual 230 million litres from a Fraser Valley BC aquifer for its bottling plant, for which the province charges them pennies. There are no restrictions on where this water goes.

The Man Who Stilled The Waters

FEBRUARY 2009

On his first official visit to Canada, US President Barrack Obama reassured America's largest trading partner that "buy American" provisions in his multi-billion dollar stimulus package do not signal an end to "free trade" between our two countries. "Now is a time where we have to be very careful about any signals of protectionism," Obama told the assembled press in a joint news conference with Prime Minister Stephen Harper. And with these words he stretched out his hands, and calmed the winds and raging waves in the Canadian political teapot.

US government contracts have always carried "buy American" provisions, both at the state and federal levels. To some extent these have been tempered by NAFTA and other trade agreements, but for the most part they include the very sensible provision that American taxpayers' money should be spent, where possible, on American goods and services. There was never any reason to panic, or even to be mildly concerned, about the latest assertion of America's desire to use American materials and labour in government projects. Not only did it reflect long-standing practice in the US, it's similar, if not identical, to Canada's own policy.

According to the Ministry of Public Works 2008 supply manual, "The Canadian Content Policy is a Cabinet-mandated policy. The Policy encourages industrial development in Canada by limiting, in specific circumstances, competition for government procurement opportunities to suppliers of Canadian goods and services." Like the American policy, the "buy Canadian" clause contains exceptions for NAFTA and other trade agreements.

Only one government agency is specifically named in the Canadian content clause. According to the policy, the Canadian International Development Agency (CIDA) is obliged to buy Canadian on purchases made "on its own account." In fact, CIDA's entire operation is coloured by a commitment to Canadian goods and services, a policy known as "tied aid."

As an example of the effectiveness of tied Canadian aid, when famine struck Niger in 2005, Canada's insistence that 90 per cent of its aid dollars be spent on Canadian produce meant that the food arrived months late. The famine was essentially over, and the influx of free Canadian food drove down prices for local farmers. In Bangladesh CIDA funded the establishment of a free-trade zone where Canadian companies can benefit from the cheapest labour in the world. In Afghanistan most of the money we claim to spend on our biggest aid recipient ends up in Canadian corporate pockets, or is linked to military spending.

In Haiti, CIDA funded the right-wing political organizations that helped the US and its allies, including Canada, to engineer a violent coup d'état that overthrew the elected government of Jean Bertrand Aristide and paved the way for an expansion of "free trade zones" where Haitian workers are subjected to such abuses as being beaten and forced at gunpoint to work beyond the ten-hour day legal maximum. This week Bev Oda, the cabinet minister responsible for CIDA, announced the names of the 20 countries in which Canada will invest the bulk of its foreign aid. While dropping far more desperate countries – Kenya, Rwanda, Cameroon – the new list adds Peru and Colombia, two states with which Harper has recently signed trade agreements similar to NAFTA.

According to Oda aid Jean-Luc Benoit, the change in aid policy is "a function of need, of the capacity to deliver aid effectively, and supporting Canada's foreign policy." In other words aid is being redirected from the most needy countries to those most likely to further Harper's political agenda of closer foreign-policy ties to the US and stronger trade agreements in the Americas.

This won't be CIDA's fist venture into Latin America by any means. During the late 1990s the development agency spent $11 million campaigning to rewrite Colombia's mining regulations to reflect a "globalized perspective." In effect, this was international aid aimed at opening business opportunities for Canadian mining companies. The North South Institute, a Canadian independent development agency, describes the result as a "regressive mining code that has weakened – rather than strengthened – democratic procedures."

Liberal and Conservative fears that the storm of US protectionism would rise up and swamp our poor little economic boat were not only unfounded, they were pure political posturing, and Obama's "peace be still" was little more. In the globalist system laughably described as "free trade," powerful wealthy nations can take whatever steps necessary to protect their own economies. It's only the poor and weak who are forced to open their borders unconditionally.

Never Mind The Human Rights, We're From Canada

NOVEMBER 2010

Last October, when the government of Honduras fell to a military coup d'état driven by powerful business interests, one of the largest piles of chips on the table, the San Martin mine in the Siria Valley, was owned and operated by Vancouver mining giant Goldcorp. For years the mine had been at the centre of protests and blockades, as well as a court case, over its alienation of indigenous land and the diversion and pollution of water needed for agriculture.

Ousted president Manuel Zelaya was about to entrench peasants' land and water rights in law, as well as a national minimum wage, measures that would have cost Goldcorp and other foreign corporations a lot of money. Backed by a program of beatings, shootings, arbitrary arrest, and torture a new president took office this January. Since then Judges who criticized the regime have been shoved out of their jobs, and seven journalists who failed to write the party line have been murdered. Zelaya's social reforms are now dead, and it's full speed ahead in San Martin.

Reports from Amnesty International, Mining Watch, The United Nations, and many others hold Canadian mining companies both directly and indirectly responsible for human rights abuses, from alienation of indigenous lands to the brutal repression of protest, to the murder of anti-mining activists in Honduras, Guatemala, Argentina, Ecuador, El Salvador, Mexico, Burma, Congo, and the Philippines, to name a few. According to a mining industry report, Canadian companies face four times as many such charges as companies from other major mining nations.

Last week, the Canadian parliament voted down a private members bill that would have enforced ethical standards on Canadian resource extraction companies operating abroad. The governing Conservatives voted against the bill in a block, while the opposition Liberals, one of whose members sponsored the bill, absented themselves in high enough numbers to let it fail.

Why did the leaders of Canada's two big-business parties shut down a bill that would have held companies responsible when they trample indigenous land rights, steal farmers' water, pillage minerals, pollute rivers and lakes, emit toxic smoke, leave behind toxic tailings, hire thugs and militias to suppress dissent, and finance repressive governments?

The Mining Association of Canada, the Canadian Chamber of Commerce, and the Yukon Chamber of Mines, speak with one voice on this question: it's all about false accusations. Perrin Beattie, CEO of the CCC summed it up: "It would encourage groups, and particularly the competitors of Canadian companies, to launch false accusations." Or as Carl Schultz of the Yukon chamber of Mines puts it, "A bad reputation can live on, if it's proven wrong."

I'm surprised we don't see more of this false accusations argument. It's a tidy answer to any kind of complaints process, indeed to regulation at all. Let's face it, if you have rules, anybody can claim that somebody broke them. Such claims can be very damaging to the reputation. Civilian oversight of police? Environmental regulations? Traffic laws? The Criminal Code? Each and every one an invitation to false accusation.

During debate, much was made of the idea that the defeated bill would have harmed mining in Canada, particularly in the North. How would a law against human rights and environmental abuses in foreign lands harm mining in Canada? Are mines here so unprofitable that they have to be propped up by offshore revenue obtained by stealing land and water, exploiting miners, and violently repressing dissent?

The Yukon Party government introduced a motion in the territorial legislature urging our MP to vote against the bill. Did they buy the argument that trying to prevent widespread pollution, land-theft, violent repression, union busting, and murder in poorer countries would somehow make it harder to extract minerals out of the Yukon's mountains? Corporations and the political parties that support them oppose accountability because it would harm profits. It costs money to negotiate fairly with farmers and peasants for their land. It costs money to reduce pollution and to treat workers decently.

This is not a story about false accusations, or about some nebulous harm that may be caused to mining in the Yukon when giant Canadian corporations are curtailed in their ability to tramp all over Third World communities. It's a story about corporate profits, and about a country that has just announced to the world we don't give a damn about human rights. Just show us the money.

Exporting Hate Speech

This week the Supreme Court of Canada upheld the hate crimes conviction of William Whatcott, a Saskatchewan anti-homosexual crusader whose pamphlets equate gay men with pedophiles, and claim that "children will pay the price in disease, death, abuse and ultimately eternal judgment" for tolerance of gays in schools. While condemning some of his works, the court found that two of Whatcott's pamphlets, though virulently anti-gay, stopped short of criminal hate-mongering.

In finding some of Whatcott's writings criminal and others not, the court helped to define what constitutes hate speech in Canada. According to this week's decision, hate speech "equates the targeted group with groups traditionally reviled in society." The offensive pamphlets are deemed to be illegal because they "delegitimize homosexuals by referring to them as filthy or dirty sex addicts and by comparing them to pedophiles." Whatcott's right to freedom of speech extends to speaking out against gay men's right to advertise for casual sex hook-ups, but does not permit him to lump them in with child molesters or describe them as filth.

Inevitably, the Whatcott decision has drawn fire from defenders of free speech. Jonathan Kay used his space in the *National Post* to describe the judgment as "anti-Christian censorship," and stands by the right of religious conservatives to see gays as "agents of civilization-destroying 'filth,' or as some sort of deadly bacillus or abomination," (though he asserts that these are not his own views).

A strong voice for freedom of speech in Canada is about to fall silent when Doug Christie succumbs to liver cancer, sometime in the near future. Christie is a lawyer who has made a career of defending those accused of hate speech. His clientele has featured some of the bright lights of anti-Semitism in Canada, from Alberta junior high school teacher Jim Keegstra, who taught his students that Jews were treacherous, sadistic, money-loving child killers who "created the Holocaust to gain sympathy," to the violent neo-Nazi leader Wolfgang Droege.

Christie has always said that his defence of Holocaust deniers and anti-Semites was about freedom of speech, and the right of accused persons to fair representation. But even he doesn't believe in untrammelled free speech; when broadcaster Barry Bannerman said, in 1990, that Christie had "aligned himself so many times with these perverted monsters that he has to be viewed as one himself," the free speech defender sued, and lost. Christie had more success in an earlier case where he sued a journalist for describing his separatist right-wing Western Canada Concept as the "Alberta version of the Ku Klux Klan."

So we can see that even the strongest defenders of freedom of speech believe that some speech should not be free. Speech which is both false and harmful can and should give rise to legal action. It wasn't true that the WCC was a version of the KKK, and the falsehood did harm by drawing unwanted attention to the group's right-wing extremism. It isn't true that gay men are filth, or pedophiles, and saying that they are can encourage gay-bashing, which too often turns deadly, or leads to anti-gay bullying in schools, which in turn can lead to teenage suicide.

Until recently the website of a group called Crossroads Christian Communications included the following list of "sexual sins" or "perversion(s)": "pedophilia, homosexuality and lesbianism, sadism, masochism, transvestism, and bestiality." This text, so similar in style and content to what the Supreme Court has just judged to be hate speech, was pulled down after the public learned that CCC had received federal funding of almost $550,000 for development work in Uganda. Uganda raised international controversy when it proposed a law making homosexuality punishable by death. According to the London Evening Standard, that law "was proposed after a visit by US Christian ministry leaders."

To his credit, Foreign Affairs Minister John Baird has taken a strong stand against the proposed anti-gay law in Uganda, but Julian Fantino, the minister responsible for foreign aid, dismisses CCC's homophobic views as irrelevant because Canada's funding of the group only extends to development work.

CCC, which produces the popular Christian TV show 100 Huntley Street, is very clearly an evangelical organization, which is to say its purpose is to spread the gospel. If the gospel according to them includes the belief that homosexuality is morally equivalent to two very serious crimes – child molesting and bestiality – those are falsehoods which have the potential to be extremely harmful in the mouths of missionaries in a country contemplating the death penalty for gays.

According to a study published in the Canadian Journal of Development Studies, Canada has increased its funding to religious aid organizations by 42 per cent under the Harper government. With foreign aid increasingly being channeled through conservative evangelical groups very much like CCC, how can Canadians be assured that the ideas we're paying to export to developing countries don't violate our own laws against hate speech?

Towards A Fair-Goal NHL

MAY 2013

A controversy has erupted in the National Hockey League over its first-past-the-post scoring system. Fair Goal NHL, a public interest group, is calling for sweeping changes to the way that goals are counted during hockey games. Currently, the winner in a game is determined solely by counting up the goals and handing absolute victory to the team that gets the highest score.

According to a spokesperson for FGNHL, only seven per cent of goals scored in play-off games last year were "successful goals," or goals which eventually lead to winning the Stanley Cup. Clearly, this disenfranchises the players who scored goals in a losing effort, or who won the game but lost the series, or who made it to the finals but lost. What to do about all those unsuccessful goals?

To address the inequity of first-past-the-post hockey, FGNHL proposes a hybrid mixed-player team-list single-transferable-goal play-off season, with the Stanley Cup shared between the first-past-the-post champions and the winners of a complex two-tiered scoring system.

Ok, for all its faults the NHL hasn't turned quite that silly yet. But in the larger arena of Canadian politics, such silliness abounds. Fair Vote Canada, a group which advocates for proportional representation, asserts that votes cast for the losing side "don't even count," that majority governments elected under the present system are "phoney," and that the way we currently elect our governments "is not democracy." But Yukon PR booster Dave Brekke goes them one better. In his view, "843 voters are NOT represented because they voted for losing candidates." (His capitals).

It is, as PR promoters like to point out, common in Canada for a government to win a majority with only a plurality of votes. Opponents of Stephen Harper are fond of saying that he holds a majority government with only 39 per cent of the vote. This complaint ignores the fact that there are more than two political parties in Canada. The NDP, with 30 per cent, came second, and the Liberals, with 20 per cent, came third. A fringe party with less than 10 per cent of the vote came last. How is this unfair?

Consider three friends voting on whether to order pizza or Chinese. If two vote for pizza, was the one who voted for Chinese disenfranchised? After all, she got 33 per cent of the vote, and no wontons. If people all over town are voting on take-out, and pizza is winning most of the time, do we need a system to reconcile the votes of all the losing voters? Observe the language: you win a vote, or you lose it. That's been called democracy for centuries.

Contrary to Brekke's claim, all Yukoners are represented in the Yukon Legislative Assembly. Many are not represented by the person they voted for, but that's what voting is about. Brekke suggests that voters are disenfranchised unless they can "point to an MLA whom their vote helped to elect and be relatively comfortable taking their complements, suggestions or concerns to." Voters, take your suggestions and concerns to your MLA, whether you voted for them or not. If they refuse to help because you're not a supporter, expose them, they are not doing their job.

Some of the imbalance in the current system is built in to protect regional interests, and we in the Yukon should be grateful for that, and wary of those who seek to change it. One thing that unites PR supporters and conservatives is the notion that to be fair, votes ought to count equally. There are six ridings in the Greater Toronto Area each with between 150,000 and 180,000 voters. In order to balance our vote with theirs, we would have to live

in a riding composed of the three territories, plus Labrador and Prince George-Peace River.

Proportional representation is fairly common around the world. It exists in Germany, and in 2004 it allowed the neo-Nazi NPD to elect 12 members with 10 per cent of the vote in a provincial election in Saxony. Under Israel's PR system tiny right wing extremist parties hold the balance of power and are a tremendous impediment to peace and democracy. There are currently 39 parties in the Italian legislature, an institution so fractious it barely functions at all.

Canada's electoral system is not perfect, but then whose is? Democracy is a messy business. There may be benefits to be gained by making the voting system more proportional, but there are also great risks. Electoral reform should be an ongoing process, and we should always be open to improvements in the system, as well as cautious about jumping into grand experiments based on silly talk. The heated rhetoric coming out of the PR camp implies that the current system is a total failure, and there's a perfect one out there waiting to replace it. Wrong on both counts.

When Friends Fall Out

AUGUST 2013

Last week the anti-feminist lobby group Real Women of Canada launched an attack on Foreign Affairs Minister John Baird who had, according to a press release written by national vice president Gwen Landolt, "awarded $200,000 of Canadian taxpayers' money by way of the Department of Foreign Affairs to special interest groups in Uganda and Kenya to further his own perspective on homosexuality."

Mr Baird's perspective on homosexuality brings him into conflict with the Ugandan government, who propose the death penalty for gays. In what Landolt describes as "the strange, intolerant world Mr Baird wishes to impose on sovereign countries" gay sex in Kenya would not be punishable by fourteen years in one of the world's harshest prisons, while in Russia, if Baird had his way, it would not be possible to jail and fine someone for speaking in favour of gay rights, holding a pride parade, or engaging in – I swear I am not making this up – "relations not conducive to procreation."

You could almost hear the shudder run through the Conservative backrooms of Canada; the staunchest bastion of social conservatism had just fired a shot across the bow of the Conservative Party. Baird is the Harper government's jewel: a dyed-in-the-wool fiscal conservative spawned in Harper's favourite pond, Mike Harris's disastrous Ontario government, he's also a personable, quick-witted partisan who, it's said, can schmooze a room in ways the wooden Harper can only dream of. Real Women of Canada is the extreme right-wing's vanguard in its desperate battle for the hearts and minds of ordinary Canadians. Should this quarrel live on until election time, it could do real damage to the Conservative brand.

For RWoC and the Conservative Party to fall out is no small matter. The two grew up together, and

> " FRINGE GROUPS LIKE RWoC TAKE A LONG TIME TO FADE AWAY. LIKE BARNACLES THEY CLING TO THE UNDERSIDE OF POLITICAL LIFE LONG AFTER THEY SHOULD HAVE PERISHED FROM IRRELEVANCE.

have faced some tough times at each other's side. Real Women had to cope with public criticism over the fact that founding director Rita Anne Hartmann was a real neo-Nazi with close ties to the Ku Klux Klan, while the young Reform Party, driven by public outcry, was obliged to dismiss several right-wing extremist candidates and MPs. In 1989, according to Murray Dobbin, in his book *Preston Manning and the Reform Party*, as founding members of the extremist Northern Foundation, Hartmann and Stephen Harper fought shoulder-to-shoulder in a losing campaign in support of the South African Apartheid regime.

RWoC was founded in 1983, largely in response to the rise of the feminist group the National Action Committee on the Status of Women. Though a much smaller organization than NAC, RWoC had connections in Brian Mulroney's Conservative government, and was influential in inhibiting progress on abortion, equal pay, universal daycare, and gay rights.

In those days, RWoC and Reform were cut from the very same cloth. Conservative pundit Dalton Camp, after attending an early Reform convention, declared "The speechifying gives off acrid whiffs of xenophobia, homophobia, and paranoia – like an exhaust – in which it seems clear both orator and audience have been seized by some private terror: immigrants, lesbians, people out of work or from out of town and criminals." In other words, the speeches were much like what you may read on the RWoC website today.

It's only a year ago that RWoC and the Harper Conservatives were still so chummy that the government gave the lobby group a box of Queen's Diamond Jubilee medallions to distribute as it pleased. How did things come to such a pass that these old pals are suddenly at odds? The rift grew from the fact that the Conservative Party has to operate in the real world, while Real Women inhabit a fantasy – a world in which theirs is the "mainstream" view, and they are the real women.

Canadians, by a huge margin, oppose everything RWoC stands for. In seat-rich Ontario and BC, 66 per cent of respondents to a survey favoured same-sex marriage. The survey didn't ask, but let's take it as given that at least that number would expect their foreign affairs minister to take a stand against the death penalty for gays. Only 5 per cent

of Canadians surveyed believe that all abortion should be illegal, and 59 per cent are opposed to "re-opening the abortion debate."

Real Women don't need to be troubled by the unpopularity of their ideas, they can operate quite nicely on the generosity of a few well-heeled members and donors. But the Conservative Party can only travel so far on the support of the far right wing. If they want to continue to govern, they can't be the government their hard-line supporters want them to be. To RWoC, "homosexual activists" are "a tyrannical minority." To the Harper government, they're a significant voting block in hotly contested urban ridings.

Fringe groups like RWoC take a long time to fade away. Like barnacles they cling to the underside of political life long after they should have perished from irrelevance. Bit by bit, Real Women are slowly slipping away into the past of their 1950s housewife fantasies. If last week's outburst helped to hasten that slide, that's cause for celebration. Canada will be a better place without them.

Preston Manning And The Wisdom Of Serpents

MAY 2013

Last week, the Manning Centre for Building Democracy held its Manning Networking Conference, an international gathering of conservative thinkers. And you'll never guess who the keynote speaker was. Oh, you did guess. Yes, it was Preston Manning himself, father of the Reform Party, the little engine that grew into the current Conservative Party of Canada. The MNC is after all Preston's party, and he'll talk if he wants to.

In proper speech-giving form, Manning began his address with a personal story to illustrate the question at the centre of his discourse: "Do you tell them what they want to hear, or do you tell them what they need to hear?" He went on to say that he would be sharing some hard truths that conservatives need to hear. But it was later in the speech that the true meaning of the introduction began to reveal itself, although the question might better have been phrased, "Do we tell the public only what we need them to hear?" The answer being a resounding, "Yes."

Having established his parameters, Manning tore into the tough fabric of green conservatism. Conservatives, he said, can draw an example from ranchers who "believe ... property rights and markets ... can also be ... harnessed ... to the task of environmental conservation as an alternative to mass governmental intervention in the marketplace ..." (Excisions for the sake of brevity only, Mr Manning's speechwriters are big fans of the adverb, and the adverbial phrase).

Manning spoke of "more effective ways" of addressing "global warming, proliferation of plastics, urban sprawl, and the loss of biodiversity" than "treaties, top-down regulations, and other approaches offered by big governments and their dependents." He offered no specifics on how green conservatives will address global warming in the absence of treaties and regulations, but the solution will involve a "multitude of local and small-scale initiatives."

The matter became clearer when he rounded out the environmental portion of his speech with the rallying cry, "Green conservatives of Canada, unite! And change the climate of environmental discourse in this country." It's simple really, the problem green conservatives face is not melting ice caps and disappearing islands, it's the overheated climate of discourse. Cool that discourse down and right-wingers can "occupy the high ground" – which is good, because that's also going to be the dry ground.

Having blazed a trail to that high green ground, Manning got down to the nub of his speech, the matter of training conservatives to "win more elections" and to "govern in accordance with conservative values." Actually, he didn't say much about the latter at all, but was quite clear on the matter of election-winning. He revealed the results of studies that prove Canadian voters aren't moved by "ideological politics" or "issue politics," so much as by "strength of character, industriousness, and civilized conduct."

This last truth was widely understood as an admonition not to deceive parliament about defence spending, take a limo two blocks from one luxury hotel to another, or shag the babysitter. But it was when he came to address the "ideological strengths and weaknesses" of conservatism that Manning's true intent was revealed. The movement's strength, he declared, is its inclusiveness; social, green, libertarian, "progressive" (Manning's quotes, not mine), and fiscal conservatives are all welcome in the "Big Conservative Tent." Its weakness is loose lips. He cited two examples.

Last year, Allan Hunsperger, Wildrose candidate for Edmonton-South West, said that gays "will suffer the rest of eternity in a lake of fire, hell, a place of eternal suffering." More recently conservative thinker and Manning protégé Tom Flanagan told a college audience, "I do have some grave doubts about putting people in jail because of their taste in pictures," even if the pictures are of child pornography. Flanagan went on to volunteer the information that he had once been on the mailing list of the Man Boy Love Association.

"A genuinely free society and the broad conservative movement itself may tolerate such comments out of our commitment to free speech," Manning told his audience, but in an era of "gotcha journalism" you don't let outsiders know that, for conservatives, free speech trumps human rights or the safety of children, for fear of providing "perverse incentives and opportunities for human rights commissions and the courts .. to further restrict ... freedom of speech."

To illustrate his point, Manning dipped into the Gospel according to Saint Mathew, and came out with a joke, calling on conservatives "when dealing with value-laden issues, to be 'wise as serpents and gracious as doves' not vicious as snakes and stupid as pigeons." In making his point, the father of modern-day conservatism in Canada seems to have missed the better joke, about a leader who stands up in a public forum and counsels his followers that it's ok to support hate speech and the freedom to possess child porn among conservative peers, so long as you keep your mouth shut in public.

He also seems to have missed the fairly obvious extension of his (or Saint Mathew's) metaphor: that whether you teach a serpent wisdom or simply stitch its mouth shut, when all is said and done it's still a snake.

Witches To Hunt? Money To Burn

APRIL 2012

This January, Natural Resources Minister Joe Oliver raised eyebrows when he declared that "environmental and other radical groups" funded by foreign special interests were hijacking development in Canada. Stephen Harper took up the same cry, speaking of a "growing concern" about foreign funding for environmentalists.

These statements were widely condemned as reminiscent of the rhetoric of dictatorships, a gratuitous attack on Canadians who hold proscribed opinions, and a patent absurdity given the billions in foreign money behind resource industries. For a while it seemed as if the Conservatives realized they had a weak case, and would let the matter drop. Last week's budget dispelled that notion.

According to the budget document, "concerns have been raised that some charities may not be respecting the rules regarding political activities. There have also been calls for greater public transparency related to the political activities of charities, including the extent to which they may be funded by foreign sources." It fails to mention that the concerns were raised and the calls made by the finance minister's cabinet colleagues.

A registered charity in Canada can legally spend ten percent of its annual budget on non-partisan advocacy work. Flaherty announced a special audit to make sure no one is breaking that rule. At the same time he created special reporting rules for charities that receive foreign funding, although foreign donations are a perfectly legal source of revenues. The estimated price tag on this charade is $5 million in the first year and $3 million in the second.

While the budget doesn't name the groups who will be the focus of all this attention, you can bet that environmental activists are much more concerned today than conservative advocacy groups. Real Women of Canada won't have to sweat over those reporting forms or bother about what percentage of their budget they spend advocating against basic human rights. They'll be too busy handing out the Queen's Jubilee Medals.

Another advocacy group that can consider itself safe is the Canadian Shooting Sports Association. Closely tied to the National Rifle Association of America, the CSSA advocates for the rights of Canadian gun owners. The association played a strong role in the fight against the long gun registry, and in the course cemented a tight relationship with the Harper Conservatives.

One of the most influential lobby groups in the country, the CSSA has the ear of cabinet ministers and the power to affect policy. Executive director Tony Bernardo was looking across at lots of friendly faces when he addressed the senate last week as it reviewed the act to repeal the gun registry. Bernardo is a donor to the Conservatives, a good buddy of MP Garry Breitkreuz, and a member of the government's Firearms Advisory Committee.

Bernardo can sleep easy, knowing that the foreign-funding police won't be bothering him about his boast that the NRA gives the CSSA "tremendous amounts of logistic support," or about the $100,000 video he made at NRA expense, opposing the Canadian long gun registry.

The CSSA's influence in government goes far beyond the national firearms registry: so far indeed that the organization is involved in writing Canada's foreign policy on small arms. Or perhaps more accurately, the NRA is writing our foreign policy through the CSSA. The CBC reports it has learned through access to information that, at the CSSA's behest, "Foreign Affairs Minister John Baird ordered last-minute changes to Canada's position on an international arms treaty, as well as to its delegation to meetings at United Nations headquarters."

Against the advice of officials, Baird decided at the last moment to include CSSA president Steve Torino as the only non-governmental representative on the Canadian delegation at last summer's UN Arms Control Treaty negotiations surrounding the international trade in small arms. Small arms fire is the leading cause of death in armed conflict around the world, causing 90 per cent of civilian casualties and killing more than 300,000 people every year.

Soon after appointing Torino, Baird unveiled Canada's new policy on small arms control, rewritten to reflect exactly the position of the NRA, including the demand that "hunting and sporting" weapons be excluded from any treaty. Mexico, where rifles and pistols are in common use by drug gangs, is one of fifteen countries who have spoken out against Canada's new position. NRA executive vice-president Wayne LaPierre spoke, of course, in Canada's support.

Measured against this and countless other examples of the Conservative Party's strong ties to Republican conservatives in the US, their feigned outrage against foreign influence should be laughable. Last week's budget took all the humour out of the situation. Even the usually staid voice of the *Globe and Mail* editorial page has blasted the budget measures against charities as a "dishonourable attack meant to intimidate environmental groups," and a "needless new cost," declaring "witch hunts don't come cheap."

Cheap was never the issue for the Harper Conservatives. Flaherty's "austerity" budget still has room to maintain $1.3 billion in annual tax incentives to the oil and gas industry – something his department advised against – and $8 million to silence the industry's critics. There may be no money for programs the government dislikes, but there's always something in the kitty to reward friends, and to persecute enemies.

Hijackers Ain't What They Used To Be

Western Canada is on hijack alert this week after two stark warnings from Ottawa. Prime Minister Stephen Harper led with the announcement that "foreign money" is being used to hijack the regulatory process for the Northern Gateway pipeline. Natural Resources Minister Joe Oliver followed up in an open letter with the news that "environmental and other radical groups ... threaten to hijack our regulatory system to achieve their radical ideological agenda."

In my day, radicals with an ideological agenda hijacked airplanes. Those were the days when radicals were radicals. I mean, what do you do with a regulatory process after you've hijacked it? Blow it up? Fly it into a building? Land it in Algeria and demand ransom? It's not exactly the terror threat of the century, but Oliver's convinced that if these foreign-funded radicals have their way Canada's economy will look like it's been targeted by the Red Brigades. "No forestry. No mining. No oil. No gas. No more hydro-electric dams." Boom! Boom! Boom! Boom!

Unfortunately Minister Oliver didn't specify who in particular advocates that the Canadian economy be bombed flat, but he was quite clear that whoever they are they "use funding from foreign special interest groups to undermine Canada's national economic interest. They attract jet-setting celebrities with some of the largest personal carbon footprints in the world to lecture Canadians."

And as if being radical and jet-setting wasn't enough, the enemies of the Canadian economy are – wait for it – quintessentially American. "Finally, if all other avenues have failed," says Oliver's letter, "they will take a quintessential American approach: sue everyone and anyone." It's just not fair: litigious radicals with foreign money and an American quintessence are beating up on defenceless multinational oil corporations for no better reason than to plunge Canada into poverty.

At one time the term radical was understood to mean communist, and given the fact that jet-setting communists with size thirteen carbon boots are busily pumping billions into Canadian tarsands development and would love to influence the regulatory process, you might think the Harper government was reverting to that old usage. But communism has been redefined in the modern era to mean capitalism without bothersome elections or charters of rights. Communism is now officially good for business, and therefore no longer radical.

The Northern Gateway Pipeline Project is a proposal to transport Alberta tarsands oil to the coastal British Columbia town of Kitimat. Its proponent, Enbridge, is a multinational corporation with a long history of pipeline construction, and a safety record it would be kind to call patchy. Among the more than 600 recorded leaks or breaks in Enbridge pipelines in the past ten years the best known is the 2010 Kalamazoo, Michigan spill where a broken pipe dumped three million litres into the Kalamazoo River.

The Northern Gateway Enquiry got underway in Kitimat this week. Foreign-funded radicals kept a low profile while the hall packed with mackinawed locals and leaders of the Haisla First Nation in traditional blanket coats and woven hats. One local showed up to voice support for the project, a plumber in a Super Mario suit. The most radical idea expressed so far has been fear of what an oil spill would do to the fishery.

The proposed pipeline route crosses the traditional territory of five First Nations, where it faces an icy welcome. It crosses the Rocky Mountains, where the pipe is in danger of damage from avalanches. It crosses hundreds of rivers and streams, including five great salmon rivers. At Kitimat the heavy crude is to be pumped into tankers. There has been a moratorium on tanker traffic up the BC coast since 1972, because the rocky coastline and high storms combine to create the extreme risk of a spill.

In short, a pipeline company with a long record of mishaps, including at least one environmental disaster, wants to convince Canadians to give it a shot at one of the most environmentally risky projects ever undertaken, reversing a 30-year old protection that has been regularly reviewed and always renewed. A word to foreign-funded radicals: don't waste your backers' money hijacking this process. It's going to take some time.

Just Say No To The Fraser

MAY 2011

The Fraser Institute's recent study on BC and Yukon schools was released this month, and as usual Yukon high schools fared badly. In fact, publicly funded schools did badly across the board when compared to private schools, a predictable enough result: Fraser Institute studies all begin with the premise that public funding is bad.

The Fraser Institute describes itself as "an independent non-profit research and educational organization." A more objective observer might describe it as an industry-dependant right-wing propaganda machine. The institute was founded in 1974 with the financial support of forestry giant MacMillan Bloedell, and has faithfully campaigned against stumpage fees, regulation, and public ownership of BC's forests ever since.

The Fraser went on to shill for the tobacco industry, taking funding from Rothmans and Philip Morris and sponsoring two conferences in 1999, titled, Junk Science, Junk Policy? Managing Risk and Regulation, and Should Government Butt Out? The Pros and Cons of Tobacco Regulation. At these conferences, tobacco industry "scientists" presented papers they could never have published in peer-reviewed journals, which Fraser propagandists re-packaged for the media.

Later, backed by donations from Exxon Mobil, the Fraser turned its attention to global warming. In this case the think-tank hired physicists Willie Soon and Sallie L. Baliunas to craft a report "debunking" climate-change science. Soon and Baliunas were well qualified for the job, being already in the pay of the American coal industry. Not surprisingly, they concluded that "There is no clear evidence, nor unique attribution, of the global effects of anthropogenic CO_2 on climate."

SADLY FOR HONEST POLITICAL DISCOURSE IN CANADA, THE FRASER INSTITUTE IS NOT GOING TO GO AWAY.

This is not to suggest that the Fraser can be bought and sold like a used car. On the contrary, the institute exists for purely ideological reasons. As their web-page states, "The Fraser Institute measures and studies the impact of competitive markets and government interventions on individuals and society," and it invariably finds that the impact of competitive markets is good, and that of government intervention is bad. If you want to buy a study showing that pollutants from Fort McMurray are causing cancers in downstream First Nations communities, look elsewhere. If you want one proving the opposite, the Fraser Institute can arrange it for you.

Stephen Harper was one of the founding members of the Fraser, and you may rest assured that he will look to its work to legitimize much of what he does with his newfound majority. So be it. Whatever you might think of our current electoral system, it is the one under which we went to the polls, and it selected a right-wing government. They will use right-wing think tanks to instruct and to justify their actions. But that doesn't mean that the media has to follow suit.

There are three ways that the media can deal with Fraser Institute canned news stories. They can run them as if they represented genuine research. This is the cheapest and easiest way to proceed, and will be the one favoured by Sun Media, the *National Post*, and the *Globe and Mail*, who share the Fraser's general outlook on politics. Anybody reading those papers or watching that news ought to be aware of their pro-corporate bias, and take it into account.

But a problem arises when the Fraser's blatant propaganda is taken up as news by media outlets whose bias is less clear. Why does the CBC still do sole-sourced, uncritical reports based on Fraser Institute studies? Why does the *Yukon News* not simply ignore rubbish like the "report card" on schools, or at least amend those reports by saying that the results of any and all Fraser Institute studies are deliberately and absurdly skewed in favour of anything done by the "private sector" and against anything achieved by government?

Sadly for honest political discourse in Canada, the Fraser Institute is not going to go away. It will continue to be the mouthpiece of big business, accepting blood money and spreading misinfor-mation to prove the unprovable, that corporate greed serves the interests of the country, and not simply of greedy corporations. One thing that could change, and it wouldn't be hard, is that those media outlets which are not financed by the same greedy cabal that funds the Fraser could put a little more effort into challenging its right-wing bunk.

Or, if it's too much trouble to critique the Fraser's work, to follow the money and the lies that it buys, there's one other solution when those press releases land on your desk, outlining yet another so-called study that proves once again how much good unregulated greed does for the world: ignore it. It won't go away, but at least one editor, one radio producer, one TV host, will have refused to legitimize a corporate mouthpiece as a "news source." It's simple: when the Fraser Institute comes to call, don't encourage them. They already have enough power and influence. Just say no.

Canada's Conservatives And Sesame Street

FEBRUARY 2011

Amidst all the furor in Ottawa over government secrecy and misinformation, one question emerges: what is it with Canadian conservatives and Sesame Street? Last week it was Mr Snuffleupagus, this week it's the interjection NOT. What's next? Jim Flaherty as the Count? John Baird popping out of a garbage can?

Some years ago the word "not" enjoyed a period of great popularity, courtesy of the kids' TV show, Sesame Street. It was the greatest giggle for the three-to-seven crowd to make a statement of fact and then contradict it by shouting, NOT! This annoying practice found its way into the common culture. It manifested itself on T-shirts, often accompanied by an insert arrow and some silly statement. Thankfully, such things are bound to pass, and this one did. By now, there is almost no one left who can hear or see that old gag without a roll of the eyes.

Almost. Somebody in Ottawa still thinks it's funny. The question is, who? Bev Oda says she doesn't know who butchered a $7 million funding recommendation by shoving in the old NOT joke. She also says she told them to do it. Don't be confused, children. Here's what happened. Kairos is a Christian aid agency with 35 years of funding from the Canadian International Development Agency. In 2009 it applied to renew its grant. CIDA put the application through the customary scrutiny and recommended payment of $7 million over four years, a 4 per cent raise "to recognize Kairos' strategic alignment with CIDA's objectives."

Oda signed the document. At some point after it had been signed by two CIDA officials, someone inserted a bold "NOT" into the final line, barely withholding the exclamation mark, upsetting the grammar of the sentence, and completely reversing the meaning of the document. Kairos got no funding. A few days later, Citizenship and Immigration Minister Jason Kenney told an Israeli audience that the government had cut Kairos off because it supported a boycott against Israel.

There's no evidence that Kairos ever did support a boycott against Israel, but neither is there any reason to doubt that Kenney was sincere, if misinformed. Something about Kairos struck the Harper government as anti-Israel, and that is something Harper will not tolerate. On three occasions during 2010 Ms Oda's parliamentary secretary Jim Abbott contradicted Kenney, telling the House of Commons that Kairos's funding was rejected on CIDA's advice. In December, Ms Oda told a parliamentary committee that she didn't know who tampered with the CIDA memo. This week she said, "The funding decision was mine. The 'not' was inserted at my direction."

The contradiction is so plain that even the government's strongest supporters are cutting Oda no slack. Bev Oda Must Go says the *National Post*. Maclean's goes so far as to invoke the usually forbidden L-word: "She lied — flat out-lied." As for their opponents, Liberal blogger Warren Kinsella has suggested that Oda's actions constitute criminal fraud that could result in a prison term of up to fourteen years. Even Peter Milliken, the Speaker of the House now called upon to judge whether Oda's actions constitute criminal contempt, has already pronounced on the matter in unusually strong language. He called the facts "troubling," saying anyone who read them would be shocked, and sympathized with the CIDA officials involved. It seems that poor Bev Oda has no friends.

Well, not quite none. She still has the prime minister and government house leader John Baird on her side. But why? Harper has shown a willingness to feed cabinet ministers to the dogs before this. Even once-favourite daughters and sons like Helena Guergis and Maxime Bernier have furnished a repast for the hounds when they became a public embarrassment, what makes Oda so special?

It was within Minister Oda's power to reject CIDA's recommendations. Standard procedure in such a case is to send the memo back with a note attached saying thanks for the good work, but for policy reasons we're rejecting the funding. Could anything other than spite have inspired the course of action taken in this case? And does anyone really believe that the spite originated with Oda?

Ok, Oda must go. But her departure won't be enough if it leaves behind these questions. When was the CIDA memo tampered with, who did the tampering, and who gave the order? And finally, who in Ottawa is the mystery Sesame Street fan?

CANADA'S CONSERVATIVES AND SESAME STREET

Hello False And Misleading News. Welcome To Canada.

JUNE 2010

Amidst all the public outcry over the Canadian Radio and Telecommunications Commission's recent decision on usage-based Internet billing, another far murkier story involving the broadcast regulator emerges. Last December, the Standing Joint Committee on the Scrutiny of Regulations wrote to the CRTC to demand that it comply with a cobweb-covered issue related to a Supreme Court decision concerning "false and misleading" statements.

In 1996 the Supreme Court of Canada, while ruling on the case of neo-Nazi Ernst Zundel and his outrageous lies about the Holocaust, pronounced that the Charter of Rights and Freedoms protects citizens from prosecution on the grounds of disseminating false information. Called upon to examine its own rules in light of that decision, the CRTC found no reason to make any changes.

Last Monday on the CBC program Power and Politics, Dean Del Mastro, parliamentary secretary to the heritage minister, appeared to confirm opposition claims that the push to change the truth in broadcasting rules comes straight from cabinet. In defence of political interference in the broadcast regulator, Del Mastro made the claim that his constituents have been complaining that "free speech is under attack in this country." No word as yet on how many calls he got on that one.

In a curious coincidence, Sun TV is set to begin broadcasting this March. If the new conservative news channel lives up to its reputation as "Fox North," it will have reason to celebrate a loosening of the rules on false and misleading statements on air. Always happy to shade the truth Fox has recently reported that President Obama is a Moslem who was raised in a radical madrasa, that Christians were being thrown in jail for praying, and that a Tea Party rally in Washington drew 1.5 million supporters – nobody else estimated the crowd any higher than 70,000. Fox even went to court in 2003 to protect its right to "distort or falsify" the news.

The Fox North tag represents more than the expectation that Sun TV will imitate the Fox style. There is evidence that Stephen Harper himself has worked toward the creation of a news outlet that will give him the coverage he wants, and that in so doing, he has looked to the ferociously Republican Fox for an example. According to The Canadian Press, during a 2009 visit to Washington, Harper and his former spokesman Kory Teneycke held an unannounced lunch meeting with Fox president Roger Ailes and owner Rupert Murdoch.

The next year Quebecor corporation announced that Teneycke would be the point person on the new Sun TV channel. There was considerable public outcry over his transition from Conservative spokesperson to head of a large well-financed news network, leading to an online petition. Somebody in Ottawa tampered with the petition, inserting numerous false names, including that of Sesame Street character Mr Snuffleupagus. Teneycke boasted on his blog of a connection to the prankster. Last September, Toronto lawyer Clayton Ruby asked the RCMP and Ottawa police to investigate the tampering. The following day, Teneycke resigned, saying the dispute had become "vicious and vitriolic" and confessing, "I have contributed to debasing the debate myself." Last month he quietly returned to the job.

Which brings us back to the CRTC. When Sun first came on the scene it applied for the class of license that would require cable providers to carry its channel. The regulator turned this application down and Sun was forced to accept an ordinary class 2 license. Having clearly thwarted the wishes of the prime minister, the agency came under new pressure. When vice chair Michel Arpin's contract came up for renewal, he was dumped, and Quebecor vice president Luc Lavoie was offered the job. Lavoie turned down the offer saying the only job he would accept is that of the chairman.

When he couldn't get Lavoie, Harper instead appointed Tom Pentefountas, a Quebec businessman with no apparent qualifications other than being a friend of the prime minister. Current chairman Konrad von Finkenstein is not facing contract renewal until 2012, but according to the *Globe and Mail*'s Lawrence Martin, "insiders report that Mr Harper now wants him out well before that date and replaced by a rubber stamper."

A tip for investors: if Lavoie gets his wish and becomes the chairman of the CRTC, put your money in Quebecor. With a ruthless former Conservative Party spin doctor at the helm and the broadcast regulator controlled by corporate insiders and government cronies, the future of Fox North couldn't look brighter. The future of truth in broadcasting is another story altogether, but who cares? There's no money in that.

Politics And The Art Of Distraction

JANUARY 2011

This just in: men absorb less news when the anchor is an attractive woman. It's not that we're not paying attention, it's just that we're paying it in the wrong place. In a recently released study, a professor and a graduate student at Indiana University found that men watching the same woman news anchor absorb less information when she's dressed in sexy clothes.

Is anybody surprised by this news? We already knew that a bit of female flesh can be a major distraction for the average male. But even if we were unaware of this shortcoming, it should be obvious to even the most cleavage-distracted observer that for the general public the news goes in one ear and out the other. How else to explain the state of the world?

Consider Canada, for instance. You can't open a newspaper today without being exposed to speculation on when there will be a federal election, who stands strongest in the polls, and what will be the deciding issues. On the latter front, the current favourite is – get this – a Liberal promise to roll back tax cuts for the rich.

Ok, take your eyes off that newscaster and think for a moment. If the Liberals get elected, will they keep this promise, or will they cave in to the onslaught of corporate lobbying that will ensue the minute they touch down in the halls of power? A Liberal leader promising to stick it to the rich has all the credibility of a fish promising to walk on dry land. It might be possible, we suppose, but where is the precedent?

But instead of laughing the Liberals off the court, the Conservatives respond to the promise as if it were believable, and trot out all their reasons for maintaining the cuts. We the electorate, if we happen to be listening at all, accept this as a real debate. Aha, we think, an election issue: corporate tax cuts.

Why are we hearing about highly improbable rollbacks on tax cuts for the rich? For the same reason newswomen are dressing up like fashion models. It's a distraction. The two big money parties want you to forget that they have been functioning as a de facto coalition for five years, every move the Conservatives made supported by a cowed and frightened Liberal opposition. They want you to forget that the Conservatives ran up record deficits even before the recession began, and the Liberals helped them do it either by voting in favour of budget after budget, or by staying home in droves.

While you're forgetting, it would be good for the Con-Lib coalition if you forgot that they managed to weasel out of the speaker's ruling that they release all the documents related to Afghan detainee torture. It should be easy enough to forget, the whole story has just about dropped off the edge of the Earth since the two implicated parties cut a deal to keep the most damaging documents secret. We may never know if senior politicians from both sides are guilty of war crimes, and as far as the coalition is concerned, that could be a good thing.

Also off the election agenda, or so it seems, is the possibility that human greed may turn the only currently available planet into an uninhabitable pile of rock in this century. Heard a Liberal reference to global warming lately? I keep hoping to hear that someone with a hope of forming a government has a plan that will actually reduce emissions in my lifetime, but if such a story has aired lately, I must have been ogling the newscaster at the time.

Don't expect senate reform, that old Conservative bugaboo, to dominate election discussion any time soon. Both sides of the coalition have packed that institute of higher gold-digging with the party faithful, and they're not about to defecate in that cushy nest. Failure to reform the senate is one of Harper's most obvious broken promises, but you won't hear a whole lot about it from the Liberals.

Canada is in the process of creating the kind of justice system the US would like to get out from under, one that swallows human beings and chases them down with million dollar bills. The system has proven itself to be cruel, useless, and absurdly expensive, but it doesn't show up as a major election issue, possibly because the Liberals already let the legislation pass. It's hard to campaign effectively against something you could have stopped by voting against, but didn't.

We stand in grave danger of returning Harper to office in the next election. The only hope offered for avoiding this possibility is that we saddle ourselves with Ignatieff instead. These are depressing times. No wonder the newscasters' legs get more attention than the news.

Let's bring back the business suit standard. From now on, let's have all anchors, male or female, dress like Peter Mansbridge. I know, I know, we will still be a thoughtless, distracted, complacent electorate, the real issues will still slip from sight while the spin-masters at Lib-Con headquarters manufacture phoney disputes, and the pace of progress on the things that should matter will still be glacial at best. But hey, you have to start somewhere.

The Importance Of Seeming Earnest

DECEMBER 2004

It seems safe to assume that, on the eve of his upcoming trip to Libya, Prime Minister Paul Martin won't be staying up late to stitch a maple leaf patch on his backpack. People can tell where he's from by the Mounties in his entourage. In this, he has the advantage over ordinary Canadians, who are easily mistaken for Americans in most of the world.

This is a problem because, although unable to tell us apart without visual aids, many foreigners harbour the notion that English-speaking North Americans are separated culturally and politically by a line as straight and true as the 49th Parallel, hockey to the north, backward thinking to the south. They tend to miss the details that blur the picture: Real Women of Canada, for instance, or the Anaheim Mighty Ducks.

Not only is it difficult for foreigners to tell Canadians and Americans apart, we're not always clear on the distinction ourselves. If George Bush put on an Ottawa Senators toque and walked around Calgary, people would hide their wallets when they saw him coming, and quite a few would relax considerably when they found out he was from Texas and not Ontario.

Our southern neighbours need not be offended by our apparent obsession with identity abroad. We know that by wandering around with our maple leaf pins we are perpetuating the stereotype that we Canadians are all earnest, peace-loving modernists, and Americans are antediluvian, imperialist warmongers. We know it's a shameful lie, but the division plays well overseas, and we exploit it, not in contempt for Americans, but out of concern for our own safety.

We wear maple leaf stickers on our luggage, Canadian flag t-shirts. Some of us have had to learn to speak what is taken for Canadian before heading out on vacation, and many an adventurer from West Vancouver has said, "Cold enough for ya, eh?" for the first time while setting up base camp on Everest. We behave in this embarrassing manner because being taken for a Yank is more dangerous than looking like an idiot. The American or apparently-American traveler may be subject to indignities ranging from poor service to car-bombs, and many Canadians are willing to risk acting like dorks to avoid these things.

So it's unsurprising, though nonetheless troubling, to learn that some Americans abroad have taken to disguising themselves as Canadians. Now, we might turn a blind eye to a few Hoosiers posing as hosers on the Champs-Élysées, we may let slip an indulgent smile should travellers from Yukon, Oklahoma attempt to pass themselves off as genuine Yukoners, but when the practice of impersonating a Canadian becomes so widespread as to be commercialized and offered on the Internet, it's time for the department of external affairs to step up – oops, pardon the Americanism – to the plate.

T-Shirt King, a New Mexico company, offers a package called Go Canadian, "the perfect disguise" for the American who wishes to reduce vacation risk. "This is specifically if you're traveling and you don't want people throwing eggs at you," said Lisa Broadbent, who with her husband Bill owns T-Shirt King. "Our American politics – we're stepping on some toes right now and there's no doubt there's some animosity."

The release of this package is of concern to Canadians for at least two reasons. First, it weakens our only protection against being mistaken for Americans, and second, it adds to our fears another possible consequence of that misidentification. We now have to worry about poor service, car-bombs, *and* people throwing eggs at us. It's not clear at this reading whether each package includes a famous Canadian surname along with the Canadian flag t-shirt, patch, and lapel pin, and the educational text, How To Speak Canadian, Eh?

We can only hope that the package will in some way be so flawed as to mark its user as an impostor: a reference, say, to President Martin, or the Vancouver Canadiennes, or perhaps the dismissal of 100,000 deaths as "stepping on some toes" – something so glaringly not-Canadian it can be spotted from the kitchen, and taken into account when the spitting-in-soup decision is made.

For the American abroad who wishes to avoid the taint of imperialist villainy, here is some advice: forget pretending to be Canadian. People abroad know a great deal about American politics – statistically much more than you know about theirs – and are quite aware that millions of Americans oppose most of the policies for which the US is currently distrusted around the globe.

So if you want to feel safe overseas, don't pose as us. Pose as, or better yet be, tolerant, peace-loving Americans. Scrap the maple leaf collar pin, and substitute a dove's foot. For that T-shirt, try Impeach Bush, or better yet that old favourite, Make Love Not War. You don't have to be Canadian to be loved.

A Matter Of Priorities

OCTOBER 2016

> *We really really wanted electoral reform 'cause we had to get rid of Stephen Harper, but now we have a government we sorta like, so electoral reform just doesn't seem as much of a priority anymore."*
> —Justin Trudeau

When the CBC comedy show This Hour Has 22 Minutes aired a video of Prime Minister Justin Trudeau saying the above words to an audience of students at Ottawa University, I thought at first they must have dubbed the speech in, for comic effect. Surely no prime minister of Canada could be that cynical. Is there a single Canadian who doesn't remember "this will be the last election under the first past the post system"? But no, he really said it, six months ago. Apparently he went on to say, "it's a priority for me," but that was then. Last week in an interview with Le Devoir, he repeated the lowered priority trope, this time without the qualifier.

Suddenly, it all becomes clear. With both opposition parties leaderless, Trudeau's popularity is off the scale. Like Harper's Conservatives, the Liberals were elected into a majority with 39 per cent of the vote, but it seems like since the election, every time Justin takes his shirt off his popularity rises. So now that we've got rid of Stephen Harper, and have a government people sort of like, all bets are off.

When the unlikeable Harper government was in power, Trudeau was promising nation to nation relations with indigenous Canadians. Now that people sort of like their government, First Nations don't seem like much of priority anymore. Justin can dump the Site C Dam down on traditional territory with a sunny smile, and refuse to comply with a Human Rights Tribunal ruling calling for an end to discriminatory spending restraints on indigenous children. Under Harper's unpopular

SURF'S UP SUNSHINE

regime, kids on reserves were dying from under-funding of schools, undrinkable water, and lack of programming. Now that we have a government that people sort of like, they're still dying, but it's not so much of a priority anymore.

Those unpopular Harperites sold weapons to Saudi Arabia to use in genocidal warfare in Yemen, but now things are different; today the Saudis are buying armoured vehicles from a government that people sort of like. Yemeni children dying under the rubble must be so comforted to know that, if they were Canadian and middle-class, our bare-chested prime minister would probably crash their wedding and let them take selfies.

Harper's unpopular Conservatives came under a lot of fire for selling access to cabinet ministers in return for contributions to the party. No problem now though, people sort of like the Liberals who are doing the exact same thing. When you consider it, if you're going to leave a trail of broken promises, it makes a lot of sense to do it during your first year in office, before the bloom wears off the rose. After the honeymoon is over, the voters start expecting you to live up to your word.

That part of the public that isn't still dazzled by Justin's sunny ways is left wondering, to what level does the Liberals' popularity have to drop before living up to their election commitments becomes a priority?

A Letter From Canada

Dear Neighbours, we've heard that many of you are worried, perhaps even afraid, of what might become of your country if Donald Trump becomes president. There's been a lot of talk about a mass migration to Canada (the home lest-we-forget of Conrad Black and the late Rob Ford). Yes, our American cousins, we too have our right-wing criminals and nutbars, and though yours may be crazier, that's only to be expected. You do things large down there. It's something we've always secretly admired, when it didn't get out of hand.

We haven't failed to notice that Trump does not stand alone, though. Those of you, the ones who seem rational from this squinty angle, the ones who are placing your hopes in fleeing over the border before we get our wall built, may consider Trump an incompetent, self-aggrandizing, racist, misogynist, bully who can't be trusted anywhere near a dollar or your daughter, but you're not in nearly as great a majority as we would like to see. Even now, after he's been outed as at the very least a wannabe sex offender, Trump is beating Hilary Clinton by 5 points among male voters. Read that sentence again.

Canada is a neighbourly place. And, for no obvious reason, we trust you guys. In the 70s, when your President Nixon was intent on flattening Vietnam if he had to sacrifice every young man in the US to do it, we took in about 30,000 of you, plus spouses in some cases, without any particular screening process, and for the most part it turned out ok for us. Draft dodgers and deserters wove themselves into the fabric of Canadian society without tearing any great holes that I can recall. Later, on September 11, 2001 we opened our airports so you could close yours. We're still not sure how that all made sense, except that our cities tend to be smaller, so if there had been terrorists aboard determined to strike somewhere, fewer people would have been killed, and they would have been us instead of you.

So don't take this personally. We like you. If you're an American who doesn't think you should ban Muslims, punish women for having abortions, and build a freaking great wall on the Mexican border, I for one would be happy to know you. In another world I might be willing to trade Ford Nation supporters straight across for you, one for one. Hell, two for one, I'm feeling generous. There are, I am sure, millions of you who are far better people than Conrad Black; Trumpworld could have him in exchange for one reasonable American if it were up to me. But you'd better stay home.

Here's the problem. It's 2016. Trump wants to drag your country back to the "good old days." Thousands cheer madly when he says this, and millions plan to vote for him. He's clear what he means about those days too: they were the days when white men could punch black protesters in the face, and if that didn't shut them up, they could kill them. And a lot of Americans are lapping it up. If the richest country on Earth, with the mightiest military machine, has millions of voters who are barking fascists, the rest of you have to stick around and make sure they don't get their hands on that big red button.

It doesn't look as though Trump will be your president now. That's a relief. But Trump Nation won't go away. There will always be millions of people in your country who believe that a loud-mouthed sexual braggart who openly advocates both racism and rape should be president, while a woman who deleted e-mails should go to jail. We're uncomfortable having these people as neighbours (though we don't mind selling them bobble-head

Mounties and painted gold pans as they drive through on their way to Alaska).

Dear, reasonable, sane, American neighbours, whatever happens down there, we need you to stay. It's not that we don't want you here. We're sure you'd fit in fine (though location is everything: I would recommend, say, Nelson over Etobicoke).

But your country needs you. It really, really needs you. Stay home.

Sigh. Trump did of course become president, and we have had a small influx of refugees from the US, though only a tiny percentage have been disaffected Americans. Now, how can we make the US pay for that wall?

The Semantics of Definitions

AUGUST 2016

Jane Philpot "could have been more clear" when she told Parliament that she had never used a limousine service. In so saying, Canada's Health Minister raises an interesting question. Is the truth more clear than a falsehood? Because it turns out that Philpot had not only used a limo service, she had spent at least $7,500 on limousines belonging to a friend who had "volunteered" on her campaign.

The Oxford English Dictionary offers several definitions of the word volunteer, but the one which applies to campaign workers reads as follows: "A person who works for an organization without being paid." This unpaid status is the very essence of an election volunteer, and extends to the non-payment of indirect benefits, such as thousands of public dollars directed to the alleged volunteer's business in the year following the election.

In the same statement, the Minister said, "I don't want to get into the semantics of definitions of types of vehicles." Returning to the OED, we find semantics defined as "The meaning of a word, phrase, or text," and it's quite easy to see why Philpot would prefer not to dwell on the meaning of the word "limousine," given that the luxury Lexus sedans she hired belonged to a company called Executive Sedan Livery Service Inc. True, the word Limo does not appear in the name, but the semantics would seem to support opposition accusations that the business is indeed a limousine service.

Prime Minister Justin Trudeau responded to questions about Philpot's spending spree as follows: "We have seen over the course of the past months, have noticed many long-standing government policies that we are questioning and that's certainly one that we are looking at as perhaps not the best use of public funds." So that settles it. Minister Philpot was simply following a long-standing practice followed by such Conservative ministers as, say, Bev Oda, who overspent on limo services and –oh wait– resigned. Maybe that's the part that the Liberals are now questioning. Philpot will be staying on.

Philpot's prevarications seem to have stirred up the scummy bottom of that shimmering pond which is the Liberal image. All of a sudden the press are following the money instead of the prime-ministerial pecs. Was it wrong for Environment Minister Catherine McKenna to spend $11,000 on a French photographer for the Paris climate talks, when she could simply have gone around photo-bombing people's weddings like Sunny Justin? Could the $275,219 spent on the Trudeau-Obama lovefest in Washington have been better directed? Is running a $113 billion deficit really going to Fix Everything, once and for all?

Taking a page out of the Justinian book, McKenna mysteriously suggested that her own use of public funds for Liberal photo-ops was the other guys' fault. "Previous governments used photographers as well but we can do better, and that's something I'm committed to personally," she said, "I think there are ways that we can reduce costs." She offered no explanation as to why she hadn't looked into those ways prior to pissing away the equivalent of an Ontario welfare recipient's annual income on glossy pics for the Internet, but never mind, Justin the Beautiful is reflecting on the practice.

"We're moving forward with a reflection on a broad range of things that are government policy that we might need to move or tweak to suit the openness, transparency and expectations that Canadians have of this particular government," the PM said during an infrastructure announcement in Toronto last week.

Dear Mr Prime Minister, this particular Canadian expects neither more nor less from your government than from any other party in power. Take the tax dollars you need to do your job, and spend it as much as possible on the needs of the country, rather than on the needs of your own party. Do this regardless of your standing in the polls, your personal popularity, your purported good looks (am I the only one who thinks you're a wee bit funny-looking?), or your sunny ways. The honeymoon may not be quite over yet, but the bills are already rolling in, and we're pretty sure we can't afford for you to party like this for four more years.

Oh, Canada!

OCTOBER 2013

Author Margaret Atwood caused some big ripples in Canada's little pond this week when she joined a campaign to return our national anthem to an earlier, gender-neutral version. For those of you, and you are legion, who don't know the words, the current official version of the song makes reference to "all our sons," replacing "all of us" in the anthem's previous, though not original, edition.

You need search no farther than the *National Post* to find arguments on both sides of this conflict. Barbara Kay takes the position that, since all our sons were inserted into the song in 1914 when Canada was sending them to die by the thousands in a foreign imperial war, it would offend "actual history and respect for our fallen" to include daughters. Kay fails to mention the 3141 Canadian women who served as nurses in that particular bloodbath, or the 46 who died in the line of duty.

Kay's colleague Jonathan Kay – I have no idea if the two are related – stays with the military angle while taking the opposing view, alleging that "all our sons" is an offence to the women who serve in the armed forces today. He refers in particular to those women who have fought in Afghanistan, pointing out that the mother of Nichola Goddard, the first Canadian woman to be killed while fighting, is involved in the campaign to restore the anthem.

To change the national anthem is a laudable goal, but the current campaign falls short, neglecting as it does the fact that, in addition to excluding girls and women and celebrating one god to the exclusion of all others, Oh Canada distinguishes itself by being an uncommonly bad song. An attempt to render a French song into English without actually translating the words, it's an appalling piece of team-writing, poorly penned in the first place and badly damaged by revisions. The lyrics are gibberish, the music a dirge.

Consider the line in contention: "Oh Canada, our home and native land, true patriot love in all our sons command." The original line was "true patriot love thou dost in us command," a clear statement of love for one's country, if somewhat marred by the 19th Century fashion for biblical language. The 1914 revision turns the song into an entreaty to the country to command the loyalty of its sons, though oddly enough the loyalty required of them was to another country altogether.

And what of those of us for whom Canada is our home, our country of citizenship, but not our native land? If we weren't born here, should we pretend we were, or mumble through that part, like the atheists in the next row singing "Mwum mwum our land, glorious and free"?

Barbara Kay believes Oh Canada's greatest moment came when it helped to inspire 600,000 young men to march off to a pointless shambles, to wager their lives against the lives of young German men over a family quarrel between royal cousins. Sixty-seven thousand Canadian men died in the Great War, 150,000 were wounded, and few indeed returned unscathed. It's very clear why we commemorate that; less clear is why we would choose to celebrate it.

Though a century old, the English version of Oh Canada didn't become our official anthem until 1980, prior to which we had to borrow Britain's, giving rise to the question, why bother to replace one rotten song with another? Is there, indeed, a national anthem that doesn't make the listener grind valuable enamel away at every hearing?

Take a look at The Star Spangled Banner. True, it has a stirringly bombastic tune, which is more than

Oh Canada can claim, but oh say, can you figure out what it's supposed to mean? Or consider God Save the King/Queen, a 13th Century polemic against the Scots that doesn't even get to retain its name when the gender of the monarch changes.

La Marseillaise, the national anthem of France, helped initiate the Reign of Terror, and asserts that only impure blood floods the country's gutters. Deutschland Uber Alles, with elegant Germanic simplicity, makes the point all the others struggle toward: we (insert country name) are "above all, above everything in the world." Perhaps if we all stopped telling each other this the world might eventually evolve into a less frightening place.

Today, the best reason for Canada to have a national anthem is that we would look stupid at hockey games if the Americans got up and sang their own bombastic rubbish and we didn't have a response. So why not ditch the song we once employed to whip a generation of young men into a meaningless mass sacrifice, and write a new one? Something that celebrates equality, diversity, peace, independence, and, oh what the hell, hockey. Hockey's what it's for, after all.

I was taken to task in the Yukon News *online comments page over a line in this column. I had originally said "The Marseillaise celebrates the Reign of Terror," but as the commenter pointed out, it was written and adopted as the anthem a year before the Reign of Terror began. And to be fair, it is a pretty good song, as national anthems go.*

OH, CANADA!

May 1917

Advertise Your Profile

Some hitherto unacceptable occupations stand poised to become listed in Canada's job bank. If a memo from Human Resources and Skills Development Canada bears fruit, the following categories will be considered newly suitable for posting at the government website: "Exotic dancer, erotic dancer, nude dancer, striptease dancer and table dancer. Escort, chat line agent, phone agent for personal services and telephone agent for personal services."

Let's not linger over the question of what possible difference there can be among some of these job descriptions – the bureaucracy must at all costs churn out words. Let us instead celebrate the very rapid enlightenment that has taken place in Canadian government circles in the scant two weeks since Ontario Supreme Court Justice Susan Himel threw out the country's prostitution laws.

At that time Justice Minister Rob Nicholson, announcing a court challenge to the ruling, told Parliament that "prostitution is a problem that harms individuals and communities." If HRDC goes ahead with the change, prostitutes will have access to such services as the Job Match – "Advertise your job profile to employers and receive a list of matching jobs," the Resumé Builder, the Career Navigator, and the job alert – "Receive by e-mail a list of job openings that match your search criteria." Hey, who needs Craigslist?

Let's assume for the sake of argument here that the government of Canada is aware that escort services don't exist simply to provide single gentlemen with suitable dates for formal occasions. Could it be that someone in Ottawa has recognized that it's safer, and better for traffic flow, to get the sex trade off the streets and under the purview of Service Canada?

There's some chance that the memo originated at the bureaucratic level and has nothing at all to do with the Conservative Party, which has not in the past shown a high degree of enthusiasm for the professions listed therein. Given that Prime Minister Stephen Harper has still not explained why he dumped former star minister Helena Geurgis from caucus, there's little left to conclude but that she fell prey to rumours surrounding her husband and "busty hookers."

Back in 2004, when Liberal immigration minister Judy Sgro signed a ministerial order to extend the work permit of a Romanian stripper, Conservatives were outraged. By coincidence, the afore-mentioned Geurgis scored the best comment on that occasion when she accused Sgro during Question Period of "dancing around the subject."

It's still quite possible that this memo will lead nowhere. Just because the Conservatives have set their foot on this path, it doesn't mean they're going to march up to the red light and knock on the door. Since taking office, Harper has displayed an ability to change direction on – well, I can't think of a specific case, but he's human, so they say, and human beings do change their minds.

But there are several reasons why the government might decide to stay the course on its new friendlier attitude toward the sex trade. There's the increase in the tax base, the expansion of opportunity for MP expense claims, and most important of all, the reduction of Canada's jobless numbers. Just let the opposition try to say the government isn't addressing unemployment now, or that all the new jobs are low-paying part-time work.

A better reason than all of these, and one we can only hope might be taken seriously in government circles, is that street prostitution is a deadly trade, and the bizarre set of laws surrounding that trade make it all the more dangerous. Justice Himel tossed out the existing laws because they violate the Charter of Rights by endangering the lives of sex trade workers. Since 1985, 300 prostitutes have been murdered or have disappeared from Canada's streets.

Whatever befalls the job bank listing, the government of Canada has a responsibility to address the Ontario court ruling, not by appealing it to the Supreme Court of Canada, but by writing new laws to protect sex trade workers from exploitation by pimps, harassment by police, and assault and murder by clients.

Prostitution won't go away because it's illegal. The circumstance most likely to diminish its presence in society is equality for women. Educated women with good employment opportunities will be less likely to choose "escort" from the job bank listings. In the meantime, choosing sex work as a way to get by is a tough enough decision as it is. Let's not make it a capital crime.

CHAPTER 8: **POP GOES THE CULTURE**

WHERE WOULD WE BE
WITHOUT SILLINESS?

No doubt there has been popular culture for as long as there have been paths between villages. One century had its story-tellers, another its troubadours and wandering players, another its books and penny dreadfuls. Video killed the radio stars and Twitter killed the paragraph, but whatever the medium, humanity will always find ways to disseminate the bizarre, the absurd, and the ridiculous. And a good thing, too. Where would we be without silliness?

Pretty Baby Goes To Dance School

SEPTEMBER 2012

Looking for a nice healthy exercise routine for your pre-school daughter this year? A dance studio in Duncan BC has a great new idea: pole dancing lessons. It's perfect. Not only can the apple of your eye shed a few unsightly pounds and tone up those buns and abs, but in the process she can gain valuable employment skills to help defray the cost of college.

Kristy Craig, owner of the aptly-named Twisted Grip Dance and Fitness Studio, dismisses the notion that she is peddling the sexualization of children. For one thing, the whole pole-dancing routine was not her idea, she was merely responding to demand. "My existing students were asking about it for their children," she explains. "They were saying, 'My daughter plays on my pole at home all the time. I'd love for her to learn how to do things properly and not hurt herself.' "

This pole dancing is not like pole dancing as you may have seen it in the local tavern or strip club or on The Sopranos, because as Craig says, "The sexuality is being taken out of it. It's highlighting the gymnastic, athletic and circus acrobatics aspect." Well whew! For a minute there we thought it was highlighting pole dancing. As in stripper pole. There is no truth to the rumour that advanced classes will highlight the gymnastic, athletic, and circus acrobatics aspects of lap-dancing.

In a related story, six-year old Alana Thompson, star of the popular American TV show, Here Comes Honey Boo Boo, has appeared on YouTube dancing for dollars on a table in a bar. Georgia Child Protection Services investigated the incident and brought it to court, but the judge threw out the case, perhaps because, as Alana's mother pointed out, "at least (the bar) wasn't one of those sleazy ones."

Here comes Honey Boo Boo is an offshoot of the program Toddlers and Tiaras, which follows the children's beauty pageant circuit in which Alana is a regular contestant. Other contestants include Maddy Jackson who at five years old has appeared as Dolly Parton, complete with padded breasts and bum, as well as in a faux-cop outfit modelled on a stripper's costume. Maddy is now the subject of a custody suit. Eight-year old pageant contestant Britney Campbell got Botox injections for her birthday last year, a new addition to her quarterly beauty routine which also includes – bafflingly – waxing.

In an interview, Britney reported that, "My friends think it's cool I have all the treatments and they want to be like me. I check every night for wrinkles, when I see some I want more injections. They used to hurt, but now I don't cry that much...I also want a boob and nose job soon, so that I can be a star." Doctors don't normally give Botox to children, but not to worry, Britney's mom buys it on the Internet, and bums the needles from a diabetic friend. No word yet on where she plans to pick up the Junior Miss Home Breast Enhancement Kit.

In a heartbreaking speech at this year's Newsweek and the Daily Beast Women in the World Summit, actor and activist Ashley Judd described Atlanta, capital city of Honey Boo Boo's home state, as "absolutely over-run with sexual exploitation of children." She might have been speaking of pageant princesses, tarted up like pedophile bait and turned out on the runway, but she wasn't. She was talking about out-and-out sex-slavery. Children are pimped out to men who travel to Atlanta for just that purpose. I wonder, could it be a coincidence that in the same state where you can toss dollar bills at a child of six swaggering in Daisy Dukes on a bar table, you can rent a child for the purpose of rape?

You can, of course, pay to rape a child in other parts of the world besides Georgia. According to a June 2012 story in the *Vancouver Sun*, 15,000 people, most of them women and children destined for the sex trade, are trafficked into Canada each year. The figure for Canadian-born victims, a disproportionate number of them aboriginal girls, is similar. A sex slave sells for as little as $5,000 in Canada, and can net her pimp as much as $280,000 a year for as long as she survives.

Vancouver parents with more money than sense who put their children into de-sexualized pole dancing classes would no doubt be outraged to find themselves mentioned in the same breath as people who pimp children to pedophiles. They would probably also balk at any comparison between themselves and mothers who exhibit their sexed-up toddlers at child beauty pageants.

But the pageant mothers don't think they're doing anything wrong either. Just like Ms Craig, most insist that the "sexuality" has been taken out of what they do. Some of them might need a little coaching in getting that message across, though. Questioned about the controversy surrounding the sexualization of junior pageant queens, one mother replied with remarkable candour, "Who cares? She's my daughter, I'm gonna do whatever I want with her. Git over it people."

Who Owns The Kids?

SEPTEMBER 2012

Steve Tourloukis has a problem. The Hamilton, Ontario dentist is a conservative Christian with two children in the public school system. His problem is that the province's new anti-bullying law calls for the schools to teach tolerance, and Mr Tourloukis finds this intolerable. He has taken to the courts in an attempt to force Gordon Price Elementary School to inform him in advance if his children will be subjected to any discussion involving tolerance of homosexuality, so that they can opt out of the class.

Tourloukis isn't acting alone in this matter. Financially supported in his suit by a five-member group calling itself PRIEDF – parents for something-or-other – he is also part of a larger movement. A campaign called PEACE Hamilton is encouraging parents to voice their intolerance by means of a form letter to the school board. The letter requests that parents be contacted "prior to my/our child's involvement in any activity or program containing the following issues and topics," followed by a checklist.

This checklist merits consideration. Parents may request to be consulted before their kids discuss witchcraft, black magic, spirit guides, Satanism, Environmental Worship, anal sex, oral sex, sadism, masochism, bestiality, fetish, bondage, and infanticide. Oh yes, and before any "discussions or portrayals of homosexual/bisexual conduct and relationships and/or transgenderism as natural, healthy or acceptable."

It's not considered likely that teachers would be much inconvenienced by the requirement to contact parents prior to discussing bestiality in the classroom. Nor does the timing of the action provide us with any obvious connection to infanticide, or anything else on the list, until we arrive at that last item, the one that this campaign is all about. It's no coincidence that Tourloukis launched his suit just days after the anti-bullying law came into force; a major component of the strategy is the portrayal of queer people and their relationships as natural, healthy, and acceptable.

Ontario has not embarked on this course to spite conservative parents, or to steal their children away. They did it because teenagers were dying. Toronto's Centre for Addiction and Mental Health reports that approximately 32 per cent of lesbian, gay, bisexual and transgendered youth contemplate or attempt suicide. Too many succeed. Jamie Hubley in Ottawa, Jeanine Blanchette and Chantal Dubé in Orangeville, Shaquille Wisdom in Ajax, all took their own lives in the wake of homophobic bullying. What PEACE Hamilton is fighting for is not just the right to perpetuate the intolerance that killed these young people, but to force schools to do the same.

At first glance the whole campaign seems absurd, the lawsuit frivolous and vexatious and sure to be tossed out the minute the judge lays eyes on it. How could you run a school that way? Would teachers have to keep a list, updated every time a new form letter came in, of which students were allowed to discuss which subjects without first consulting their parents? What if a proscribed subject simply came up while the class was talking about something else? Should the teacher call for silence and start making phone calls?

Sad to say, it's no fantasy. In Alberta, a teacher runs the risk of facing a human rights complaint if gay marriage or aboriginal spirituality comes up in class. According to Toronto Star columnist Gillian Stewart, the law, brought in by former premier Ed Stelmach, has "caused quite a chill – reluctance on the part of many teachers to include anything in the curriculum that might upset a parent and provide the basis for a complaint." Dale Wallace, former head of English literature at Lord Beaverbrook High School in Calgary wrote in Alberta Views, "Teachers started to change how they taught, with English teachers realizing they'd have to send letters home for almost any literature they studied. The quality of English education started to fall – and has continued to fall in the two years since."

Wallace goes on to say that "challenging novels

" ONTARIO HAS NOT EMBARKED ON THIS COURSE TO SPITE CONSER-VATIVE PARENTS, OR TO STEAL THEIR CHILDREN AWAY. THEY DID IT BECAUSE TEENAGERS WERE DYING.

such as 1984 are replaced with safer ones, like Pride and Prejudice." Since the odds of a modern-day high school student actually reading Pride and Prejudice are low in the extreme, it sounds like literature is all but off the program in Alberta, along with tolerance, and the science of natural selection unless presented as conjecture.

It may be that the people spearheading the campaign against tolerance in Ontario schools don't actively hate gay kids, or at least not to the extent that they are consciously trying to drive them to suicide. Maybe it's not about homophobia at all. Maybe it's all about control. Last week, writing about abuses on the child beauty pageant circuit I closed with this quote from a pageant mom. "Who cares? She's my daughter, I'm gonna do whatever I want with her. Git over it people." It's almost eerie a week later to be closing with these revealing words from Steve Tourloukis: "My children are my own, I own them."

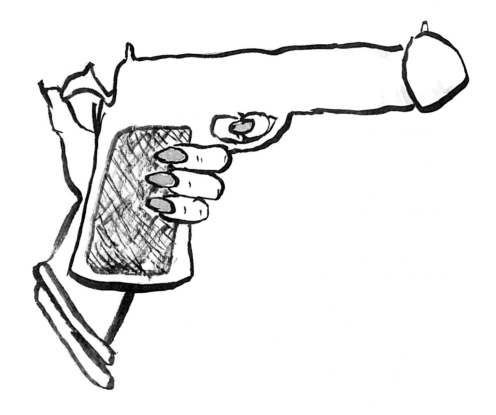

All Rise – Silence In Court

Oklahoma State Judge Donald Thompson retired last month amid allegations that he had kept and employed a penis pump under his robes during court. The judge admitted owning the device, a gift from a hunting buddy, but denied using it while court was in session, though lawyers complained of "the swooshing sound of a penis-pump coming from under the bench during trials."

At press time, *Nordicity* had yet to confirm the rumour that the judge stands accused of handing out overly-stiff sentences. "The allegations are bizarre and preposterous," Thompson's lawyer said. "Recently, some members of local law enforcement that are upset with a number of his rulings, used this situation to embarrass and attack him."

Sometimes I wonder if I've lead a too-sheltered life; maybe my hunting partners have all been social conservatives. Before I could even approach the obvious question – how were the lawyers able to recognize the swooshing sound? – I first had to find out what a penis pump is. Which meant that I had to learn to adjust the security settings on my computer.

According to the web site Sex Toys Pro, "Penis pumps were originally developed to help men with erectile dysfunction achieve and maintain an erection. This is the only medically endorsed use of penis pumps, and it has been made all but obsolete by Viagra, Levitra, and other drugs."

With the popularity of these drugs the penis pump, formerly a perfectly respectable piece of medical equipment consisting of a plastic tube with a squeeze-bulb on the end, now falls exclusively into that far less noble category, the sex toy. So it's

a good thing for Judge Thompson that he served on the bench in Oklahoma, and not in Alabama, where sex-toys are banned, unless they have "other recognized medical or therapeutic uses."

Actually, it's not entirely clear that His Honour's little friend would be illegal in Alabama and the other southern states with similar laws, since these seem to be directed primarily at devices designed to stimulate women. Last week, the US Supreme Court declined to review Alabama's so-called vibrator law, claiming that to do so would open the door to similar challenges of the laws governing "incest, prostitution, obscenity, and the like."

Sex store operators in states with sex-toy bans are currently said to be discussing strategy. Plans for a Million Dildo March to Washington, followed by a Vibe-In on Pennsylvania Avenue, have been shelved while organizers concentrate on a marketing strategy to redefine the product, to make it more palatable for conservative lawmakers.

Several ideas have already emerged. The classic or "lifelike" silicone dildo might be marketed as "the Maxi-Gavel," the latest power-enhancing device for judges whose authority has been undermined by suspicious whooshing sounds. Thump this baby on the bench a couple of times and you'll be amazed at the attention it gets.

Vibrators will be remodelled and sold throughout the South as the all new Home Missile Defence Model Kit. The devices will come in packages of two, with instructions. The game requires three players, and one very large room. Player one takes one vibrator and moves to the far end of the room. He or she turns the vibrator on and throws it as hard and fast as she or he can at player number two.

Players two and three sit down at a table together and consult as to what action to take.

When they reach an agreement, player two gets up, turns on the second vibrator, and throws it at the first. (You do need a very, very long room for this one). In order to win, a player must "shoot down" the other player's vibrator before it hits him or her in the head. Don't be discouraged if you can't make this work, neither can the Leader of the Free World.

But if the way to market dildos in the anti-sex toy states is to convert them into a more socially acceptable device, why not choose one of the two most respectable items in those locales? Of course, converting your toys into bibles would be impractical and may cause offence, so let's turn to our second choice. For states such as Alabama, Texas, Georgia, and Florida, the possession of vibrators will be legal if the device has been bored out to at least .22 of an inch, and a firing chamber, firing pin, and barrel have been installed.

Sales projections for the new "hot pistol" model are extremely optimistic. The market is ready for a light, convenient firearm designed to fit snugly in a ladies' purse. Just don't tell the Texans what it was originally designed for: you know how deeply moral they can be.

Frack The Peel And Pass The Tofu

FEBRUARY 2014

On the advice of a helpful reader – I would say a fan but modesty forbids – I've been considering a vegan lifestyle. Since a large part of my diet consists of meat, eggs, and dairy from my own farm, becoming vegan will require a great deal of consideration.

To begin my vegan education I turned to the Vegetarian Resource Group, where I learned that, "Vegans, in addition to being vegetarian, do not use other animal products and by-products such as eggs, dairy products, honey, leather, fur, silk, wool, cosmetics, and soaps derived from animal products."

So as a vegan I will need to find new clothing options, as well as a new diet. Gone my leather boots, my wool sweaters, my down parka, my felt boot liners and silk underwear.

OK, I don't actually have any silk underwear, but I can strike it off the list of future possibilities.

I understand that veganism is not simply a lifestyle choice, it's a philosophy. As a vegan, I can't just eschew the use of animal products for myself, I must embrace the belief that the world will be a better place without animals, other than vegan pets.

Farm animals will naturally be the first to go. When no one is eating animal products we will quickly turn the age-old question on its head, asking which became extinct first, the chicken or the egg? What place will there be for pigs in a world without pork? For cattle in a milkless, beefless society? For sheep when no one wants wool?

You might think that wool would be an exception to the proscription on animal products, since it can be taken from a live animal without inflicting injury, other than to the dignity of the sheep. But vegans do not cull, and shepherds must. Every time you breed a ewe, there's a 50-50 chance you will get a male lamb. Allow them all to grow to maturity and your flock will be about as manageable as a convention of soccer hooligans.

And anyway, the very existence of livestock is unethical, and their extinction will be a great leap forward for vegans. Next to go will be the wildlife, their habitat destroyed in the endless search for petroleum to make nylon, polyester, and polypropylene clothing to replace wool, feathers, silk, felt and fur. Petroleum will be in great demand in a vegan world, not only for clothing, but for the manufacture of fertilizers to replace all that lost manure.

Not all ethical clothing will have to come from oil. Many vegans will turn to cotton. But cotton is grown using vast quantities of chemical fertilizer and pesticides – so back to the oilfields again – and even more water. According to the Environmental Justice Foundation, it takes "about 2,720 litres of water to produce one cotton T-shirt, equivalent to what an average person might drink over three years."

Also according to EJF, "In 2008, 2,890 billion litres of water was used in Pakistan to grow the cotton needed just to make products sold by the homestore Ikea – equivalent to the volume of drinking water consumed in Sweden over 176 years." Over the past 50 years cotton production has turned the vast teeming Aral Sea into the vast lifeless Aral Desert. But then of course, in a vegan world, who needs fish? Does seem a shame about the water though.

As a vegan, I'll have to forego the use of working animals. As the Vegan Society puts it, "Vegans oppose all forms of exploitation of animals." No more plough horses, carrier pigeons, or guard dogs (though vicious dogs will be protected by law, so long as they only bite in an amateur capacity). On the plus side, there will be no exploitation of honey bees, which will create millions of jobs hand-pollinating all that vegetation.

As I consider a vegan lifestyle, it is this prohibition on beasts of burden that gives me the greatest pause. You see, my vegetable garden is quite dependant on the exploitation of earthworms. These are not naturally-occurring earthworms, and can in no way be considered pets, or as vegans would say, companion worms. I introduced them to my garden to work for me. In the fall I bring as many as I can recover indoors for the winter so that I may turn them out and exploit them again next year.

When I stop eating dairy, meat, and eggs I'll be needing a lot more veggies, and as a conscientious vegan I'll have to try to grow them without manure, and without exploiting earthworms. Just as I was starting to close in on self-sufficiency, it appears I'll be back to depending on diesel trucks to supply my food. As a vegan, I'm really going to have to learn to love the tar sands. But of course it will all be worth it if we can save the animals from being unethically exploited, or born, so having given it full consideration, count me in.

Out with the down parka, in with the fleece jacket. Frack the Peel and pass the tofu burgers. Nobody said ethics come cheap.

A Horse Is A Horse

JULY 2005

Maybe it was the name that did it. This month, Canvas, a restaurant in Hamilton, New Zealand, served horse meat steaks as its entry in the annual Montrieth Wild Food Challenge, an event in which eateries compete to serve the most "out-of-the-ordinary" dishes. Perhaps if they hadn't named the item Mr Ed is Dead, the offering might have caused less controversy.

Mr Ed, for those readers challenged in years, is a television character from a popular 60s comedy. He was as I recall a tall, handsome palomino, distinguished from other palominos by the fact that he talked. Not to be misunderstood: Mr Ed wasn't just one of those horses which can communicate by the use of strong body language, such as kicking you on the shin with an iron shoe. Nor was he a human-whisperer like his forerunners, Trigger and Champion the Wonder Horse. Mr Ed talked American, with just a touch of horse. Think of Bill O'Reilly on Fox News, or the RV'er at the laundromat who can't understand why the machines won't take his coins.

Now, I was a very young person during the 60s, and not yet a tough investigative reporter, so I'm not able to say with absolute authority that the actor who played Mr Ed was in fact a talking horse, but the character certainly talked, and the actor's lips moved, which is about as much as could be said for most of the bipedal actors on television.

One of the distinguishing marks of the recovering television addict of a certain age is that he or she is incapable of learning and retaining new information, due to the fact that her or his brain's memory storage is filled to capacity with jingles and theme songs from some of the silliest entertainments ever devised.

That's why I'm able to relate, without looking it up, that the show Mr Ed began each week with the musical affirmation that: "A horse is a horse, of course of course, and no-one can talk to a horse of course, unless of course the horse of course is the famous Mr Ed." Long after the demise of the show, the entire situation-comedy genre died giving birth to "reality TV," a kind of semi-scripted sitcom, adding fuel to rumours that 60 Minutes had for years been involved in an illicit relationship with Cheers.

A Reality TV version of Mr Ed has been in the planning stages for some time now, and has only been prevented from producing a pilot by a shortage of suitable participants. Inappropriate as the menu item at Canvas might be, Mr Ed is indeed dead. So is Francis the Talking Mule. Bill O'Reilly, though technically alive and able to mimic human speech, doesn't quite meet the communications standards implied by the expression "talking."

In a competition devoted to unusual recipes, it's unlikely that horse steaks would have generated "lots of complaints and abusive phone calls" which were "pretty lively and disgusting and not comforting for the staff" if the dish had been named something innocuous, like say for instance, "dead horse" or even the elegantly simple "horse steaks," but really, was it necessary to invoke the name of a great equine superstar?

What's next? The Barbecued Hillbillies? Three's Compote? Eat Smart? Bewhisked? I Cream of Genie? The restaurant-going public can only be expected to ingest so much darkness with their meals.

New Zealand's leading race horse breeder, Sir Patrick Hogan, has been an outspoken critic, not of the dish's name, but of its contents. A traditionalist who was knighted by the Queen for his contribution to the Sport of Kings, Sir Pat subscribes to the view that human consumption offends the dignity of the horse. "My life with horses has been my passion," he told the New Zealand Herald. "I'm not impressed at all that horse meat is available as a kind of delicacy."

What breeder of thoroughbreds wouldn't rage at the thought of the noble steeds dished up on a plate with two veg., salad, and a choice of baked potato or fries? Surely the kingly creatures are destined for greater things, things like a racing career that begins with the onslaught of adolescence and ends at the knacker's yard before the beast reaches adulthood. Anyone whose lifelong passion has been horse racing knows that a horse must be treated properly, according to the best race-track traditions – drugged into submission, overworked, kneecapped for the insurance money, and finally given a dignified burial in a can of cat-foot.

Despite the best efforts of the neigh-sayers, Mr Ed is Dead sold quite briskly during the Wild Food Challenge. So much so that the restaurant's owner is already planning its next entry. Although a dark veil of secrecy has been drawn around the mystery dish, rumours have begun to leak out. We don't know the name of the dish yet, but it's almost certain that one of the ingredients will be sacred cow.

What A Wonderful World

This month, in an unprecedented technological breakthrough, a fridge took part in a spam attack. The campaign consisted of about 750,000 junk messages, routed through personal computing devices, including laptops, wireless routers, TVs, and at least one refrigerator.

If you've never thought of a fridge as a computing device, welcome to the 21st Century, the brave new world of smart technology. The word smart has been redefined since 1966, the year my Pocket Oxford Dictionary was printed. At that time the adjective meant "Of some severity, sharp, vigorous, brisk, quick-witted, clever, dextrous, quick and precise in movement, spruce, of fresh or bright or well-groomed or well-dressed appearance, of the latest fashion, setting the fashion."

While it's true that smart technology is of the latest fashion, hence clever from a retailing point of view, the modern world does not understand the word "smart" to refer to fashion, or indeed to cleverness. Editors at the Oxford are said to be considering the following new entry: "Smart. adj.: stupid."

This definition would encompass the smart car, not to be confused with the Smart Car. The latter is a supremely fuel-efficient television set on wheels, while the former is a car that can drive itself – over a cliff if so commanded. The smart category of objects also includes the smart phone, which erases every trace of privacy you ever had, and the smart fridge which, as we observed, sends unwanted e-mails to your friends, causing any who manage to trace the message to believe you are secretly a pornographer, a stockbroker, or a Nigerian prince.

It's easy to see why the modern consumer would want to own a car that drives itself. When have you ever heard a Yaris argue back over whose turn it is to be the designated driver? On the other hand, the

> **JUST AS HIP CONSUMERS IN THE 1970S LINED UP TO BUY FISHING REELS TESTED ON THE MOON, SO WILL MODERN-DAY TECHNOPHILES JUMP AT THE CHANCE TO BUY FRIDGES THAT WORK ON MARS.**

car is a car. Trusting your life to 500 kg of metal and a computer chip is only marginally less stupid than trusting it to yourself after two margaritas. As for smart phones, they exist to settle arguments. Can't agree on who won the FA Cup in 1976, or who really said, "In the morning I shall be sober?" No worries, not only is your phone smarter than you are, it's in touch with that incontrovertible arbiter of truth, the World Wide Web.

But why a smart fridge? To judge by the Samsung Wi-Fi enabled RF4289, the function of the net-connected fridge is to part fools from money. At $3,499 for a device that allows you to tweet while grabbing a sandwich – in case you happen to have left your smart phone on the couch – there can be few surer ways on Earth of ridding oneself of unwanted coinage.

If, on the other hand, you choose to leave the planet Earth, the sky, so to speak, is the limit. Planners at Mars One, the project to put a human colony on the Red Planet by 2023, estimate that it will cost $6 billion to send the first four astronauts, who will live together in a giant dumpster surrounded by uninhabitable desert, and then die. Mars One organizers report that more than

165,000 people have applied to be Mars colonists. This outbreak of acute technophilia is believed to be brought on by over-exposure to smart (in the sense of stupid) technology. Americans make up 23 per cent of all applicants, and an estimated 99 per cent of those either own or wish they owned a smart fridge.

On Mars, everything will be smart. Tight energy supply will require the lights, fridge, furnace, and toilet to be in constant communication with each other. No word yet on contingency plans for when the appliances begin to squabble over resources. No matter. The uber-nerds who will be chosen for the suicide mission of the century won't mind a little adversity. And for those still earthbound who crave the latest in technology, what could be more appealing than appliances which have been tried on Mars?

Just as hip consumers in the 1970s lined up to buy fishing reels tested on the moon, so will modern-day technophiles jump at the chance to buy fridges that work on Mars. Whether product testing will help to cover the cost of the mission remains to be seen, but organizers do have a plan to defray expenses. The whole mission will be one big reality TV show.

Picture the future. Your smart couch detects that you are thirsty, and relays a message to the smart fridge. The fridge, mindful of your calorie count, selects a low-cal beer. The TV lets the fridge know that Big Brother on Mars is at a turning point – Tiffany is mad at Mindy for flirting with Max – so the fridge sends a robot with your beer so you don't miss anything. The couch, the fridge and the TV are all in communication with your personal robot-trainer, which makes a note to give you extra treadmill time. A computer at CSIS registers all of the above and determines that you are unlikely to be a terrorist, and the drone of death passes over your house.

As the Mars colonists wait to die, their labours will help to make life on Earth safer, more comfortable, and more predictable for everyone. Ain't technology wonderful?

Smoking For Health

APRIL 2011

Try this for a novel experience. Ask your doctor to prescribe smoking as a cure for what ails you. What do you predict will be the outcome?

That's the dilemma faced by would-be medical marijuana users in Canada today. Cannabis has been found effective against a list of ailments, from fibromyalgia to the nausea associated with chemotherapy, but smoking is a killer, associated with heart disease and cancer.

True, smoking is not the only way to ingest cannabis. It can be eaten or vaporized, eliminating the massive ingestion of tar that is the nastiest element of smoke inhalation. The trouble is, nobody knows the health implications of nonsmokeable dope. When doctors prescribe drugs, they're supposed to know what risks are associated with their use, in order to balance the potential harm they might do with the benefits they offer.

Canadian law permits the use of weed for certain medical conditions, if it's prescribed by a doctor. Many people suffering from those conditions have no hope in the world of finding a doctor to write that prescription.

The Canadian Medical Association's position on the matter is that "The same safety and evidence standards should apply to medical marijuana as to pharmaceutical products."

In the absence of testing to establish those standards, a lot of doctors are unwilling to prescribe marijuana. So as a patient, your access to a drug that may be the only relief you can get from sometimes unbearable symptoms is determined by where you live, and whether you are able to travel and shop around for a sympathetic doctor.

This is the situation faced by fibromyalgia and scoliosis sufferer Matthew Mernagh, who was busted in St. Catherines, Ontario for growing his own weed after he couldn't find a doctor to prescribe the government-supplied variety. Mr Justice Donald Taliano of the Ontario Superior Court found that the arrest violated Mr Mernagh's constitutional right to liberty, and struck down Canada's laws against possession and cultivation of marijuana.

Don't rush out and stick your hitherto clandestine pot plants on that sunny window ledge facing the street just yet, the ruling gives the government 90 days to rewrite the law. Should they fail to do so, there will be no law against owning or growing dope, at least in Ontario. Given that laws can't be written and passed that quickly, it's more or less certain that the government will appeal the decision, to buy themselves more time.

When the Conservative government was defeated a couple of weeks ago, it was pushing its "anti-crime" Bill S-10. If passed, S-10 would create a mandatory minimum sentence for possession of as few as six pot plants. Stephen Harper has promised that if re-elected with a majority his first act will be to push that bill through the House.

In Harper's well-financed, tightly controlled campaign, you may be sure that he wouldn't be making this promise unless it had been studied and found to be popular with his conservative base. By way of an interesting contrast Alaska, one of the more conservative states in the US, has decriminalized possession of under an ounce of pot on strong libertarian grounds: the constitutional right to privacy in one's own home.

It's unreasonable to expect doctors to prescribe an untested drug. It's even more so when that drug is normally smoked, an activity only slightly less unhealthy than jumping off cliffs. It's even more unreasonable to lock people up (at the taxpayers' expense, don't forget) for using a substance that brings relief from some of the nastier ailments around. The solution seems simple enough, and should be palatable to conservatives and socialists alike. Never mind the medical marijuana quagmire, just legalize it.

Some people find that marijuana alleviates their symptoms, others enjoy it as a recreational drug. It's not a particularly healthy thing to do, but if you don't smoke it in public places or in homes where there are nonusers or children around, who does it hurt? Prohibition isn't a conservative value, it's just stupid. The Conservative party wants to waste your money locking people up, not only for treating themselves when they're ill, but for one of the most basic individual freedoms a conservative ought to support: the right to go to hell in whatever damn handcart you choose.

Stop! Don't Feed That Child!

JANUARY 2012

Picture the loveliest thing you know. Now picture it with a beautiful baby nuzzling at it, those soft, translucent little eyelids closed in ecstasy, and a doting mother's face smiling down on the whole scene. Ok, if you started out picturing sailboats and sunsets the whole thing falls apart, but if you did, reconsider; they're only boats and clouds after all.

The online community birthday-sharing thingy Facebook was in the news this week – when is it not? – this time because the company that operates it doesn't allow members to post photographs of breastfeeding. That's right, peek-a-boo, embarrassing-pictures-of-drunks-in-their-underpants, oops-career-wrecking-one-there Facebook does not permit depictions of the fully naked female breast. They don't insist on a great deal of clothing, but a certain amount is considered de rigueur, and the feeding breast, most commonly seen nude, is unacceptable.

Vancouver mother Emma Kwasnica has had her Facebook account embargoed four times for the sin of posting pictures of herself nursing her babies. A breastfeeding activist and mother of three, Ms Kwasnica has been trying for six years to share her pictures with the world, or at least with the 500,000,000 or so who use Facebook to, er, do whatever Facebook is for. Thwarted at each attempt she recently coaxed an apology out of the company, though other women report that the harassment continues.

In Canada, the right to breastfeed in public is entrenched in law, as indeed is the equal right to toplessness. Once in a while someone ignorant of this fact tries to interfere with a breastfeeding mother, and lives to regret it. For example, in 2008 a clerk at an H&M clothing store in Vancouver asked Manuela Valle to step into a change room to feed her baby. A few days later hundreds of breastfeeding moms and babies packed the store during lunch hour.

Store employees probably learned at least three things that day. One: breastfeeding is nice. It's kind of cozy and sweet and makes everybody happy. Two: you can't really ogle with the baby's head in the way. The average baby's hungry lips and chubby cheeks, never mind its big bald head, obscure more of the breast from view than many popular clothing options. Three: it's embarrassing and bad for business to be on the wrong end of a public protest.

Joining a social Internet site like Facebook is a bit like hanging out at the mall. You feel like you're in a publicly-owned space, but you're not. Just like the mall, that web site is private property. Unlike the mall, that property exists in the legal wasteland that is Cyberspace, so your right to be protected against discrimination is a lot less clear. If Facebook decides that a breastfeeding mother is obscene while saucy hen-night pictures are not, it's difficult to get the Canadian Human Rights Commission after them, and you can't fill their business space with breastfeeding mothers on a busy lunch hour.

Facebook is not unique in its bipolar attitude toward breasts. It's reflecting the whole culture's peek-but-don't-look fixation. Used to sell everything from cars to whiskey, the female breast as sex object is ever present. We even have the means to surgically mutilate breasts to look bigger, or younger, or whatever you desire and can afford. Breasts are popular. They're hip. Much hipper than hips. But the breast itself is to be kept covered in public. Or partly covered. At least a tiny bit.

The sheer volume of traffic on Facebook makes it influential, regardless of how trivial the whole business is. By the time your "friends" – many of whom you don't know from Adam – have posted a hundred or so pictures of themselves doing silly, embarrassing things, they don't seem so silly any more, and you might be persuaded to post similar pictures of yourself. Bad things can result. Teachers lose their jobs for appearing in pole-dancing pictures. Students get suspended for those very arty shots of themselves using drugs. Rioters post pictures of each other rioting and end up in jail.

If, in addition to legitimizing self-destructive behaviour, Facebook was shining the light of its approval on breastfeeding, this too would become a totally normalized activity, just as acceptable to society as beer-bonging and birthday spankings.

And once normalized on Facebook, how much longer before it became normal on the street? Oh, it's just another breastfeeding mum, Mum. No reason to gawk, or to complain to the management.

By encouraging rather than banning breastfeeding, Facebook would be contributing to a more equal and sensible society, where the rights of mothers and babies are respected, and where public spaces would be enhanced by lots of examples of the loveliest thing you know. Unless, that is, you're a die-hard admirer of sailboats and sunsets. There's no accounting for tastes.

Glam And Boredom On The Campaign Trail

OCTOBER 2012

Two new stars, both of them hunky athletic guys, made their entry onto the Canadian reality TV scene this week. Brad, a former football player, will star in the Canadian version of The Bachelor, while Justin, a one-time boxer, will play the lead role in an upcoming special called the Liberal Leadership Race.

The Bachelor Canada is an offshoot of an American TV show, in effect a drawn-out beauty pageant in which the prize is not a purple sash and a golden crown, but a man, in this case Brad Smith of Hudson, Quebec.

Brad is the Bachelor, while the women are collectively known as the Bachelorettes. This custom of feminizing nouns by adding a trivializing suffix has fallen out of use over time, except in a few special cases, and it's a pity, because it could be used to explain so much.

Consider, for instance, Stephen Harper's recent decision to abandon the modern practice of striving toward gender balance on the Supreme Court. When he chose to promote a man over a similarly qualified woman at a time when the bench already had a male bias, his motivation would have been so much clearer if he had simply said he preferred to advance the career of a judge, rather than to indulge the ambition of a judgette. But I digress.

The Liberal Leadership Race is another drawn-out beauty pageant, and again the winner doesn't get to sport the sash and crown, but instead receives the dubious honour of carrying the Liberal banner into a second round of voting, called a general election.

It's a bit like being crowned Miss Papineau, and going on to compete for the Miss Canada title. This is where Justin's path diverges from Brad's, for while Brad is the prize, Justin is a contestant. Nonetheless, the two have similar tasks. Each must present himself as a desirable object to a select group while entertaining a broader public. Let's take a look at how they're doing so far.

In the Age of Google, it was a safe bet that both Brad and Justin would turn up on YouTube. I found several clips from interviews with Brad, and I must say I was disappointed. While each and every interviewer came across as predictably vapid and silly, Brad seemed personable, intelligent, and completely at ease. In vain I sifted his answers for a quote that would make him sound suitably idiotic, given the enterprise on which he is embarked. In Justin's case, I had no trouble at all.

Justin Trudeau launched his campaign for the Liberal leadership in his home riding of Papineau, and on YouTube. I did my best to watch the whole thing, but the entertainment value of any political gathering being inversely relative to the number of times the crowd breaks into the iambic chanting of the candidate's name, I failed. Only notable on this occasion was the fact that, eschewing the custom of given-name chanting, the Liberal crowd was using Justin's surname. Still it drove me off, but not before I had time to glean a couple of facts.

The first thing I learned was the nature of Justin's great vision, his Just Society, as it were. It is this: "hard, honest work." Hard honest work cropped up early in the speech, and it was clear from the delivery that this is Justin's bold new plan, like nobody ever thought of hard honest work before, except maybe Plato.

Having delivered his dream of the future, Justin went on to outline his equally dreamlike vision of the past. "This magnificent, unlikely country was founded on a bold new premise," he said, "That people of different beliefs and backgrounds, from all corners of the world, could come together to build a better life for themselves and for their children than they ever could have alone."

Really, Justin? Is that how it was? In the 19th Century, were we all about founding a nation on co-operation and diversity? So what was all that talk about the degenerate Irish, the treacherous Chinese, the primitive Indians? How to account for the two wars with the Metis, the broken treaties, the stolen land? And then it came to me: Justin wasn't talking about the 1860s. He thinks his dad founded the country in 1982.

A week ago, a poll conducted by Forum Research for the *National Post* found that if Justin Trudeau were their leader, and the vote had been held on that day, the Liberals would have been elected to government with 39 per cent of the popular vote. Not to fear, there is plenty of time yet for Justin to correct the misapprehension that he is the second coming of Pierre Trudeau. If his maiden speech was anything to go by, now that people are actually paying attention, he's more likely to follow Michael Ignatieff's footsteps than his own famous father's.

Breaking into metaphor, Justin promised his listeners a Canadian highway with "breathtaking vistas and a few boring stretches." I like to imagine Brad and Justin getting together for a beer to talk over their respective careers in reality TV. "Dude," Brad might say, offering some friendly advice, "Boredom is a total turn-off. The Bachelorettes hate that. If you're bored, you might as well get into a new line of work."

Ok, so Justin defied expectations and went on to become Canada's hugger-in-chief with a resounding majority. Your point?

If She's Hungry: Celebrating Rape

SEPTEMBER 2013

This week three stories appeared in the national press about university students, both men and women, using frosh week as an occasion to celebrate rape.

The first story to break concerned "student leaders" at St. Mary's University in Halifax who encouraged new students to chant a rhyme about raping underage girls. Next we learned that business students at the University of British Columbia had latched onto the same rape chant, while Engineering students at Newfoundland's Memorial University passed out mugs proclaiming, "If she's thirsty, give her the D." The phrase derives from the name of a porn site.

In a recent survey of undergraduate students at Canadian universities, 4 out of 5 women reported that they had experienced violence at the hands of men they were dating. Of those, 29 per cent had been the victims of sexual assault. In a separate survey, 60 per cent of college aged males said they would rape a woman if they were certain they could get away with it.

How have we arrived at a place where young men take the idea of rape so casually, where even young women in the highest-risk age group think it's ok to celebrate rape in public? Matt Gurney has it all figured out. According to the *National Post* columnist, "An investigation into these incidents is wasted effort because everyone knows full damn well what the problem is: teenagers are idiots. ... Investigation complete!"

Gee, thanks Matt, that clears everything up. Well, almost everything. We understand that, as you say, "Teenagers are impulsive, have lousy decision-making skills and are highly vulnerable to peer pressure." There's nothing like a good stereotype to put things in perspective. But there is just the small question of context. In 1914, youths were expressing their idiocy by volunteering to go to a war they knew next to nothing about. In 1970 idiotic teens were trapped in the delusion that sex, drugs, and rock and roll could put and end to war, famine and school. In 2013, they're chanting about raping each other's little sisters.

These are all excellent examples of the dangerous stupidity of the young, but they're hardly interchangeable. We're still left with the question, why this idiocy, and why now? In 1914, young people were influenced by a culture of imperialism, in 1970 by a culture of self-indulgence. Today it would appear they live in a culture that says rape is cool if you can get away with it.

Where a mature society might promote the freedom to follow one's sexuality, the duty to play responsibly, and the joy of sharing good sex with an equal partner, today's advertising-driven pop culture teaches success through sexual conformity: men be macho, women be available, girls be women before your time, boys start learning sexual opportunism long before you're ready to understand what that means.

In support of his tidy explanation for rape chants on campuses, Gurney offers the evidence that he himself was an idiot as a youth, guilty of "stupid pranks, minor trespassing," lots of "stupid, hurtful" remarks, and at least one act of drunkenness serious enough to involve the police. He produces no evidence in support of the claim that idiocy was a function of his youth, and has since passed, but let's take that as a given. At least one of the things he confesses to – binge-drinking on over-proof alcohol – has proven fatal for a number of young people, tragedies which might have been avoided if the young weren't socialized to drink like fools.

By the same token, if young men were not social-ized to see women as commodities, and themselves as consumers, they might be less inclined toward rape. But what is to be done? Censorship is neither a desirable solution, nor possible in this mass-media age. People young and old will continue to be exposed to images of women and girls as sex-toys, and men as careless little boys who may be forgiven for misusing their playthings.

All we can do is offer a counter-narrative, one in which young people are not assumed to be idiots, and the presumed impulsive foolishness of youth is not made an excuse for self-destructive or criminal behaviour. As soon as they are capable of under-standing, children need to begin a comprehensive sex education, one that teaches them that sex between equals is a beautiful and desirable thing.

We can't ban rape language. No law will change the fact that, in pop culture, the word "bitch" means both a woman and a slave. But we can make a counter-offer. We can present the language of love, and of equality. We can also be honest and frank about rape, be clear that it's not a joke but a horror, an assault from which few ever fully recover, and a very serious crime.

Here's a tiny first step down that road we media types could take. Almost every news story about the college rape chants refers to child rape as "non-consensual sex with minors." That's like calling murder non-consensual death. If we want to build a culture that discourages rape, let's start by calling it what it is.

CHAPTER 9: SCANDALS, COVER-UPS, AND LIES

 YOU SEE, MUM WAS RIGHT, YOU CAN FIND SOMETHING GOOD TO SAY ABOUT ALMOST ANYONE.

Nothing spices up a columnist's life like a nice juicy scandal, and for that reason I might have come to love Brian Mulroney, if only he hadn't been such a smarmy toad. Paul Martin, Jean Chretien, and Stephen Harper all provided their share of scandal stories too, though they lacked Mulroney's talent for oleaginous self-congratulation. Trudeau the Younger hasn't been around long enough yet to judge, but at the time of publication no fat cash-stuffed envelopes have appeared to stain his good-boy image. You see, Mum was right, you can find something good to say about almost anyone.

The Scent Of A Cover-Up

DECEMBER 2007

From the sleazy heart of the military industrial complex, where quiet money seals the deals and success depends on good connections and a low public profile, Karlheinz Schreiber sprang into the Canadian limelight last month. Schreiber is an old Conservative backroom boy, as well as an international arms dealer, and a professional greaser of the wheels of commerce. His wheeling and dealing helped bring former Conservative leader Brian Mulroney to power.

Mulroney was prime minister for nine scandal-ridden years, from 1984 to 1993. In 1988 Air Canada – then a crown corporation – purchased 34 airliners from German manufacturer Airbus Industrie. Schreiber brokered the deal, and claims to have spent $20 million in Schmiergelder, or grease money, (his term) to defeat a bid by British competitor Boeing.

In 1975, Mulroney learned that the RCMP was investigating the Airbus contract, and had named him in a request for information to Swiss authorities. The former prime minister sued the Canadian taxpayer for $50 million, claiming damage to his reputation. He finally settled out of court for $2.1 million. During that court case, Mulroney claimed that he hardly knew Schreiber, had met him once or twice for a cup of coffee, and had never had any dealings with him. In fact, Schreiber had met Mulroney in three separate luxury hotel rooms, handing over $100,000 in cash each time.

Mulroney had known Schreiber for more than a decade by the time he pocketed those envelopes. Schreiber had raised funds for Mulroney`s campaign to become prime minister, and helped engineer his defeat of Joe Clark for the Conservative leadership in 1983. It's hard not to be reminded of the Liberal sponsorship scandal at this point. If there was one thing that brought down the Martin government, it was the stink of cash. There was just something so underworld about all those fat envelopes. The Mulroney story reeks of cash too, tinged with a strong hint of cover-up and lies.

According to Stevie Cameron`s 1995 book, On The Take, Mulroney was the recipient of regular cash payments throughout his term as prime minister. Delivered to his wife, Mila, the cash came from the Conservative Party, as a top-up to the prime ministerial salary. Every week or two, the

Mulroneys' chef would pick up an envelope of cash, usually between $8,000 and $12,000, and deliver it to Canada's Shopper in Chief. Mulroney flat denied that the Conservative Party was supplementing his salary, so where was all this cash coming from? Is this what Mulroney means when he speaks of protecting his family?

Only a few cabinet ministers still remain from Mulroney's days, only a handful of the old power-brokers still broker power. If only they hadn't tried to cover it up, the Airbus scandal might have passed today's Conservatives by altogether.

But they did.

Karlheinz Schreiber is awaiting extradition to Germany on Schmiergelder charges there. If he is extradited now, the entire affair will be swept back under the rug. Canada will never know where Schreiber's $20 million went, why he paid Mulroney $300,000 in cash, or what he means when he says he has a story to tell that's "bigger than airbus."

Canada's minister of justice has absolute power over who is and is not extradited. The current justice minister, Rob Nicholson, spent last week trying his hardest to get Schreiber out of the country as quickly as possible. Nicholson's claim that he has no power to prevent the principal witness from leaving the scene defies credulity.

Had it not been for unrelenting pressure, applied mainly by the media and the NDP's Pat Martin, Schreiber would be in a German jail this morning, and that would be the end of that, as far as Canada is concerned. Instead, he's testifying before a Commons standing committee. The Conservative-dominated ethics committee will never get to the bottom of Schreiber's story, but at least it's keeping him in Canada. What remains to be seen is how far the Conservatives will go to get rid of him before they're forced to call a proper judicial enquiry.

Unless there's a very full public hearing, with a mandate to dig all the way back into Schreiber's earliest dealings in Canada, and to trace all of the grease money and where it ended up, we will never know why the Harper government tried so hard to stifle this investigation.

Bumper Stickers Threaten Our Way Of Life

APRIL 2013

Those radical environmentalists are at it again. Taking time out from scheming against the prime minister's pipelines, foreign-funded ecoterrorists have set their sights on the Yukon, and according to the premier, when they get done with their preservationist agenda you won't recognize the place.

This time the radicals aren't just plotting to stall development by making presentations at environmental reviews: they're out to destroy the territory by preserving it, and make no mistake, they have the bumper-stickers to do it.

Premier Darrell Pasloski dedicated a bit over two pages of his recent budget address to warning Yukoners of the threat posed by environmentalists in general, and in particular by the more than four members of the Yukon board of the Canadian Parks and Wilderness Society. In a shocking revelation, the premier uncovered CPAWS' secret agenda: they're out to create parks and protect wilderness.

Fantastic as this allegation might appear, Pasloski based his case on cold, hard facts. Consider for instance that "protection of additional lands in the Peel watershed region will likely make Yukon the leading jurisdiction in Canada in terms of environmental protection of its land area." With only his political staff and the Yukon civil service to draw on, the premier hadn't the resources to establish that this is indeed the case before using it in his budget speech, but he knows it's likely. He also seems to know that it's a bad thing.

Reaching back into his bag of hard evidence, Pasloski reported that "whatever the amount of land that the Yukon government protects in the Peel watershed region, it will never be enough to satisfy the demands of the Canadian Parks and Wilderness Society."

Never mind that CPAWS endorsed the Peel planning commission's recommendation for permanent protection of 55 per cent of the Peel, and interim protection of 25 per cent more. You can't take radical environmentalists at their word. As the premier pointed out, CPAWS' "next targets for protection include the Wolf Lake Ecosystem in south-central Yukon, including Teslin and the entire Upper Liard Basin."

This is the kind of unrestrained extremism you can expect from radical environmentalists. You protect habitat in the northern Yukon, but are they satisfied? Oh no. Now they want habitat protection in the south, even "including Watson Lake." Does it get any more subversive? Let the fanatics get away with protecting wildlife corridors around Watson Lake and, as Pasloski so eloquently puts it, "Yukon as we know it today would cease to exist." And, the premier tells us, the campaign to destroy southeast Yukon is set to begin in earnest, or in his own words, "You can bet the bumper stickers are already prepared."

This is how the radicals operate. Fuelled by massive influxes of foreign money, they print bumper stickers which – and this is the devious part – enable Yukoners to make a clear public statement on a matter of deep general concern. And there's no measuring the extent to which these tactics skew the debate.

If you were to believe the profusion of bumper stickers, the great bulk of letters to the local papers, the results of an opinion poll, the protests, the First Nation position statements, or the conclusion of the Peel Planning Commission, you could be misled into believing that the vast majority of Yukoners oppose widespread mining activity in the Peel watershed.

Welcome to Yukon
FREE TO EXPLORE!

The Yukon Party can play at that game, too.

The premier knows better. What the Yukoners who matter care about is the economic potential of an iron ore mine in the middle of nowhere. As he points out, the Crest deposit, some 350 kilometres northeast of Keno City, contains 1.68 billion tonnes of ore, valued at $83 a tonne, and if the government would just build a multi-billion dollar railroad 1,000 kilometres to tidewater, Chevron could sell the works on the open market for $139.7 billion.

This is the kind of clear-eyed economic leadership the Yukon has come to expect from its eponymous governing party: if you can't give it away, pay someone to take it. That's how you keep the economy rolling.

None of this should be taken to imply that the Yukon Party is unconcerned about the environment. Indeed, says Pasloski, "we do support environmental protection and are committed to preserving Yukon's wilderness beauty." So much

so, he tells us, that regulations currently place 12.68 per cent of the territory under some kind of environmental protection. This leaves only 87.32 per cent of the Yukon open to free-entry mining, threatening the very existence of the territorial economy, or at least of the 23 per cent of it that relies on resource extraction.

The Yukon government has tabulated the results of its Peel consultation process, and revealed that 80 per cent of the 10,000 responses originated outside the Yukon. No word yet on what the responses were: we can only conclude from the silence that they favoured CPAWS' vision more than the premier's.

To keep us informed the government has commissioned a pamphlet, about which only the name was known as of this writing. Shakespeare aside, the name tells us quite a lot. It will be called not "What You Said," but "What We Heard." I think we can already guess the answer to that.

Dump The Bums

MARCH 2013

So here's the deal. We're going to give you a job that pays an annual salary of $130,000. If you're coming from more than 100 kilometres away, we're going to give you $22,000 for living expenses. We'll put up $161,200 a year to run your private office and hire staff. We'll throw in a first-class travel allowance you can run up to at least $175,000 a year with a little juggling, and you can share it with family and friends. We'll top that off with a great pension plan, and free haircuts. All we expect in return is that you work toward abolishing the job.

Officially this is the deal between Stephen Harper and his 58 Senate appointees. The question now is, who had their fingers crossed behind their backs? Harper built his career on the promise: "I will not name appointed people to the Senate." Now that he is naming appointed people to the Senate, it's ok because as Conservative Senate Leader Marjory LeBreton tells us, "they all support Senate reform."

At present counting, 64 out of 105 senators are Conservative, Senate reformers every one. Harper has a majority in the House. So where's the bill creating that Triple E Senate? The Conservatives' proposal currently before the Supreme Court calls for relatively tame reforms – eight-year term limits, and the opportunity for provinces to hold elections to nominate appointees, if they choose.

Could it be that as prime minister Harper has realized what a royal pain an equal, effective, elected Senate would be, with its own politics, its own agenda, and its own leader? Eight-year term limits and kinda-sorta elections must seem like a far safer option.

Still, term limits do limit terms. If you were planning to ride that gravy train till you turned 75, leaving it, say, 10 years early could be a $2 million

kick in the pants. It looks like in the not-distant future those 64 Conservative senators will be faced with the responsibility to vote themselves out of the cushiest job in the country. There's no empirical evidence to back me on this, but just on a hunch I'm predicting the longest, soberest second thought the upper chamber has ever seen.

The Senate is a child of the 19th Century, when democracy was still a dangerous and radical idea. Although only white men of property could vote in any election, it was still a threat to stability for the elected Commons to be in control of the King's dominion. The Senate existed to oversee democracy and make sure it didn't overstep its bounds. That's where the expression "sober second thought" comes from. Appointed by His Majesty, senators had to prove that they were of a certain worth, both in land and capital. A title or knighthood and a luxuriant growth of white whiskers didn't hurt either.

What function does this 1860s institution have in a modern democracy? It serves as a vehicle for the prime minister to reward the faithful; Conservative Senator Irving Gerstein, with remarkable candour, spoke for a number of his colleagues last year when he told the Senate, "I look back over many years of working as a party bagman." The Senate is also used as a gold-plated parking lot for political candidates; three of the Conservative senators who resigned to run in the last federal election failed to win a seat, and were immediately reappointed.

The Senate makes a great retirement job for Conservative journalists – even though they're notoriously clueless when it comes to filling out the necessary forms. Sometimes it even indulges in good old-fashioned sober second thought, like in Black November, 2010, when appointed Conservative senators broke seven decades of democratic tradition by voting down the environment bill passed by the elected House of Commons.

None of these are necessary, or even defensible, functions of an appointed body in a democracy. A democracy has no need of a system to channel public funds into the hands of party bagmen, a place to reward large donors to political parties, or a golden parachute for failed political candidates.

Most of all we don't need another level of Parliament to supersede the elected House of Commons.

In short, we don't need a Senate. It's an outdated idea and a huge waste of money. There are many better things the country could do with $90 million a year. Whether they fudge their expenses or not, senators are a disgrace to democracy. The solution is simple. Never mind limiting terms, dump the bums.

Detainee Transfers: No Fuss, No Muss

APRIL 2010

Then said they unto him, Say now Shibboleth: and he said Sibboleth: for he could not frame to pronounce it right. Then they took him, and slew him at the passages of Jordan: and there fell at that time of the Ephraimites forty and two thousand." — Judges 12–6.

One of the greatest challenges in fighting a war against a guerrilla resistance movement is that it's almost impossible to tell enemy fighters from ordinary civilians. Wouldn't it be handy if all your enemies had a speech impediment? Just like the Israelites in the Book of Judges, you could simply line 'em up and cull out the lispers.

Canadian forces in Afghanistan face this problem every day. Taliban fighters look a lot like ordinary Afghans, because they are. And unfortunately for our side, they not only look like everybody else, they talk like them too. What the army needs is a magic fairy dust they can sprinkle on suspects that can tell them who is good, and who is evil. Enter the gunshot residue test. Canadian soldiers carry in their kits a simple swab that can be used to tell if a person has been handling guns or explosives. It makes identifying insurgents quite simple: you swab all the men and boys, and detain whoever tests positive.

This term 'detain' has a rather special meaning for Canadians in Afghanistan. There are no prisoner of war camps, no Canadian detention centres, and our senior ally, the US, has enough on its hands abusing its own detainees without having to worry about ours. Canada solves the problem by handing suspects over to the Afghan authorities, in the person of the National Directorate of Security.

The system has all the no-fuss-no-muss convenience of disposable paper towels. Just swipe the handy GRT, and toss the insurgent in the trash! It works so well that, according to the Afghan Independent Human Rights Commission, Canadian troops hand over twice as many detainees as any of our NATO allies. There are a few minor flaws in the GRT system. Most men in Afghanistan handle guns, whether for hunting, self-defence, insurgency, or in the service of the local warlord. The country has been at war for so long that residue from guns and explosive is everywhere, and finally, farm fertilizers may cause false positives.

When our troops do hand prisoners over to the NDS, there are a number of things that may happen. The most likely first step is that they'll undergo a money residue test. If they are found to be capable of paying a bribe, they have a good chance of going free. There's no evidence that this test distinguishes between ordinary civilians and Taliban any better than the gunshot residue test, so it's quite likely that some legitimate detainees are quickly back in action, shooting at Canadians again.

If a detainee fails to pass the money residue test, he may face criminal prosecution, or he may be tortured, or he may just disappear. Reports from AIHRC, Amnesty International, Canadian diplomats, and others describe a smorgasbord of interrogation techniques which includes electric shock, beating with electrical cables, and rape. A US State Department report from 2006 describes as common such practices as "pulling out fingernails and toenails, burning with hot oil, beatings, sexual humiliation, and sodomy."

There are secrets yet to learn about Canada's actions in Afghanistan, and the Harper Conservative government is determined not to let those secrets out. This week Peter Milliken, speaker of the House of Commons, ruled that the government must obey Parliament and hand over all documents related to detainee transfers in Afghanistan. The Conservatives are not going to heed that ruling. Whatever is buried in those heavily redacted files, the government has done everything in its power, and a few things not technically within its powers, to prevent it from coming to light, and you can rest assured that they will continue to do so, even if it means forcing an election with their own popularity at its lowest level yet.

As the political parties battle it out you will hear a lot of talk about parliamentary privilege, contempt of parliament, national security, and constitutional crisis. These are all matters of the gravest importance, but they are apt to become a smoke screen for the real questions that those hidden documents have the power to answer. There are now clear allegations, substantiated by many observers, that Canada callously delivered men into the hands of torturers who would have done the Holy Inquisition proud. It's also alleged that we still do. There are further allegations that we have deliberately used the NDS as surrogate torturers.

If we do end up in an election because Harper flat refuses to turn over the documents, Conservative politicians and spin doctors will do everything they can to divert attention from the real meaning of that election. They will try to make it an election about gun control, or crime, or Ignatieff's years abroad. Don't let them get away with it, Canada. If Harper won't answer to Parliament, he'll have to answer to the people. Not about the long gun registry, not about his phoney war on crime, not about the bogus recovery supposedly created by his corporate bail-out schemes: it's about the careless handling of human life, about complicity in torture, about horrible crimes, about cover-up.

If we're heading into an election over this, let's call it like it is: it's an election about war crimes.

Dude, Where's My Gazebo?

SEPTEMBER 2011

On Monday, the Yukon Conservative Association held its annual charity barbecue. MP Ryan Leef, joined by Tony Clement, President of the Treasury Board, manned the coals to raise some very badly needed funds for the Whitehorse Food Bank.

Praiseworthy as it is for politicians to mix with the folk, to don the apron and to dish out the burgers for a worthy cause, I must say that, as a supporter of the food bank, I'm a little disappointed. When I heard Tony Clement was on the program, I was hoping for bigger things. They say around Parry Sound that when Clement takes it into his head to spread the cash around, you'd better duck.

When Canada hosted the G8 Summit in 2010, the Conservative government chose the Ontario cottage country town of Huntsville, in Clement's riding of Parry Sound–Muskoka, as the venue. The area was looking a little run down, so the government decided to invest some money to spruce the place up for their important visitors.

It put $1.14 million into sidewalks in Parry Sound, which nobody from the summit ever set foot on because it's too far away.

It put $3.5 million into prettying up the Huntsville airport, where the world leaders neither landed nor took off. It built the famous $745,000 gazebo in Orville, a tiny, out-of-the-way place that would rather have had a skating rink. All of this could be dismissed as bureaucratic bungling, except that the bureaucracy had very little to do with it. An auditor general's report released this June found Clement and Conservative party staffers spent $45.7 million of public funds in Parry Sound–Muskoka, without leaving a paper trail.

Not only did the Conservatives cut out the boring paperwork, they managed to avoid all that messy business of parliamentary oversight. The $50 million Clement and his political aides splashed around the riding came from an infrastructure fund to reduce congestion at the border. It's fortunate there wasn't too much reporting required, it would have been a nuisance trying to explain how a gazebo in the Muskokas would reduce congestion 300 kilometres away.

The Harper government dismissed the findings in the June AG report as evidence of nothing more than sloppy bookkeeping, and promised to do better next time. Others saw the misappropriation of public funds as a violation of the Criminal Code of Canada. The Appropriations Act forbids governments to spend money without parliamentary approval, and no such approval was ever given for the G8 spruce-up. It's not likely that Harper will call the Mounties in to investigate though; he promoted Clement to the Treasury Board after the controversy surfaced. So guess who's in charge of investigations into misuse of public funds?

A couple of weeks ago, NDP researchers, using access to information requests, uncovered new details about the G8 spending. According to Muskoka municipal documents, during the 2008 election Clement went around the riding holding meetings with mayors and councillors to identify suitable projects for the G8 slush fund. Within days, he had posted video endorsements on his campaign website from "local townspeople, mayors and council members."

Tony Clement's entry into national politics wasn't a smooth one. He was soundly defeated in Brampton in 2004, and squeaked in by 28 votes in

Muskoka in 2006. Still, as a graduate of the Mike Harris provincial government he was welcomed into the Harper cabinet. As health minister, he was on point for the government's anti-harm-reduction policies, and took the boos at international conferences for the Conservatives' backward views on drug addiction and AIDS.

Naturally, the party wanted to give his chances a little boost at election time. But did they have to be so blatant? The highest amount spent on civic improvements for a G8 summit in the past has been about $5 million, or one-tenth the amount spent by Clement's political staff. Just for the sake of comparison, the public funds involved in the Sponsorship Scandal that brought down the Martin Liberals was $150 million, or just three times the Clement slush fund.

There are a lot of people in need in Whitehorse, and we're glad to see the food bank get all the help it can. The barbecue really was a good and generous gesture on the part of a busy man like Clement. I'm sure Leef appreciated the exposure he got from flipping burgers with the Treasury Board President. As a matter of fact, next time Clement wants to impress his own constituents he might try putting on that blue apron in Orville. Barbecuing's not as splashy as a $50-million giveaway, but at least it's honest work.

The Fix Is In

Senator Mike Duffy says he's "pleased" that the Senate's internal economy committee will re-examine his expense accounts. I bet he is. That's the same committee that exonerated him less than a month ago. It's a committee dominated by his old Conservative pals, and it stands accused of altering documents in his case. It sits in camera, and its minutes are sealed. If you ever have to face a jury, I wish you one like that.

The alternative, presented by dissenting Liberal senators, was to have the matter referred to the RCMP. No, no, no, no, no, that's not the way we treat senators in Canada. Particularly not if they come from the ruling party. Although access is no longer restricted to white males, the Canadian Senate is still a 19th-Century gentlemen's club, and the decision to refer the peccadilloes of its members to the constabulary is not taken lightly. Far better to settle such things behind closed doors, out of the distracting eye of the rabble. Or to quote section 4 of Chapter 1:02 of the Senate Administrative Rules, "senators act on their personal honour and senators are presumed to have acted honourably."

Here is a story about privilege. Canada conferred great privilege on Mike Duffy. Or to be specific, Stephen Harper did, by appointing him to the Senate. Duffy earned that privilege by being a loyal Conservative, a well-known TV reporter, and a great schmooze artist. Installed in the red chamber he became a popular speaker at fundraisers and campaign events around the country. This is the Senate at work for you: providing handsome salaries and expense accounts for party operatives, at the taxpayers' expense.

When someone hands you a sinecure like a Senate seat, you hand over something in return. Let's call it your loyalty. For $132,000 a year and free travel, you dance with who brung you. Which means that the Senate is effectively a branch of the Prime Minister's Office. Senators can soberly second-think all they like; in the end they vote the party line. That goes for Senate committees too, of course. So when Chief of Staff Nigel Wright wrote a cheque to cover a little accidental overcharge on expenses (those forms are so confusing) he didn't have to speculate on whether it would shut down the forensic audit of Duffy's affairs. He simply had to decide.

Which brings us to the question of what Harper knew, and when. The PM insists he learned of the cheque from media reports, and that he is "very upset." A collective snort went up all over Canada at this, but it may be true. It is one of the principles of good politics that the leader should be insulated from scandal. When you're doing something that runs a bit close to the edge, you don't tell the boss, especially at the prime ministerial level.

But there are levels of not-knowing. There is the kind of total ignorance that comes from being deceived. This kind of not-knowing leader is duped by his or her staff into believing that everything is on the up-and-up, while underhanded underlings are secretly up to no good. At the other end of the not-knowing stick is the hands-over-eyes "I see nothing" maneuver, also known as willful ignorance. Between these two extremes are shades of naïveté.

Suppose a prime minister said at his first staff meeting, "You may have to bend the rules sometimes. If so never, ever tell me." He would in that case be guilty of a kind of general complicity, a Nixonian acceptance that dirty tricks must be played, but there would be nothing to tie him directly to the writing of questionable cheques or interfering with audits. He would in that case be guilty of nothing more than a kind of general sleaze, a moral wishy-washiness.

But suppose a leader lets it be known that he wants something done about a specific case, but doesn't say what. Suppose he makes it clear that he doesn't want to hear how his directive was fulfilled. A new picture begins to emerge. Now we've come beyond sleaze and all the way to complicity. When the Godfather tells his minions to reason with somebody, they know he doesn't mean talk.

When Harper asserts that he knew nothing about Wright's gift to Duffy, which of these characters is he claiming to be? The good and moral but slightly dopey chief duped by unscrupulous staff? The powerless official with no choice but to cover his eyes and pretend he doesn't see? The sleazy boss who lets it be known in advance that the moral code is elastic so long as his deniability is preserved? Or the compromised leader who said, 'Fix this, and don't tell me how'?

You can hear the silence all over the country as Canadians hold their breath in anticipation of the answers to these and all the other questions surrounding the Senate expenses scandal. After all, as Minister of Foreign Affairs John Baird has told us, there are two "independent enquiries" into the affair. One is being conducted by ethics commissioner Whitewash Mary Dawson, who never met a Conservative she couldn't exonerate, and the other by a Conservative-dominated Senate committee which is itself a suspect in the case.

Yes, Mike Duffy has reason to be pleased. The fix is in.

Don't Let It Bring You Down, It's Only Trousers Burning

DECEMBER 2011

Peter Mackay's dog is loyal. Fortunately for the Minister of National Defence, so is his boss, for now at least. Otherwise the Member for Central Nova might find himself hoisted out of his cabinet seat and sent on a quick, low-cost trip to the back benches, as befits a minister caught misleading the House.

Mackay's original sin was not a major one. On July 9, 2010 he was at a remote fishing camp in Newfoundland, enjoying a bit of vacation time. It's a big job, being Canada's defence minister, and who could begrudge him the opportunity to catch a few fish and hoist a few beers on his days off? But duty called, in the form of a funding announcement in London, Ontario, and the Challenger jet which is the minister's preferred mode of transportation doesn't land in remote fishing camps.

To reach Gander, the nearest place the Challenger can land, by boat would have taken three hours of precious fishing time, so Mackay commissioned a Canadian Forces Search and Rescue helicopter to taxi him to the airport. It must have been quite an exciting ride, since he had to be hoisted out of the camp in a sling, there being no suitable landing site available.

The whole matter might have passed un-remarked, but Mackay was already taking flak from opposition members over his alleged overuse of the Challenger. He's spent $2.9 million on flights in the government jets in the past four years. This figure does not include trips to Afghanistan, for which he uses military aircraft.

It's not the kind of issue that brings down a government or even a minister, but for a ruling party trying to pass itself off as penny-pinching it's an embarrassment they could do without. The real problem began when opposition members called Mackay on his high-flying ways. On the Challenger bill, his office released a statement declaring that "In approximately 50 per cent of the total Challenger flights Minister MacKay has taken, he has taken these flights to attend the repatriation of fallen military personnel."

Oops, or as Mackay's colleague Bev Oda might say, NOT! The record shows that out of thirty-five Challenger flights, only nine offered the minister opportunities for photo-ops with flag-draped coffins. But the fallen-troops claim came from an underling, and at any rate is almost true except for the arithmetic. It's not until we come to Mackay's response to questions around the helicopter flight that the stench of burning ministerial trousers becomes overpowering.

Mackay told the House that the only reason he took the helicopter instead of a much cheaper boat was that the forces wanted to give him a long-delayed SAR demonstration. As it turns out, there's not a word of truth in that claim. For one thing, he'd had that demonstration the previous year. Military communications reveal that the request for the flight came from Mackay's office, and that reluctant officials first considered sending a transport helicopter from CFB Gagetown, or from Goose Bay, finally settling on the SAR chopper because it was closer.

Confronted with these facts, and with e-mails showing that the military strongly advised against using a SAR helicopter for a shuttle bus "under the guise" of a training mission, the Conservatives changed tack. Defending his defence minister, Prime Minister Harper told reporters that the flight was "appropriate" because "the minister was called back from vacation and used governmental aircraft only for government business."

Does this mean that in the future SAR helicopters will be at the disposal of cabinet ministers who are suddenly called away to make emergency funding announcements? Because if so, your chances of survival in a nautical emergency off Canada's coast just got a lot slimmer. It's sheer good luck that the chopper in question wasn't needed for real search and rescue work while Mackay was using it for a taxicab.

Now it seems that in addition to covering Mackay's $16,000 heli-cab ride so he could spend a couple more hours with his fishing buddies, the taxpayers are footing the bill to re-cover the minister's fire-ravaged posterior. According to the *Globe and Mail*, Department of National Defence officials "have been aggressively searching for ammunition against the opposition" and have so far turned up the fact that Bob Rae once traveled in an OPP helicopter, back in 1992.

By Conservative standards, Mackay's misuse of a military helicopter is a mini-scandal. It didn't cost $50 million, like the Muskoka boondoggle, it's unlikely to result in a criminal conviction like the in-and-out election fraud, and it doesn't involve proroguing parliament to escape allegations of complicity in war crimes. On the other hand it does give off the strong scent of mendacity on the part of a cabinet minister. There used to be a remedy for that. They used to resign.

Elections Canada Reports Smear Campaign In 200 Ridings

MARCH 2012

During the 2011 federal election, I received a number of robocalls. But I didn't inhale. Nor will I be reporting the calls to Elections Canada, the *National Post* or the Council of Canadians. It's not that I don't care about the integrity of the election, it's just that I have no idea who the calls were from or what they were about.

This gap in my knowledge isn't a result of my being forgetful – I am, but in this case it would make no difference as there's nothing to forget. I didn't listen to the messages. I never listen to a recorded message on the phone. Frankly, I wonder who does. When you pick up the receiver and an obviously-recorded, over-cheerful voice says, "Hi! I'm calling from ..." what could possess you to let the precious minutes of your life tick away finding out who they are, let alone what they want?

When a real human being is on the other end of the line, it's different, but not by much. True, it's rude to hang up on someone, but you needn't linger long if you're not interested. The proper response to an unwanted, "Hi, my name's Tiffany, and I'm calling from the Conservative (Liberal, New Democratic) Party of Canada, how are you today?" is a pleasant, "Fine, thank-you, goodbye." That way you don't waste Tiffany's time, and better still, you don't waste your own.

Now that robocalls are such a hot-button issue, you might want to hang in there long enough to see if someone's trying to scam you out of your vote. But last year when most of us didn't even have a name for pre-recorded political messages, surely nothing but desperate loneliness could have induced anyone to keep the receiver to their ear long enough to discover that some robot wanted them to vote at the Long Lake sewage lagoons.

I raise this point in reaction to the news that the Council of Canadians has asked the Federal Court of Canada to overturn election results in seven ridings, including the Yukon. According to a story in the *Yukon News*, the alleged Yukon robocalls employed the now-famous Pierre Poutine Gambit, in which someone purporting to be the Conservative Party calls asking the recipient for their support, and if the answer is "no," "Elections Canada" calls up and sends the voter to the wrong polling station.

The Conservative Party and MP Ryan Leef deny any connection to the calls, and who could doubt their word? Calls intended to misdirect non-Conservative voters could have come from any number of sources. The government has concluded its internal investigation into the matter and found itself completely innocent of all charges. It even knows who the real culprits are. According to Conservative findings, the evidence points to sore losers.

It appears that during the last election sore losers in the opposition parties knew in advance they were going to lose, so they engaged in dirty tricks to provide themselves with evidence for a post-election smear campaign. They harassed voters, using their real identities, hoping they could later pass themselves off as Conservative impostors. They tried to send their own voters to the wrong polling stations. Sore losers have tried to attach significance to the fact that all the evidence in the Pierre Poutine affair points to a Conservative database, a contractor hired by the Conservatives, and a former Conservative staffer – that's him over there with all the others, trying to avoid the bus wheels.

Chief Electoral Officer Marc Mayrand appeared before the House affairs committee on Thursday to address the sore losers' allegations. He reported that his office has 800 complaints under review, in 200 ridings, which are "sufficiently founded to spark initial investigation," and 250 have gone on to become open case files. Multiply that by a thousand for all the people that had the sense to hang up before they heard the message, and these become serious allegations.

The government scheduled Mayrand's appearance on budget day, and put out just four seats for members of the press, because who cares about a few mistakes that may or may not have been made at election time? But the sore losers' smear campaign has proven so effective that the room was packed with both journalists and members of the public.

It's got to stop. This campaign is diverting attention from the government's great accomplishments in – well, see? It's such a distraction I can't think of one. Mr Prime Minister, put a stop to it now. You know you love royal things. Create a Royal Commission to Investigate the Sore Losers' Robocall Smear Campaign.

Clear your name. The country needs to know the truth.

Left-Leaning Council Goes To Court

DECEMBER 2012

If you've been paying attention to the news lately you could be forgiven for believing that there's an organization in this country called the Left-Leaning Council of Canadians. The COC's challenge of federal election results in six ridings came to trial this week, and it seems that nothing is more relevant to the case than the sinister tilt of the organization representing the plaintiffs. Apparently there is no need to remind readers of the fairly pronounced list to starboard of the other major player in the story, the Conservative Party of Canada.

The purpose of this battle between left and right is either to unmask the culprits who tried to subvert the 2011 general election, or to prevent that unmasking, depending on which side you're following. The applicants are eight Canadians in six federal ridings, each won by a Conservative candidate in 2011, all by small margins. During the election, each of the eight received a phone call purporting to be from Elections Canada, attempting to send them to the wrong polling station. Supported by the COC, they allege that these calls were sufficiently widespread to call into question the results of the vote. Here in the Yukon, Ryan Leef won his seat by 132 votes – not a particularly small margin by Yukon standards, but small enough to be in question if there was in fact a campaign to suppress the vote.

Some of the facts in the case are out of the realm of debate. For sure, somebody put time, money, and effort into a campaign of prank calls designed to keep non-Conservative voters out of polling stations. Many of those who received the now notorious robocalls (though not all the calls were automated) say they had earlier identified themselves to Conservative canvassers as supporters of other parties. Elections Canada is investigating a similar pattern of events in Guelph Ontario, where the misleading calls have been connected to a robocall company often used by the Conservatives, and from there back to the local Conservative campaign office.

Since the Guelph story broke in February, voters from all over the country have reported receiving the misdirecting phone calls. Lawyers for the COC are in possession of Elections Canada documents detailing 87 such complaints deemed credible enough to be used in court. There is also evidence that, during the election, officials from EC contacted the Conservative Party to raise concerns about deceptive calls originating from its campaign.

The evidence is damning, and Elections Canada is conducting an investigation which ought to result in criminal charges, but it's unlikely the COC's civil case would ever have come to court without the testimony of pollster Frank Graves. That's because even if one party is convicted of conducting a criminal campaign of voter-suppression, the results can't be overturned without proof that the campaign succeeded, and enough people were prevented from voting to affect the outcome of the election.

President of the polling firm Ekos, Graves conducted a poll which found that voters in the six ridings in question were significantly more likely to have received the misleading phone calls than those in other ridings. He also found that those who had identified themselves to the Conservatives as non-supporters were much more likely to receive the calls, and that on a statistical balance of probabilities the deception is likely to have skewed the election results.

Conservative Party lawyer Arthur Hamilton spent part of Tuesday trying to attack Graves's credibility. This is a common tactic in court, but according to the COC's lawyer Steven Shrybman,

Hamilton went above and beyond the norm. "I can't imagine a more egregious form of character assassination," said Shrybman, complaining that his adversary had taken "almost an hour of this court's time … to assail Mr Graves's integrity."

If Shrybman had ever been a criminal lawyer he might be able to imagine a more egregious form of character assassination. It's standard practice in sexual assault cases to attack the character of the complainant, almost always for much more than "almost an hour." In many cases, after the defence lawyer gets done attacking her character, a woman has to listen to the judge do the same. In one high-profile case here in the Yukon a judge tossed out a rape charge in part because the accuser had sat on an exercise ball with her legs apart. (Try crossing your ankles on one of those things some day.)

To be fair to Shrybman, the attack on Graves's credibility did reach near exercise-ball-like levels of absurdity at times. Hamilton grilled the pollster on his firm's donations to the Liberal Party, alleging anti-Conservative bias, and not backing down even after Graves pointed out that he donated a larger amount to the Conservatives. The whole line of questioning really went down the rabbit hole when the Tory lawyer pointed to one of Graves's tweets critical of a neo-Nazi mass murderer in Norway as proof of the pollster's anti-Conservatism. Did his employers really want him to make that association on their behalf?

As an MP, Leef has proven himself to be nothing more than a Harper yes-man. Even the Yukon's former member, Liberal seat-filler Larry Bagnell, looks like a star by comparison. If a by-election was held today it's likely that the incumbent would come in a distant last. But let's not get our hopes up. The burden of proof in cases of election fraud is heavy, as it should be. Unless there's evidence that 133 Yukoners couldn't find their polling stations, we're probably stuck with what we've got. But only till next election.

Robocalls: Another Blow to the Brand

MAY 2013

Last week, Federal Court judge Richard Mosley handed down his decision in a lawsuit led by the Council of Canadians against the Conservative Party of Canada, in the so-called Robocalls case. Though he found that there was an attempt by someone to subvert the last federal election by preventing non-Conservatives from voting, evidence that the attempt succeeded was inconclusive. After the decision was made public, Yukon MP Ryan Leef told reporters he felt vindicated.

The Concise Oxford defines vindicate as "clear of blame or suspicion." Leef finds vindication in Mosley's ruling that, although somebody with access to closely-guarded Conservative Party records attempted election fraud on the Conservatives' behalf, there was no proof that the attempt succeeded, or that candidates or their agents were directly involved in the crime.

Let us pause for a moment to admire Mr Leef's capacity for self-vindication. Judge Mosley found that somebody used the CIMS database – accessible only by a tightly-controlled Conservative inner circle – to prevent voters from reaching the polls, after they had identified themselves to party canvassers as non-supporters. In the Yukon, survey data indicates that 36 per cent of all voters received robocalls intended to direct them to the wrong polling station. As a measure of comparison, Leef's share of the vote was 32.7 per cent.

When the robocalls story broke, the Conservatives went into full lock-down mode, doing everything in their power to prevent the facts from coming out. This Tuesday Marc Meyrand, Canada's chief electoral officer, told the House of Commons procedure and House affairs committee that the Conservatives took three months to respond to an initial request for facts surrounding the case.

Meyrand later pointed to a pattern of Conservative Party workers either refusing to cooperate with his investigation, or agreeing to interviews and then canceling at the last minute.

In his judgment Mosley observed a similar pattern, complaining that "the stance taken by the respondent MPs from the outset was to block these proceedings by any means." It began when lawyers for Leef and his fellow defendants tried to stop the trial before it began with a motion that the suit was "frivolous and contemptuous." They tried repeatedly to have the case thrown out on such obscure and inapplicable grounds as "champerty and maintenance" and asserted that it would "interfere with the case timetable" to ask Elections Canada for details behind 800 complaints of fraudulent calls.

This week the Hill Times is reporting that Conservative caucus members are feeling "horrifically depressed" about the other big Conservative scandal in the news, the Senate expenses cover-up. According to an anonymous insider, "It's hurting the government, it's a distraction. It's hurting the Conservative brand and the party more than the government because it's a fundamental to who we are as Conservatives. It's a blow to the brand because we actually care. We came to Ottawa to fix this."

There is a mystery here. We know that the members of the Conservative caucus are so sensitive as to be driven to horrific depression over the cover-up of a case of expense-fudging. How do they preserve their mental health in the face of news that their party is implicated in massive election fraud? Is Mike Duffy's creative accounting really a bigger distraction than the attempt to steal a general election? Isn't tampering with the vote as much of a blow to the brand as writing questionable cheques? Or is it that in this case, they don't actually care?

In the aftermath of Mosley's ruling, Leef told the *Yukon News*, "I was really clear when this all broke that I didn't think that this case was going to answer the questions that Canadians deserve answers to." Could this be because he knew that the Conservative Party would use all of its power to block the facts of the case from coming to light? As Leef went on to say, "Here we sit, a full year later, having the exact same questions we had when this was first undertaken."

What he didn't say is that his party is sitting on the answers.

Have A Couple Brews

NOVEMBER 2013

This just in: beer is good for you. A study published in the journal Angewandte Chemie International Edition has found that humulones, the compounds in hops that give beer its bitter flavour, may have a positive effect on such ailments as cancer, diabetes, and inflammation. In a separate study Robin Dunbar, director of Oxford University's social and evolutionary neuroscience research group, has found – this is true – that men's health is dependent on getting together with the guys for a beer at last twice a week.

The first report cautions that beer also contains alcohol, which has been found if overdone to contribute to the very ailments humulones protect against. The latter study was commissioned by Guinness and other beer makers in an effort to counteract reports by beer drinkers' spouses that too many pub nights have a negative effect on domestic harmony.

The question for Canadians is, what role did beer bro nights, or the lack thereof, play in the senate expenses scandal? Having attended one or two single-gendered pub nights in the past, I'm able to say that, at least in my experience, two things are expected of the attendee that seem to be missing from the Conservative playbook: plausibility, and discretion.

After a couple of pints, the gang down at the pub are likely to greet any dubious statement with loud references to cattle excrement. Similarly, when the suds flow, it's assumed that what is said in the pub stays in the pub, even when delivered at full volume. Failure to observe this rule can result in summary expulsion from the group.

So the question is, when Stephen Harper, Nigel Wright, and Mike Duffy discussed the question of Duffy's senate expenses, were they drinking beer? Did the PM pop the top on his third brew and shout, "Mike, shut up and pay the 90K. Our base are too dumb to understand the truth, go with the optics"? Did his chief of staff chime in with an expansive sweep of the arm and slur, "No prob, Duff. I'll write you a cheque right blanking now"? Because if so, that's privileged information. It's very bad form to be talking about it outside the pub.

Harper once insisted that no one else in his office, himself included, knew that Wright cut Duffy that infamous cheque. Now that the RCMP reports the PMO is crawling with people who knew all about it, informed observers are suggesting that the PM was simply observing the code of pub night. If all of this information was exchanged under dim light around a wooden table and a jug of draught, it would be dishonourable to divulge it to anyone, let alone the Canadian public.

Plausibility is not the same as truth, and let it be said that throughout history the pub night has seen its share of untruths. But whether it is the size of a fish, the length of a putt, or the provenance of a cheque, the bar is no place for the bad liar. The pub night fabulist quickly learns to tell it well, or stay home.

There is no better training ground for a storyteller than a gathering of friends who have been conscientiously attending to their humulone count. If you're making it up, make it good, or the boys, or girls, will catch you out. Someone will push their chair back, make the traditional reference to bovine manure, your friends will laugh at you, and attention will turn to a new storyteller.

Picture Harper down at the local on Friday night telling the gang, "I obviously would have never approved such a scheme." No claque of 163 trained seals behind him to thump their desks and bark every time his lips move, just a bunch of tipsy friends, all with their own stories to tell, ready to take over as soon as someone drops the ball. How far do you think he'd get? This is not to suggest the prime minister is departing from the truth when he claims to have known nothing about a transaction that was common knowledge among senior members of his staff. With the evidence available at present, who's to say? It's just that, if he is telling the truth, he's not doing a convincing job of it.

What Canada needs is a constitutional amendment making twice-weekly pub nights mandatory for the prime ministerial inner circle. The benefits are clear. It would help protect the country's most powerful people from disease, promote their overall good health, and most important of all, it would help to keep them honest.

HAVE A COUPLE BREWS

Tory Toast

The promises of yesterday are the taxes of today.
~ William Lyon MacKenzie

Responsible Spending, Conservative Style

NOVEMBER 2013

Last October the Conservative Party of Canada's web page carried an article praising Finance Minister Jim Flaherty's handling of the economy, under the title, Focused on Responsible Spending and Economic Growth, a commitment the party demonstrates at every turn. For example, this September the Toronto Star reported that the government has responsibly spent "well over $100 million" in public funds to promote its Economic Action Plan.

The Conservatives are so focused on responsibly spending public funds to make the action plan look like a success that this May they put out a tender for three more years of advertising, despite the fact that the March 2012 budget included "a final report to Canadians" on the stimulus program.

This March, an internal government poll contacted 2,009 people after a multi-million dollar ad blitz. Six had visited the website tagged at the end of the ads, which according to The Canadian Press is "the Finance Department's key yardstick for measuring success." No one called the toll-free hotline.

So why does a government focused on responsible spending keep throwing millions after an ad campaign that fails to attract any attention, for a program that was officially declared finished last March? It's a matter of focus. According to CBC News, "an analysis last year by the Privy Council Office ... found those who saw the ads were more likely to approve of the overall performance of the government."

What focused, responsible, governing party would throw away an opportunity like that? It's free political advertising, bankrolled by the taxpayer. It's almost as good a scam as appointing dozens of senators to campaign on the public dime. And both are money well spent, because everyone in the Harper government knows that the best path to economic growth is to re-elect focused responsible spenders like themselves.

Whatever else befalls them, the Harper Conservatives stand on their reputation as managers of the economy. This week The Toronto Star reports that the government has spent so wisely, and managed the economy so well, that 800,000 Canadians now rely on food banks to survive, up 23 per cent from 2008, during the worst recession since the 1930s.

According to Food Banks Canada's Hunger Count, 18 per cent of employed Canadians earn less than $17,000 per year. A growing number of food bank users are working poor, and others struggle with "meagre social assistance benefits" and "inadequate pensions." Young people make up a disproportionate number of food bank users, as do the very old.

Statistics Canada reports that new job growth in the post-recession period, beginning in 2011, occurred largely in the low wage service sector, which grew at four times the overall rate. But even a 10.9 per cent increase in the Mcjob rate doesn't bring us back to pre-recession employment levels. Canada's employment rate in 2008 was 73.6 per cent. Today it sits at 72.2, ranking us 20th out of 34 OECD countries, behind even some of the alleged basket cases of Europe.

There are 300,000 more Canadians unemployed than before the recession. The country did create jobs, but not enough to keep up to the number of Canadians growing up and entering the labour force, not to mention the more than 300,000 temporary foreign workers currently in the country, who have a competitive edge because they can be paid 15 per cent less than Canadian workers.

According to the *National Post*, the Harper government has responsibly spent $60 billion giving tax cuts to corporations since coming to office, "reducing the country's corporate tax rates to some of the lowest in the world." By a strange coincidence, they responsibly spent the $14 billion budget surplus they inherited and replaced it with a record breaking deficit of $56 billion, which Flaherty now congratulates himself for carving back down to $29 billion.

In 2006, when Harper and Flaherty began responsibly spending, the national debt stood at $467 billion. In 2011, they had managed to spend it up to $586 billion. When Stephen Harper was out of power, deficits, debt, and low employment were bad economic indicators. But those were Liberal deficits and debts, and Liberal low employment rates. Today we have a Conservative government focused on responsible spending and economic growth, so you can ignore the deficit and the low employment rate.

Focus instead on economic growth, or at least on the promise of economic growth, some day.

Currently the growth rate is dropping swiftly, year by year. Every year that the Conservatives have been in power, the growth rate has dropped, except for the radical leap up from a 2009 low of −2.7 per cent to the 2010 peak of 3.22 per cent, brought on by stimulus spending. Today, with the exception of that 2009 bottoming out, growth is at a ten-year low of 1.8 per cent, and dropping.

Don't be deceived by the bleak economic news, the responsible spenders in the Conservative Party know just what they're doing. In 2008, Ian Brodie, one of Harper's former chiefs of staff, explained exactly what responsible spending means to the Conservatives.

"Despite economic evidence to the contrary, in my view the GST cut worked," Brodie said, fending off criticism from economists and tax specialists. "It worked in the sense that by the end of the '05-'06 campaign, voters identified the Conservative party as the party of lower taxes. It worked in the sense that it helped us to win."

It's All Very Clear

Somewhere in the great book of Conservative Party strategy it is written that, when muddying the political waters, members shall in all cases employ the expression "very clear." It's rumoured that the marketing group considered using "perfectly clear," but rejected it for its Nixonian association. In any case, informed Ottawa-watchers know that whenever Stephen Harper or any of his cabinet ministers declare themselves to be very clear, a gob of bitumen to the eyeballs is sure to follow.

Maxime Bernier pronounced himself very clear when he, Harper, and Peter Mackay were denying all knowledge that the notorious torturers of the NDS were torturing prisoners handed over to them by Canadian troops. Less clear was why they ever believed that the Afghan secret police would make an exception for Canada's detainees. Peter Mackay was again very clear about the F-35 fighter jet, as the price played billion-dollar leapfrog with itself.

Jim Flaherty wants to be "very clear" that he is "committed to balancing the budget in 2015. Period," though he was equally clear in the past that it would be balanced by now. At press time, teams of researchers were still busy tabulating the number of times Harper has declared himself very clear while ducking questions on the senate scandal. Most recently, according to Foreign Affairs Minister John Baird, the government has been "very clear" about its position on Israeli settlements on the West Bank, despite the fact that it's impossible to tell what that position is.

The web site of the Department of Foreign Affairs makes the following declaration. "As referred to in UN Security Council Resolutions 446 and 465, Israeli settlements in the occupied territories are a violation of the Fourth Geneva Convention. The settlements also constitute a serious obstacle to achieving a comprehensive, just and lasting peace."

The occupied territories are lands taken by Israel during the Six Day War in 1967. Settlements are illegal Israeli housing projects on those lands, as well as in annexed territories in East Jerusalem and the Golan Heights. Leaders of the settler movement are unequivocal about its purpose, which is to extend Israeli sovereignty into areas claimed by the Palestinians, to make it impossible that the land will ever be returned. In condemning this act of aggression, the DFA joins not only the UN Security Council, but the International Court of Justice and almost every other country in the world.

But while the Canadian government officially opposes the settlements, Harper and Baird have been very clear that they will neither engage in nor tolerate public criticism of this or any other action taken by the Israeli government. During his recent love-fest in Israel, Harper told the Knesset that criticism of Israeli policy is "the face of the new anti-Semitism." Baird told an appreciative crowd at the American Israel Public Affairs Committee that there would be "consequences" for the Palestinian Authority if they file an international legal complaint against Israel's settlement program.

Though loath to criticize Israel for its deeds, Baird has no problem with issuing sharp criticism of the PA for its words. When Abbas made his successful bid for UN recognition of Palestinian statehood, Baird was there to oppose him. The General Assembly overwhelmingly supported Abbas, but the Canadian government didn't like his speech. "He could have been generous, and we didn't see any generosity in his remarks," Baird told the AIPAC convention. "And that deeply, deeply concerned many of us."

In response to Abbas's speech and the decision of the UN to recognize the existence of a Palestinian state, Israel announced that it would build 3,000 new illegal homes in the West Bank and East Jerusalem. Canada of course officially opposes this development, but neither Baird nor Harper has made any public expression of deep concern. In fact, according to Baird, the Palestinians themselves are to blame for this appropriation of their territory. Had Abbas not made such an ungenerous speech, Baird explained, Israel would not have had to retaliate.

NGOs who take steps to oppose the settlements cause the Conservatives concern too, as Oxfam Canada was just reminded. Oxfam opposes international trade with the Israeli settlements, a fact which came to light recently when the international development agency fired its "global ambassador" Scarlett Johansson. Johansson came into conflict with Oxfam policy when she took a job representing Sodastream, a gadget manufactured by an Israeli company on occupied Palestinian land.

Jason Kenney, Canada's minister of employment and one of the most powerful figures in the CPC, responded with a tweet announcing that he had "bought a nice Sodastream" and thanking Oxfam for the tip. For a Canadian NGO, such a jab is not to be taken lightly. In 2009, the church-based aid group Kairos lost its government funding for exactly this: opposing the illegal settlements that the DFA also opposes.

Canada opposes Israeli settlements on occupied land. We also oppose opposition to those settlements, whether by word or by deed. We recognize that the settlements are in violation of the Geneva Conventions and an obstacle to peace, but we can't say so out loud, and there will be consequences for anyone who does. In the Conservative Party of Canada, this is what passes for clarity.

This column earned me the distinction of a response from Honest Reporting Canada, an organization dedicated to rooting out criticism of Israel in the Canadian media. I was quite flattered to be included in a company that includes CBC anchor Anna-Maria Tremonti, Globe and Mail *columnist Doug Saunders, and even Daniel Shapiro, former U.S. Ambassador to Israel.*

The Buck Stops Way Before Here

NOVEMBER 2013

Last month, Toronto City Councillor Giorgio Mammoliti circulated a fuzzy photograph he claimed was taken by a member of his staff, appearing to show a city employee at a North York recreation centre with his head down on his desk, as though taking a nap. Mammoliti and Mayor Rob Ford are close allies in the fight to privatize city services, and the councillor quickly put the picture to work for the cause, sending out a press release tagged, "Wake up and get to work 'Or Parks and Rec staff to be laid off next'."

Ford was swift to jump on the bandwagon. Without waiting for further evidence he declared the incident "an embarrassment and a black eye" for Toronto, and proclaimed, "If this is the case, I'm going to ask for the manager and the employee to be dismissed. We cannot tolerate this. I want people to show up to work and do their job."

Here is the basis of Ford's popularity, the thing that makes him click with the voters: when it comes to slacker employees and civic waste, he is vigilant, unwavering, and unforgiving. He has a mandate and a duty to protect the people of Toronto from black eyes and embarrassment, and to make sure that every penny of the city's payroll is well spent.

Having built his political career on the rock of other people's accountability, the mayor now faces the disturbing fact that, once in a while, sauce for the goose is sauce for the gander. When confronted with the existence of a video apparently showing him breaking the law by smoking crack, Ford bravely stepped up and lied. "I do not use crack cocaine," said the crack-smoking mayor, "nor am I an addict of crack cocaine. As for a video, I cannot comment on a video that I have never seen, or does not exist."

That's the kind of leadership Ford has demonstrated throughout his term in office, leading by example, putting his mendacity where his mouth is. After he cleaned out the overpaid slackers in the garbage department, the mayor went on to demonstrate his personal commitment to his $170,000 per annum job by showing up for work most days, often before noon, and sometimes visibly sober.

When the existence of the crack smoking video could no longer be denied, Mayor Ford forthrightly changed his position to reflect the new facts. He could not defend himself because "it's before the courts," but despite the "allegations" against him he planned to "go back and return my phone calls and be out doing what the people elected me to do and that's save taxpayers money and run the great government that we've been running the last three years."

Now that it's impossible for the mayor to deny that he smoked crack, hung out with gangsters, and made some very indiscreet remarks on video, he has taken the high road once again, coming clean with the facts as a responsible politician should. Yes, he has smoked crack, but only when "extremely, extremely inebriated." No he's not a drug addict, nor an alcoholic.

Like the mayor, his friends and supporters are committed to accountability in office. Just as a recreation centre employee who was seen in an unclear photograph with his head apparently down on his desk should be summarily fired along with his supervisor, so a mayor who gets extremely extremely drunk, poses for pictures with known criminals, and lies about his illegal drug use should take a little time off, and maybe get some help.

Canada's tough-on-crime justice minister, Peter Mackay, didn't mince words: the mayor who admits to breaking the law while in office "needs to get help" (although the people who sold him the crack need to get mandatory minimum sentences). Finance Minister Jim Flaherty took a similarly strong stand against crime in office when he said, "at the end of the day, (Ford) has to make his own decision about what he ought to do."

In the strict mathematics of accountability to which Ford, Mackay and Flaherty subscribe, an eye equals an eye, and a tooth a tooth, though some eyes and teeth are more equal than others. Crime must be punished, and those who abuse their jobs must be held accountable. Low level employees who appear to put their heads down on desks should be fired, and their jobs privatized. Conservative mayors who commit crimes and then lie about them also need to be punished, with time off and "help."

Even the mayor's mother believes her Robbie should face the consequences of his crimes, going so far as to suggest he should "smarten up," get a driver, and lose weight. This is a sterling idea. Surely all of Rob Ford's sins will be forgiven if he only sheds the *avoirdupois*. In fact, the entire city of Toronto could stand to lose a bit of weight. Currently experts predict the city will see instant benefits from an initial weight loss target of about 250lbs.

The Artfulness Of The Apology

DECEMBER 2013

In the December 2012 issue of Psychology Today, psychoanalyst Joseph Burgo discusses the art of the apology. He lays out some simple rules, starting with "genuine apologies never contain the words 'if' or 'but'". Those words, Burgo explains, are qualifiers, and the best apologies are unqualified.

The news this week presents two very public apologies, one of which meets the Burgo test of unqualified simplicity, and one of which fails. The latter is Toronto Mayor Rob Ford's attempt to avoid being sued for implying that Toronto Star reporter Daniel Dale is a pedophile. More on this anon. The better-worded apology came from Canada's Industry Minister, James Moore.

Moore had a lot to apologize for, though perhaps not as much as Ford. Last week a BC radio host questioned him about child poverty and hunger. The minister replied, "The government says it's my job to feed my neighbour's child? I don't think so," and then laughed.

Moore is the senior federal cabinet minister for BC, the province with the highest rate of child poverty in the country, at 18.5 per cent. Needless to say his jocularity didn't go over well with anti-poverty activists, or just about anybody else. Adrienne Montani of First Call summed it up when she said, "It's a very callous statement. It is his job as a federal minister to look after the welfare of some of our most vulnerable citizens and that would include children."

At first it appeared that Moore would choose self-justification over apology. On Sunday he tweeted, "it is a ridiculous 'story' that completely takes a comment out of context." By Monday, however, he seems to have realized that there was no extenuating context, no way to blame the press for his own gaffe, nothing for it but to apologize.

> " THERE'S A LESSON HERE. WHEN YOU OWE SOMEONE AN APOLOGY, DON'T STALL. SAY YOU'RE SORRY BEFORE YOU DIG YOURSELF A DEEPER HOLE.

That's where the minister finally got it right. He posted an apology on his website, with a shorter version on Twitter. Neither edition of the apology contains a single if or but. Here is the tweet: "An apology. The cause of fighting poverty is not helped by comments like those I made last week. I am sorry." If he'd said that right away, instead of trying to bluster and shift the blame, it would have scored an A+. Given the timing, it's looking more like a C at best, hardly a passing grade for a cabinet minister making more than $230,000 a year, but better than F for Ford.

On May 2, 2012, Daniel Dale was on the public land behind Ford's house, photographing a piece of green space the mayor was trying to buy. Ford accosted the reporter and called the police, who found no evidence to support any of his accusations. In a recent cable TV interview with Conrad Black, Ford had this to say about the incident. "I guess the worst one was Daniel Dale in my backyard taking pictures. I have little kids. When a guy's taking pictures of little kids" – pause for insinuating snicker – "I don't want to say that word but you start thinking, 'What's this guy all about?'"

None of this was true. Police have confirmed that Dale was not in Ford's backyard, nor did he take any pictures except of the public land. But Ford didn't stop there. He accused Dale of climbing up on cinder blocks and "leering" over the fence.

He stood by that story long after the cops found that there were neither cinder blocks to stand on, nor anyone in the yard to be leered at, nor any evidence that Dale was near the fence at all.

Faced with a lawsuit, Ford stood up in council chambers to deliver a statement he claimed was an apology. He apologized, not for what he said, but "for the way in which the media has interpreted my statements." He denied calling Dale a pedophile, though he didn't offer an alternative explanation for his remarks. He repeated the "leering" accusation. He repeated the unsubstantiated claim that he found Dale "very far from the land Mr Dale advises he was researching a story about" and used the statement as an opportunity to accuse the Toronto Star of an "incredible assault on me and my family."

In short, although Ford's statement made use of the word "apology," it didn't include an actual apology. It was in many ways a restatement of the original accusation, and it made an absurd attempt to accuse the media of making the whole thing up. If Ford was trying to put an end to Dale's defamation suit, he failed. The suit proceeds. This outcome was so predictable that it's hard not to think the mayor wanted his day in court.

If so, it was a bad idea. Court is not a good place for someone who is inclined to play fast and loose with the truth; unlike the loyal dogs of Ford Nation, judges take offence at being lied to, and the consequences can be severe. Perhaps someone reminded Ford of this. On Wednesday, the mayor made a second apology to Dale, one in which he acknowledged that almost every word he's said on the subject to date has been false. Dale responded by dropping the lawsuit.

There's a lesson here. When you owe someone an apology, don't stall. Say you're sorry before you dig yourself a deeper hole. And leave out the ifs and buts. Otherwise, instead of appearing sincerely apologetic, you're just another sorry-looking fool.

Happy Birthday, Mr President

JULY 2013

Jennifer Lopez is suffering the scorn of the US media this week after she capped off a performance in Turkmenistan by singing Happy Birthday to President Gurbanguly Berdymukhamedov. When Lopez learned that Berdymukhamedov is that most terrifying of creatures, a dentist turned dictator, she offered a public apology. According to her publicist "had there been knowledge of human rights issues of any kind, Jennifer would not have attended."

It would appear that nobody on the star's staff bothered to google Turkmenistan before sending her to perform there. But then, the Central Asian dictatorship wasn't her real host; the show was booked by the Chinese National Petroleum Corporation, so why would anyone suspect that there'd be human rights issues?

Had they checked, J.Lo's handlers might have saved themselves and their client a lot of embarrassment. Human Rights Watch describes Turkmenistan as "one of the world's most repressive countries." The entry goes on to say "Media and religious freedoms are subject to draconian restrictions, and human rights defenders and other activists face the constant threat of government reprisal. The authorities continue to use imprisonment as a tool for political retaliation and to restrict peoples' right to travel freely."

Turkmenistan is often compared to North Korea, with its brutal repression of dissent and its personality-cult government, but there is one clear distinction between the two countries. While North Korea's economy is based on handouts from China, Turkmenistan has the world's largest identified reserves of natural gas. The past decade of war in Afghanistan has been fought in large part along the corridor of the proposed $7.6 billion TAPI pipeline, destined some day to carry Turkmen gas to tidewater in Pakistan.

North Korea is such a repressive state, run by such a demented government, that the US will have nothing to do with it. There is no US embassy in Pyongyang. There is one in Ashgabat, Turkmenistan, though; the world of international diplomacy is all about subtlety, and there is a subtle yet significant difference between a brutal dictatorship mired in poverty and a brutal dictatorship with proven reserves of gas. If Ms Lopez had made her Turkmenistan debut a couple of months earlier she could have gone to see the American Cowboy Show, sponsored by the US Embassy and billed as "an authentic introduction to the cowboy way of life in the American west, including music and poetry, slide shows and films, demonstrations of horse training techniques, and ranching handicrafts."

For some reason, neither the American cowboys nor the American Embassy have taken the kind of heat Lopez has over working in Turkmenistan. Perhaps it's because neither is as famous as she. Nor, it appears, is Deepak Obhrai, parliamentary secretary to Canada's minister of foreign affairs. His 2010 visit to Ashgabat to meet with representatives of the Turkmen oil industry passed uncriticized by the press. J.Lo only missed running into Israeli Ambassador Shemi Tzur at the airport by a few days. Tzur presented his credentials to President Berdymukhamedov on June 20, becoming his country's first ambassador to Turkmenistan. Again, Mr Tzur must lack the public stature of Ms Lopez, because his arrival in Ashgabat stirred no controversy at all.

On reflection, though, an imbalance of fame by itself isn't enough to explain why Lopez is the only one getting trashed for dealing with

Berdymukhamedov. She's no more famous than Coca-Cola, Caterpillar, or Halliburton, all of which are listed on the US embassy website as "doing business with Turkmenistan."

Reports have surfaced that Lopez was paid $1.5 million for her appearance at the despot's birthday party, a figure which may help to explain her lack of curiosity about the host country. Now that the story is out there's a great cry for her to donate that money to charity. By contrast, no one is calling on any of the above named companies to give away whatever profits they've made selling soft drinks, bulldozers, or oilfield services to the Turkmen. Clearly the star needs a strong public relations strategy to combat the bad press.

What no one seems to have noticed is that with the possible exception of Coca-Cola all of the above-mentioned companies, countries, and individuals are in Turkmenistan on the same business as Lopez herself: the oil business. All the star was doing was shaking her million-dollar money-maker to promote good company-dictator relations for CNPC, her employer for the evening.

So lighten up on J.Lo already. The name of the game in Turkmenistan is oil and gas, not human rights. One day, the US will negotiate a deal with the Taliban that will let the Turkmen gas flow through Afghanistan, and on that day all will be forgiven. We will conveniently forget Berdymukhamedov was ever anything but a kindly, fabulously wealthy, ex-dentist. Everyone who collaborated with him, whether in ignorance or in greed, will be absolved of guilt and remembered as free trade pioneers. Even if all they did was sing happy birthday.

A Few More Questions

AUGUST 2013

According to the *National Post*, "Regina is the latest community to be fooled by a white supremacist group into declaring a 'European Heritage Week'." Mayor Michael Fougere told the Regina Leader Post that when he signed the proclamation announcing the now cancelled celebration he had no idea who was behind it.

How did this happen? The NP article offers no clue. Somehow this request passed through the bureaucracy at City Hall, reached the mayor's office, was voted on by council, and proclaimed under the mayor's signature without a single soul saying, "Hey, wait a minute. Isn't European heritage a white supremacist buzz-word? Shouldn't we be checking up on who's requesting this?"

Maybe Regina is just a really nice place, where the people are innocent of such matters. Maybe the same is true of the other cities that have been taken in by the European Heritage Week scam, including Halifax, Victoria, and Fredericton. When they heard European Heritage they no doubt pictured a week of bocce and brie, of great wine, beer and sausages, a celebration of pierogies, coureurs de bois, and early Scots colonists reading the bible in buffalo-chip cabins.

Or maybe the trouble is just that the idea was submitted by a guy named Bob Smith. Bob Smith is a Google-proof name. If indeed anyone at the City of Regina took the trouble to look Mr Smith up they were undoubtedly overwhelmed with information about car salesmen, athletes, and pastors named Bob Smith.

The Bob Smith who promotes European heritage takes a tiny bit more digging to track down. You need to search for "Bob Smith neo-Nazi," or "Bob Smith convicted hate criminal" to narrow in on Bob Smith of the Nationalist Party. That Bob Smith was convicted, in a case that he fought all the way to the Supreme Court of Canada, of promoting hatred in the neo-Nazi magazine the Nationalist Report. All of the headlines say Smith "tricked" or "fooled" Regina and numerous other cities and towns into proclaiming this racist celebration. If so, it's about time Canadian municipalities started to pay a little more attention.

For instance, Mr Smith has a middle name. It's Wayne. Search the Internet for Robert Wayne Smith Canada, and you will quickly discover the NPC website, the first paragraph on the entry page of which contains the following: "...globalist elites run all the countries of the world. Call them what you want – Bilderbergers, Jews, Zionists." A few paragraphs down the text descends into slavering gibberish with, "even weird dictatorships like Gaddafi's green Revolution is only tolerated for a while before foreign "rebels" of NATO are created to oust politically-corrected leftists out of step with pro-Jew globalist elites."

The Nationalist Party lists 27 Canadian cities that "have officially declared European Heritage Week in perpetuity in their municipalities as of 1994-2013" including "Rock Mountain House Alberta" and "Whitehorse, NWT." (The *Yukon News* checked, the City of Whitehorse, Yukon does not celebrate European Heritage Week.) The racist group also sponsors the Canadian Flag Perpetual Pride Campaign. It makes much of the "white background" on the Canadian flag, interpreting it as a racist symbol, and claims its "flags have been reported ...now in Whitehorse, Yukon," getting it right that time, geographically speaking. I wonder, do they think there are two Whitehorses?

Attention, municipal governments of Canada: there are certain catch phrases that ought to alert you to the fact that you may be dealing with right-wing extremists. If someone approaches you with an idea to celebrate white people's rights or white nationalism or European heritage, take a second look. There's a better-than-even chance you're dealing with someone who believes Hitler was onto something. You could end up with skinheads and swastikas when you thought you were signing up for Tyrolean hats, accordions, and great pastry.

Anita Bromberg of the Jewish advocacy group B'nai Brith offers some advice for Regina that all municipalities might want to consider, whenever they are approached with an idea for a celebration. "Maybe." says Bromberg, "the application form might need a few more questions."

Bringing In The Sheaves: Mining For Gold The Modern Way

SEPTEMBER 2017

According to Klondike Placer Miners' Association president Mike McDougall, there is no reason to update the placer royalty rate in the Yukon. In fact, based on McDougall's logic, even the 37.5 cents per $1600 ounce of gold they already pay is an unfair burden. After all, as McDougall points out, "Does a family farm pay royalty on the wheat they produce? No." So clearly the family gold mine shouldn't pay a royalty on the gold they produce either.

Pity the poor gold farmers. Every year they cultivate the ground, plant the little gold seeds, and pray for rain. It matters not if they are organic gold miners, lovingly saving the same gold seed their parents planted year after year, or if they are giant producers whose seed comes genetically engineered from Monsanto, every gold farmer lives poised between hope and fear. What if there's a drought? What if there's mold in the seed and the year's crop of gold is lost? What if, just as harvest approaches, there's a killing frost and all the gold they have painstakingly produced is lost? No matter what the Miner's Almanac has to say about the chances for the year to come, the gold farmer has no choice but to plant the seed and hope for the best.

And yet, come good year or bad, come hail or sleet, come rain or drought, the poor miner must pay through the nose, 37 and a half cents gouged out of every 1600 bucks by the heavy hand of the tax man. It's criminal. Placer mining has existed in the Yukon since the late 19th Century, and so has the current placer royalty rate. The rate was set at a time when gold was valued at $15 per ounce, and in those days miners were able to pay a royalty of 2.5 per cent of the actual value of the gold they produced and still make a living.

But today's miners don't mine the way their forefathers did. They use modern, efficient, methods, which cost a lot of money. True, they also produce more gold of higher value in less time, but every ounce comes burdened with that usurious 37 cent royalty payment, leaving only $1599.63 to cover mining costs and patch the children's clothes. If today's miners had to pay the 2.5 per cent royalty those old Klondike miners paid, they would only have $1540 left for each ounce. True, the old timers were left with only $14.63, but the cost of living was much cheaper then.

Now certain radical elements in the territory are clamouring for miners to pay royalties at the same rate miners paid in 1898. They don't understand the difficulties the modern miner faces: it costs a lot of money to maintain one residence on the creeks and another in Arizona. And for all their hard work, placer miners produced a mere 66,000 ounces of gold a year, grossing only $105 million before taxes. They don't, as McDougall points out, "have a roomful of gold they can roll in." And yet the extremists would have them pay more than symbolic royalties.

And for what? Updating the placer royalty regime would net the Yukon Government only about $2 million a year which, as MacDougall points out, is "not even a revenue stream." What good would a paltry two million bucks be to the Yukon public? Mind you, it would be a crushing loss to the cash-starved mining industry, but to the rest of us wealthy Yukoners who don't have to mine for a living? Peanuts. Forget about it. Not worth the bother of collecting.

If you need evidence to support the proposition that a mine is just like a farm, and should be taxed accordingly, the air coming out of that Dawson meeting room says it all. Go ahead, breath deep, and tell me that ain't fertilizer.

" DO NOT BOTHER CLIMATE
CHANGE DENIERS WITH THIS FACT:
IT IS ONLY MORE EVIDENCE OF A
GLOBAL SCIENTIFIC CONSPIRACY
TO DUPE A GULLIBLE PUBLIC INTO BUYING
SOLAR PANELS AND WINDMILLS…

A *2015 review published by the Journal of Theoretical and Applied Climatology examined the 3 per cent of published climate studies – a total of 38 papers – that challenged the evidence of anthropogenic climate change. They were unable to replicate the results on even one, meaning that all 38 are now debunked. So, while the glaciers melt and the wildfires rage, 100 per cent of valid studies support the theory of a human-caused climate crisis. Do not bother climate change deniers with this fact: it is only more evidence of a global scientific conspiracy to dupe a gullible public into buying solar panels and windmills, in which presumably all the world's climate scientists have invested heavily.*

It Will Come Up

After *Nordicity* has spent a week on the op-ed page of the Yukon News, it appears on the paper's web site, where readers are offered the opportunity to comment. Yukoners are a busy lot, and it's not every week that anyone troubles to respond. Much depends on the topic.

Local issues tend to inspire more replies, as do certain key subjects. Chickens, cats, and proportional representation usually strike a spark, and breasts, religion, and marijuana seldom miss, while columns about politics often receive several "recommends" but very seldom any actual response. There is only one subject guaranteed a reaction, and that is global warming.

Climate change deniers are not shy, nor are they tormented by doubts. The International Panel on Climate Change may be 95 per cent certain that humanity is on a collision course with anthropogenic climate change, but deniers are 100 per cent sure that it's all a hoax designed to cow the masses and rake in a fortune selling solar panels to the deluded. Somewhere, they know, on some grassy knoll, a secret team of greenwashing pseudo-scientists concocts fake studies which, through the machinations of a giant conspiracy, pass the rigours of scientific peer-review and become one with the mass delusion. The rest of us, those who rely on the word of climate scientists for our information on the subject, are lefties, fools, and sheep.

Comments are often peppered with links to web sites where we can discover the real science. The London tabloid The Daily Mail is presented as a source of the real dope on the myth of global warming, as is the web-based Canada Free Press, whose masthead motto is "Because without America there is no Free World." So far, no offers of links to peer-reviewed scientific journals where I might become properly enlightened on the great climate change hoax.

I don't mean to suggest that the web page is overwhelmed by these responses: I get one, two, maybe four or five at best. It's not as though deniers are desperate for a place to air their views. For those who wish to refute the Great Hoax, there are a host of hosts for their opinions. In the world of climate change denial, *Nordicity* is small cheese, but my numbers may be about to go up, because this week there's one fewer high profile venue in which to expose the conspiracy: Paul Thornton, letters page editor of the LA Times, has revealed that he no longer accepts letters claiming that anthropogenic climate change does not exist.

The statement was, in fact, an aside in a piece about the Tea Party's shut-down of the US government. Mr Thornton was explaining that he will not publish letters alleging that Congress exempted itself from the health care law, because the allegation is false, and the paper does not print letters which present untruths. He offered as an example letters "that say there's no sign humans have caused climate change."

This is a most unfortunate policy. One of the keys to a good newspaper is a lively letters section, and there is nothing like an obsession with the facts to take the wind out of a good argument. Having a fact checker on the letters page is like putting a soccer referee in charge of a hockey game. By the second period he's red-carded all the tough guys out of the game, and the stands are rapidly emptying.

If a newspaper doesn't get your blood boiling at least once in a thorough reading, you've missed an important part of the experience. What's a Saturday morning behind the paper if you don't get it shaking in outrage at some point? And while you can always take exception to the view expressed in a column or an editorial, there's nothing quite gets the caffeine pumping like a total departure from the known facts.

Another experience your newspaper should provide is a good laugh, and again, there's nothing like an unrestrained letters section or comments page. And since one of the best gags going is somebody failing to see what's staring them in the face, the LA Times is doing its readers a great disservice by blacking out the climate change deniers and other fact-changers.

So please, if you believe that climate change is a religion, that Al Gore made it all up so he could get rich trading carbons, or that the Daily Mail is a better source of accurate science than the journal Nature, don't hold back. Our readers need you to complete the newspaper experience. Give us both barrels, every time the subject of global warming comes up. And there will be no shortage of opportunity. With the glaciers melting and the waters rising, rest assured, it will come up.

Laughter Is The Best Medicine

AUGUST 2013

Currie Dixon, the Yukon's Minister of the Mining Environment, finds it "laughable" for Robert Kennedy Junior to suggest that the Yukon Party government's approach to the Peel Watershed Regional Land Use Plan has been undemocratic. This is a good thing. Laughter is, so they say, the best medicine, and Mr Dixon must be in the pink, for surely he has been laughing his head off for months.

Immediately after the last election, having campaigned on the claim that it would be "irresponsible" to take a position on the Peel Watershed Planning Commission's report, the Yukon Party government took that position. And it turned out that they had campaigned truthfully, because the position they took could hardly have been more irresponsible. Good thing they waited till the voting was over to break it to us.

Dixon probably got his first medicinal chuckle from Dave Loeks, the chair of the Peel Planning Commission, who described the government's counter-plan thus: "either a misunderstanding in the planning process or it's an attempt to circumvent it," which, when you break it down is a pretty clear description of undemocratic behaviour.

Let's hope the minister had a good healthy guffaw when Tourism Industry Association chair Neil Hartling accused him and his party of the highly undemocratic practice of "Changing the principles after seven years of public consultation and planning." Na-cho Nyak Dun Chief Simon Mervyn must have done Dixon's health a world of good when he announced that his legal team had "guns loaded and ready to go" to challenge the government's rejection of the Peel plan. The press release from Tr'ondek Hwech'in, the Vuntut Gwitchin First Nation, the Gwich'in Tribal Council and the First Nation of Na-cho Nyak Dun stating that "Yukon's

introduction of sweeping new proposals at this point in the plan approval process is not consistent with the process set out in our final agreements," must have been a real side-splitter.

Kennedy came to the Yukon to campaign against hydraulic fracturing, the process of pumping millions of gallons of water contaminated with toxic chemicals deep into the earth to extract petroleum products. Before he spoke at the Yukon Arts Centre on Monday evening he had already suffered a blow from Dixon's cruel wit. We hope the New York lawyer, activist, radio host and law professor wasn't too bruised when that famously sharp tongue brushed him off with the following:

"We're always happy to have rich tourists come to the territory and spend their money. But I have to say I think it's a little bit hilarious and embarrassing that a rich, elitist, celebrity, activist lawyer from the lower 48 would come up here and spew such ill-informed nonsense about an issue and a process about which he clearly has no understanding."

Ouch! That had to hurt. But Kennedy should take comfort in knowing that when Dixon calls him elitist for opposing the Yukon Party's rejection of the Peel Planning Commission's Final Report, the minister is casting him among an elite that includes the vast majority of Yukoners, all of the First Nations whose territory intersects with the Peel Watershed, all of the members of the Peel Commission, the Tourism Industry Association, both opposition parties, and pretty much any honest observer who actually knows what the term "democracy" implies.

Kennedy may be a high priced out-of-town lawyer, but when he decided to tackle Currie Dixon, he clearly didn't know who he was dealing with. According to the *Whitehorse Star*, "Dixon went on to say that Kennedy was factually incorrect on a number of his statements. However, he refused to list which ones, saying he hadn't seen a transcript of the lawyer's comments." See, that's the kind of tough operator we have in the Yukon, who can dismiss your facts without even knowing what they are. Rich tourist activists beware.

And all of you rich, celebrity, elitist, ill-informed Yukoners who still believe the Yukon Party behaved undemocratically when it g-filed a five-year $1.6 million compromise on the Peel and replaced it with a road map for mining companies, don't make Minister Dixon laugh, ok? His sides hurt already.

Global Warming Is Boring

JUNE 2013

In a newly-released report the International Energy Agency warns that "the world is not on track to limit the long-term rise in the average global temperature to two degrees Celsius." Since the 2009 Copenhagen Climate Change Conference, the IEA's twenty-eight member states are in official agreement that the average global temperature must be held to two degrees above pre-Industrial Revolution levels to prevent environmental collapse. The trouble is that few of them are doing anything about it.

Or that's one of the troubles. Another is that the two degree target itself is completely bogus. Thomas Lovejoy, one of the world's leading experts on biodiversity, wrote in the New York Times this January, "It is abundantly clear that the target of a two degree Celsius limit to climate change was mostly derived from what seemed convenient ... A two degree world will be one without coral reefs (on which millions of human beings depend for their well-being)."

In 2011, climate scientist James Hansen, director of NASA's Goddard Institute for Space Studies, said that "two degrees of warming is actually a prescription for long-term disaster," including an ice-free Arctic and a rise in ocean levels "in the tens of meters." The climatologists at realclimate.org warn that two degrees of warming would mean "... drought and storm responses that could challenge civilized society ... the conflict and suffering that go with failed states and mass migrations ... the Earth warmer than it has been in millions of years."

Fortunately, world leaders are already planning to plan to act to keep global warming from exceeding that cataclysmic rise. In 2015 they are to meet to develop a plan to cut emissions, to be implemented in 2020. And if those leaders do what has never been done before, that is to say sign a meaningful, binding agreement on greenhouse gas reductions and then stick to it, the IEA says they'll already be too late to meet that woefully inadequate target of two degrees.

According to the IEA report, two degrees "remains technically feasible, though extremely challenging." It "will require determined political commitment to fundamental change in our approach to producing and consuming energy." The report calls for "an energy sector revolution ... very strong policy action. ... (Moving) the abatement of climate policy to the very core of economic systems."

The IEA report is a call to arms, a desperate cry for one last hope that the world's richest countries might meet their own self-imposed targets for greenhouse gas reductions. On the off-chance that world leaders have the wit and the will to listen and act, those targets lead to a world with flooded cities, lost islands and coastlines, massive species extinctions, widespread ecosystems collapse, and no coral reefs. And that's the good news.

The bad news is, we're not going to make it. According to IEA Executive Director Maria Van Der Hoeven "This report shows that the path we are currently on is more likely to result in a temperature increase of between 3.6 °C and 5.3 °C." Although she went on to say that it is still possible to turn around, neither she nor anyone else is predicting that leaders such as Stephen Harper are about to wake up and hit the brakes before we go over the petroleum cliff.

I learned of the IEA report from David Crane's column in the Hill Times, but it doesn't seem to be a big enough story to excite the national daily papers. The report was mentioned as a brief aside in the Ottawa Citizen, in a story about Resources Minister Joe Oliver, who asserts that despite his recent comments to the contrary, he still considers climate change "a serious issue." I could find no mention in the *Globe and Mail*, the Toronto Star, or the *National Post*. Then again, they do have to prioritize. What's the looming end of the world as we know it when the latest details of the Ford Family Saga are battling Justin Trudeau's charity-chiseling for the front pages?

Climate change has a hard time making traction in the media. It lacks the makings of a good story: known timelines, a clear narrative, an easily identifiable villain, some good guys. It also lacks the extra trappings that make a story juicy: cocaine, bikers, and busty hookers, for instance, or politicians on the take. People get bored with graphs and numbers and dire predictions and flip the page to Its Highness the Royal Bump. This may help to explain why governments pay little more than lip-service to an issue that threatens our survival as a species.

Not to worry though, there are bound to be plenty of spin-off stories as time goes on. Forget the dull mathematics of carbon reduction, the Sydney Opera House disappearing under the foam is going to make incredible video. Chasing down the last living members of dying iconic species – the last polar bear, the last elephant – will be brilliant reality TV, and once the food supply crashes there should be enough famine stories to keep the front pages filled till there's no one left to read.

The truth is, global warming is boring. A two-degree rise in temperature isn't even a decent heat wave. To make the front pages it has to be warm enough to bring out the bikinis, or kids playing with fire hydrants. Fear not. Climate change may be a snoozer today, but if the word of the IEA is anything to go by, it's about to get very newsworthy, very soon.

Since this column appeared in 2013, the US has seen three consecutive years of the worst drought and wildfires in history. In 2016 Alberta oil-patch town Fort McMurray burned to the ground. The Syrian War, which was born out of the 2011 Levant drought, has cost half a million lives. Here in the Yukon, the Kaskawulsh Glacier has retreated so far that the Simms River dried up. This phenomenon, known to geologists as "river piracy" is last known to have happened on Earth billions of years ago. Oh, and the US has elected a president who believes that climate change is a "hoax" being spread about by China to destabilize the American economy.

No Turning Back

JUNE 2013

A few weeks ago, the Wall Street Journal hailed tiny Barnhart, Texas as "an unlikely hub of the new American oil boom." The writer, Russell Gold, waxed eloquent at how fracking had "given new life" to the unincorporated town, population 200, now "chock-a-block with rail cars" eighty of which will carry "about $5.5 million of oil".

Elizabeth Grindstaff, a vice president of sales at Texas Pacifico Transportation Ltd, owner of those life-giving rail cars, told WSJ, "(Barnhart) is the centre of our petroleum universe ... My bosses call it the belly button". The belly button isn't growing in population, but, says Gold, "... businesses benefit from a workday surge in population as workers drive in from places like San Angelo and Big Lake". So things are really booming for workers at "a post office, one taco truck and a filling station called the Big Red Barn".

But oil giveth, and oil taketh away. This week, Barnhart ran out of water. The local water commission hopes to have a back-up well in service soon, but in the meantime the town is trucking in bottled water. Barnhart isn't the first town in Texas to run dry, and it likely won't be the last. The Texas Commission on Environmental Equality lists 30 communities that are in danger of exhausting their water supply.

According to the US National Weather Service, reservoirs across Texas are at their lowest levels ever for this time of year. Most of the state has been in drought for the past three years. Farmers and ranchers have lost an estimated $8 billion. In one year, 2011, wildfire consumed 2,862 houses, and millions of acres of land. Trees are dying, roads are breaking up, the electrical grid is stretched, food prices fluctuate wildly, and unplanted fields have resulted in record dust storms.

Fracking a well takes between one and eight million gallons of water, which is mixed into a slurry along with sand and chemicals. About 80 per cent of the oil and gas wells in Texas are fracked. According to WorldOil, Texas has "over 156,000 and counting" viable, producing oil and gas wells. Some municipalities have restricted or banned the use of municipal water for fracking, driving drillers to shop around. One company paid $68,000 to truck 3.5 million gallons of water 50 miles.

The current drought is predicted to intensify this year. It might ease up next year as a result of El Nino, the cooling ocean current. Or, El Nino might fail to appear, as it did last year. In either case, water is not a commodity Texas can afford to waste. This presents a conundrum because the state has committed itself to an oil and gas economy, which today means a fracking economy. Oil and gas production is using up precious water resources, while consumption is driving global warming and contributing to the drought, but what are Texans to do? Throw their whole economy out the window? Do they even have that choice?

There is a lesson here for Yukoners as we consider whether to pursue a future in fracking. Disallowing fracking would mean the loss of millions of dollars worth of oil and gas revenue. We could be tossing away a chance at decades of prosperity, jobs for our kids, revenue for territorial and First Nations government programs, a way out of poverty for many. Allowing fracking would mean committing ourselves to an oil and gas economy from which we might never be able to withdraw, no matter what the consequences.

Here in the North we're quite familiar with the boom-and-bust nature of the resource extraction industry, and we know the temptation to follow the boom, because it's a better time than the bust.

But what happens when the boom turns sour, when the law of unintended consequences kicks in, when going forward spells disaster, and there's no way to back out except by pulling the plug on your entire economy? We might never face a drought here like the one in Texas, but what if ten years down the line the caribou are threatened with extinction, or our groundwater is contaminated with methane and toxic chemicals?

If oil and gas exploration was a universal bad, there would be no need to discuss it. It isn't. People need fuel, and people need jobs. These arguments will be raised in favour of allowing fracking in the Yukon. But it's the very prosperity that the oil patch brings that makes it so dangerous. Once we open the door to fracking, does anyone really believe we'll ever be able to close it again?

CHAPTER 11: YULETIDE BRIGHT

" … WHAT IS THERE TO SAY
THAT HASN'T ALREADY BEEN
SAID IN THE TWO MILLENNIA SINCE
WHATEVER ACTUALLY HAPPENED
IN PALESTINE THAT LED TO
THE ERUPTION OF CHRISTIANITY?

In nearly two decades of Nordicity I seldom attempted a special Christmas column. Something more interesting usually came along on deadline day, and really, what is there to say that hasn't already been said in the two millennia since whatever actually happened in Palestine that led to the eruption of Christianity? Herewith, the three columns I could find in the archives that acknowledged Christmas in some way, two of them appropriately bleak and cynical, the other quite the opposite. What can I say? Who doesn't get caught up in the spirit of the season at least once in a while?

A Warm Christmas Tale

Once upon a time, there was a beautiful, cold country, where all the Christmases were white, and all the children were good.

As well as being cold and beautiful, the country was also very rich, and lots of people lived happy comfortable lives. Lots of them lived miserable uncomfortable lives too, but only a few of these insisted on living on the streets where the happy people could see them and feel a little bit miserable and uncomfortable too, for a minute in passing.

It was a country of nice people, who gave each other nice presents, and made tax-deductible gifts to charity every December, when reminded by their accountants. They believed in nice things, like Peace on Earth and Goodwill to All, but being very happy and comfortable they tended not to pay much attention when their government waged war and squandered good will around the world.

The happy comfortable people were very clever, and because it was a cold country they developed lots of good ways to keep warm, and to travel about in comfort. While other countries only knew how to get oil out of a simple well, the rich cold country learned ways to get it from the ocean, and out of tarry ground under its northern forests. This made the country richer, and the people more happy and comfortable.

And then one day, the world's leading climate scientists announced that the world was getting steadily warmer. This sounded nice at first to the people in the cold country, but the scientists said no, it's not nice: people in low-lying islands are being flooded out of their homes. Hurricanes are getting worse, there's terrible drought and wildfires, and the polar ice caps are melting. Soon coastal cities will be flooded, polar bears and penguins will be extinct, and your rich, cold country won't even be all that cold.

Hm, said the happy comfortable people. Will we still be rich?

Well, said the scientists, if you keep polluting the atmosphere with dirty oil and doing nothing to cut back on your consumption, you'll be very, very rich in the short term. Your children will be poorer, and your grandchildren may face extinction, but for you, for the foreseeable future, it's happiness and comfort all the way. The happy comfortable people thought this over for a while and said, sounds good. Let's run with it.

Things went well for the happy comfortable people. They made lots of money, owned lots of toys, and consumed as much energy as they wanted. They cut down millions of acres of forest to get the oil out of the tarry ground, and sold it to the even richer country next door for oodles of money, which they spent on lots of fun stuff made in foreign factories where the people worked for next to nothing. It was a great deal!

Then something strange happened. When the happy comfortable people travelled around the world – and they travelled a lot because they could afford to – they were used to being greeted warmly. Foreign people knew that the rich cold country was a nice country, and the happy comfortable people were nice people. But all of a sudden, foreign people started saying not-nice things about the rich cold country. They started to call the happy comfortable people fossils, and to blame them for the floods, famines, droughts, wildfires and hurricanes.

The rich country's government didn't like being bossed around by a lot of poor countries that can't even afford proper armies, so they got mad and said, if you're going to be like that, we're going to cut down even more trees to make even more dirty oil, and burn as much of it as we want, and get really, really rich.

And that's what they did. They cut down all the trees that were on top of the tarry ground, took out all the oil, filled the atmosphere with carbons, and made the planet much warmer, which felt kind of nice to the happy comfortable people, who didn't like having to shovel snow off their pickup trucks all the time. People in other countries got flooded out, or died from droughts, or had their houses blown down, but the happy comfortable people just kept getting happier and more comfortable.

Then one day the government of the rich not-quite-so-cold country announced that it had run out of tarry ground. There would be no more oil, and no more money to be made. The government had no money to spend to help keep the people happy and comfortable, because they'd given it all to big corporations to help them get the oil out of the tarry ground. The people had no money left to keep themselves happy and comfortable because they'd spent it all on giving each other gifts made by the unhappy uncomfortable people in foreign countries.

At the same time the formerly rich, formerly cold country started to experience drought, wildfires, and famines of its own. Now all the people were miserable and uncomfortable, and the Christmases were no longer white. But the saddest thing of all was that nobody in the world sympathized one bit. Get used to it, they said. We've been suffering for years.

Merry Christmas, Jerome

DECEMBER 2010

In more than a decade of writing this column, I don't believe I've ever marked the year's end by declaring a top story or a top 10 list of stories, events, newsmakers, or any of the usual foolishness that plumps out the pages of the press at this season. But this week a major international news event recalls a story which appeared in the Yukon News a couple of months ago, and it leads me for the first time to declare my candidate for hero of the year.

First, the big story: this week US President Barrack Obama signed an order to end the military's Don't Ask Don't Tell policy, which forbade gays and lesbians from serving openly. News coverage of the event made it sound as though, by the stroke of that pen, gay American soldiers, sailors, and airfolk could suddenly come surging out of the closet, but sad to say, it ain't so.

On Monday, Pentagon press secretary Geoff Morrell told reporters, "I don't think anybody has any idea how long this will take." First, Department of Defence staff will comb through a mountain of regulations to see how they affect, or are affected by, the ruling. After months of this, the president, the secretary of defence and the chairman of the Joint Chiefs of Staff will (or will not) agree that the repeal will have no negative effect on the functioning of the military. After all this there will be a 60-day waiting period for the bill to take effect.

Despite the delays, the signing of the bill is a great moment in history, and a step toward curing the US of a powerful hangover resulting from a centuries-long binge of religious conservatism. Like any other hangover, this one leaves the country's bloodstream still polluted by the drug, so much so that a hate cult describing itself as a "church" still gets away with demonstrating at the funerals of gays with signs that read, "God Hates Fags."

Although Canada's military does not officially discriminate against homosexuals, we suffer from our own version of the same hangover. To be openly gay in Canada is still an act of courage. Despite laws to the contrary, it can still cost you your job, your safety, or even your life.

Which brings me to the local hero. This October the *Yukon News* ran a story about Jerome Stueart, a Whitehorse writer and teacher who came out as gay to his fellow congregants at the Riverdale Baptist Church. He began to do so in 2009, not with any fanfare, not in a confrontational way, but by quietly speaking to other church members, and letting them know that he was no longer prepared to cover up his sexual orientation.

Stueart suffered some fairly predictable consequences for this act. Called before the elders board, he was required to take a vow of chastity, even to promise not to date, if he wanted to remain a deacon of the church. He was refused permission to explain himself in the parish newsletter or to speak in church about his decision to come out. Sometime later he was dumped from the church choir.

In a follow-up letter to the editor, Stueart explained his reasons for approaching the Yukon News with his story. Though church leaders discriminated against him and did their best to silence him, he remained in the church "for the hope of discussion and out of love."

After months of silence, he finally got his discussion, in spades. One Sunday this October, he sat through what he describes as a "toxic anti-gay sermon."

"I needed to do something," he said in his letter. "Lives are at stake." So Stueart came out again, this time to the readership of the *Yukon News*. Again he demonstrated his courage, even telling the reporter that he had come within a hair's breadth of taking his own life last year. Throughout the story, he has been magnanimous, even loving, in his attitude toward his fellow parishioners.

Taken by itself, Jerome Stueart's action changes nothing. The Baptist Church will continue to discriminate against homosexuals, coming out in public as he has done will continue to be a risky business, and institutions such as the US military will keep dragging their feet as they are forced to join the 21st century. But it is by the accumulation of small actions that big change is affected. It may take a million such acts of courage to conquer homophobia, but each one makes the next a tiny bit easier.

So here's to you, Jerome. You were brave and forthright without being harsh and hurtful; you suffered quietly through months of harm before you were pushed to go public, and even then you spoke with moderation and love. I hope you are able to celebrate the birth of your religion in the spirit of comfort and joy that it purports to deliver. In short, I wish you a Merry Christmas. You deserve it.

No, Virginia...

DECEMBER 18, 2007

" *I am 8 years old. Some of my little friends say that there is no Santa Claus... Please tell me the truth.*" Virginia O'Hanlon, 1897, a letter to the New York Sun.

Virginia, I only wish that I could tell you your little friends were wrong, that God is in his Heaven, Santa in his workshop, and all right with the world of good girls and boys. Nothing could be farther from the truth. Every day while you play, good girls and boys around the world suffer and die in prisons, brothels and labor camps. Across the sea, good little children shiver in their beds at the sound of an airplane, and wonder when their turn will come to die under the rubble of their homes.

What, Santa Claus real? You might as well say that there is no such thing as hunger, that poor children never sleep on the street while bankers bloat themselves on six-figure salaries. Virginia, some people even complain that not enough children are in prison. They say this though they know that to imprison a child is the surest way to turn a single mistake into a life of crime. Why do they want to lock away the children? Because they are so poor in spirit as to hate and fear the young.

What a world it would be, if only a jolly elf could come down once a year, and bring sweetness, light, and plum pudding to all the children of the world, one half of whom go without enough to eat. What a better place if one magic sled could do the job that a hundred aid organizations can never manage, because there are never enough resources.

Santa Claus won't be coming to the murdered children of Fallujah this year, nor to the little sex-slaves of Bangkok. He won't be visiting the children crippled by cluster bombs or torn open by shrapnel.

There will be no Santa for the orphans of Afghanistan or Palestine. In the birthplace of the Prince of Peace, there will be no peace this Christmas.

Santa Claus does not exist, as surely as hatred and greed and violence rule the world. Alas Virginia, how dreary life is for Santa's real helpers, the Asian children who labor to manufacture the war toys under your tree. There's no childlike faith on the factory floor, no poetry, no romance to make tolerable their daily existence.

Every day around the world, the lights of childhood are snuffed out by war, famine, and disease. Children go without education, without proper clothing, without clean water, without homes, without medicine or food. Without a safe place to play, away from the guns and the tanks. Without a childhood.

No Virginia, there isn't a Santa Claus. He is only a part of our annual pretence that the 19th Century, century of poor-houses and public hangings, was a better, more innocent time than this. We play this charade although we know it was in fact a brutal era of unconscionable wealth for a few made possible by the slavery of many, a time in which much of the world still lives, and back toward which the rest of us are rushing at ever increasing speed.

Santa Claus real? If he were, what a back-breaking load of coal his poor reindeer must carry to the rooftops of those corporations that employ third-world children in airless factories, guzzling the earth's resources and destroying its atmosphere to create useless junk you and your friends will break and throw in the landfill before the new year. Alas, Virginia, such children as these will not be placated with the charming myth of an infinitely generous bearded gnome who brings the fruits of their slavery into the homes of more fortunate children.

Believe in Santa Claus! You might as well believe in the hypocrites who use religion to justify war, who celebrate the birth of Jesus and fatten their wallets on the murder of innocents and the enslavement of the poor.

Fight, Virginia. Until your childish frame grows old, until you stretch it out for its last sleep, fight. Fight against militarism, greed, and indifference. Fight against charming lies and ugly truths. Never cease demanding that every day for every child be, if not Christmas, then at least a decent day on earth.

No Virginia, there isn't a Santa Claus, just yet. But there can be if we try hard enough. Let's start by making a big wish, not for lots of presents, or a glimpse of magic reindeer, or fairies on our lawn, but for something even more fundamental to the spirit of Christmas.

Let's wish for Peace on Earth, and Goodwill to all. And then for once let's act like the words mean something.

EPILOGUE ... BECAUSE ALL THINGS MUST COME TO AN END.

No, Virginia has always been a favourite column of mine. It won me my first Ma Murray Award, and I later found it on an extreme right wing web site called, I believe, The New Republic, with the headline, A Canadian Liberal's Lament at Christmas. It was of course greeted in the comments section with gleeful derision. I'm not sure which made me happier, the Best Columnist Award or knowing that those poor souls got the fleeting satisfaction of deriding a 'liberal' for Christmas. I think of it as my gift to them.

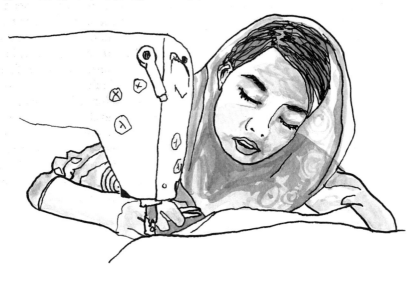

NO, VIRGINIA

About Al & Heidi

AL POPE

Bad Latitudes, Al Pope's novel of love and adventure in the bad, bold Yukon of 1978, was published in 2004 to favourable reviews in the *Globe and Mail*, Vue Weekly, the *Yukon News*, and Books in Canada, where W.P. Kinsella called it "an enjoyable page-turner." Ivan Coyote, writing in the *Globe and Mail*, called it "a great read."

Al's column, *Nordicity*, appeared in the *Yukon News* between 1995 and 2014, winning three Ma Murray Gold Medals for Best Columnist in BC/ Yukon, and two George Cadogan Prizes for Outstanding Columnist in Canada.

Al has written for magazines, newspapers, and literary journals. He has dabbled in theatre, and two of his plays and several of his stories have aired on CBC Radio. He lives on a small acreage in the Yukon's Carcross Valley, where he has variously raised sled-dogs, chickens, turkeys, pigs, and goats, as well as three children. When he can find the time he is at work on another novel.

SOCIALIZE

www.facebook.com/TheBorealCurmudgeon

ORDER THE BOOK

alpope.com

HEIDI MARION

Heidi Marion has fallen back into artistic ways after having a family, being a farmer, food sovereigntist and women's advocate. She enjoys pen and ink for its directness and has worked in printmaking and collage. Heidi remembers reading drafts of Al's first stories at his kitchen table on One Bucket Creek back when they both had radio phones. (They still use wood stoves.) Heidi graduated from the University of Toronto with a degree in Fine Art (studio).